The Situational Mentor

THE
SITUATIONAL
MENTOR

An International Review of Competences and
Capabilities in Mentoring

Edited by David Clutterbuck and Gill Lane

GOWER

Published by
Gower Publishing Limited
Gower House
Croft Road
Aldershot
Hants GU11 3HR
England

Gower Publishing Company
Suite 420
101 Cherry Street
Burlington, VT 05401-4405
USA

British Library Cataloguing in Publication Data

The situational mentor: an international review of competences and capabilities in mentoring
1. Mentoring in business
I. Clutterbuck, David, 1947– II. Lane, Gill
658. 3'145

ISBN: 0 566 08543 7

Library of Congress Cataloging-in-Publication Data

The situational mentor: an international review of competences and capabilities in mentoring/edited by David Clutterbuck and Gill Lane
    p.cm.
Includes bibliographical references and index.
ISBN 0-566-08543-7
1. Mentoring. I. Clutterbuck, David. II. Lane, Gill.

BF637.M48S56 2004
158'.3--dc22

2003056982

Typeset by Sparks, Oxford, UK – www.sparks.co.uk
Printed and bound in Great Britain by MPG Books Ltd, Bodmin, Cornwall

Contents

List of figures

List of tables

List of contributors

Liz Borredon
Professor, EDHEC Business School, Lille, France

David Clutterbuck
Mentoring and Coaching Research Group, School of Business and Finance, Sheffield Hallam University, UK

Ann Darwin
Management And Research Centre (MARC), Adelaide, South Australia

Professor Ellen Fagenson-Eland
Associate editor, Academy of Management Executive, Oxford Journals, UK

Truls Engstrom
Assistant professor, Stavanger College, Stavanger, Norway

Dr Bob Garvey
Mentoring and Coaching Research Group, School of Business and Finance, Sheffield Hallam University, UK

Stephen Gibb
Department of Human Resource Management, Strathclyde Business School, University of Strathclyde, Glasgow, UK

Anthony M Grant PhD
Coaching Psychology Unit, School of Psychology, University of Sydney, Australia

Marc Ingham
Professor, EDHEC Business School, Lille, France

Gill Lane
Executive coach and mentor, Gill Lane Executive Development, Northamptonshire, UK

David Megginson
Mentoring and Coaching Research Group, School of Business and Finance, Sheffield Hallam University, UK

Margaret Parkin
Training consultant and author of Tales for Trainers *(1998) and* Tales for Coaching *(2001)*

Ekin K Pellegrini
Department of Management, School of Business Administration, University of Miami, USA

Terri A Scandura
Department of Management, School of Business Administration, University of Miami, USA

Paul Stokes
The Mentoring and Coaching Research Group, Sheffield Hallam University, UK

Rachel Yan Lu
Centre for Research on Continuing Education in Professions and Organizations, Catholic University of Leuven, Belgium

Foreword: the making of a mentor

During the past two decades we have made considerable progress in understanding the nature of mentoring. What was first identified by Dan Levinson and his colleagues in *Seasons of a Man's Life* as a critical relationship for men in early adulthood has captured the attention of scholars and practitioners in fields that have in common the concern for individual learning and development. Many of us have worked to develop a clear understanding of the nature of this developmental relationship, under what conditions such a relationship will flourish or be thwarted, its potential consequences for individuals and organizations, and the various strategies that can be employed to make this kind of developmental relationship readily available.

My own interest in mentoring began in the mid-seventies when I was in graduate school, having already spent a few years working in industry as a human resources specialist. The challenge involved in making the transition from school to work in my own life, combined with my academic study of career dynamics and adult development, led me to focus my first research on relationships that young adults have with older, more experienced adults that facilitate learning and development in the first decade of their careers. This first study of pairs of managers involved in mentoring relationships with each other, combined with subsequent studies of peer relationships and formal mentoring programmes, led to the publication of *Mentoring at Work*.

During the eighties there was a proliferation of research on mentoring, which resulted in a relatively complex view of the nature of mentoring. By the end of that decade, a number of scholars (for example, David Thomas, Belle Rose Ragins, Terri Scandura, Raymond Noe, David Clutterbuck, Michael Zey) confirmed that mentoring relationships offer a range of career and psychosocial functions that foster individual outcomes including increased self-confidence, clarity of professional identity, increased competence and career advancement. In addition, empirical studies began to shed light on how such developmental relationships unfold over time, and how these relationships necessarily ended or transformed as protégés' learning needs evolved or organizational circumstances changed. Researchers and practitioners began to document that the organizational benefits of mentoring included increased performance, increased loyalty, enhanced individual and organizational learning, and reduced turnover.

As this knowledge began to be disseminated, human resource practitioners and organizational leaders concerned with developing talent began to question how they could create conditions for mentoring relationships to flourish in their particular contexts. In the US, Affirmative Action and the Equal Employment Opportunity Commission (EEOC) stimulated interest in making mentoring available to women and other minority group members who heretofore had been disadvantaged in their efforts to establish mentoring relationships that would advance their careers. At the same time, a number of scholars (including David Thomas, Belle Rose Ragins,

Stacy Blake-Beard, Ronald Burke among others) illuminated unique dynamics that characterize cross-gender and cross-race mentoring relationships, and pointed out the challenges posed to individuals interested in developing relationships with individuals of backgrounds different than their own. A convergence of social, political and economic forces resulted in significant efforts to make mentoring available to diverse groups of employees. And this interest has persisted around the world.

As a consequence, we have learned much about formal and informal mentoring, and particular strategies that individuals and organizations can employ to foster this developmental alliance. There are no simple recipes. Perhaps the most important lesson from all of these programmatic efforts is that the most effective strategies for fostering mentoring depend on the context in which they are implemented, the purpose for such initiatives, and the values, skills and attitudes of potential participants. There is now a generally well-accepted continuum of strategies ranging from creating a reward system and culture that encourage mentoring, to formally assigning mentors and protégés and providing extensive training on the requisite skills for making such relationships work. Debate continues as to what conditions are necessary in order for formal initiatives to be effective.

During the most recent decade, the landscapes of careers and organizations have changed dramatically. Stable, hierarchical organizations have given way to more flexible, team-based structures in order to meet the changing and complex demands of an increasingly global and technologically sophisticated marketplace. And, as the pace of change has increased, individuals in business, non-profit, and government sectors have had to face steep learning curves on a regular basis. This rapid pace of change in technology, jobs, workforce demographics, and organizations' structure and processes now require everyone to be a good learner, and to be able to cope and adapt to uncertainty and turbulence.

This dramatic change in context has had significant consequences for mentoring. The instability of organizations and jobs has been disruptive to the more stable developmental alliances that we had observed in the past. Potential mentors are necessarily living with far less job security, and also finding that their years of wisdom and experience don't necessarily inform current challenges the way that they did before. Similarly, young individuals seeking mentors are encountering work and life challenges that are quite different from those that their seniors encountered earlier in their lives, leaving them to wonder if potential mentors really understand their circumstances. Everyone is busier, more challenged to be a continuous learner, and in need of support.

Fortunately, recent research on mentoring, careers, and executive development has taken these dramatic changes in context into account. We now know, for example, that relationships are a key source of learning at all stages of careers, not just for the newcomer, and not just in the traditional hierarchical mentoring relationship. Instead, there is considerable evidence that individuals learn in relationships with their peers, as well as in relationships with their bosses, other senior managers, and even in relationships with their subordinates (see, for example, much of the research on leadership development completed at the Center for Creative Leadership in Greensboro, North Carolina). Thus, while the traditional mentoring alliance (defined as a hierarchical relationship that provides a range of career and psychosocial functions) still exists, several of us (including Monica Higgins, David Thomas, myself and others) have reconceptualized mentoring as a network of developmental relationships.

Whether individuals are protean or organizational in career orientation (as defined by Douglas T Hall), they will necessarily be confronted with the challenges posed by frequent change and the need to continuously learn. As career theory is revised to take into account this increasingly turbulent environment, it is now anticipated that individuals will necessarily have more than one career in a lifetime, and will be better able to navigate more frequent transitions if they have strong developmental networks. We are just beginning to understand how the diversity and strength of ties that characterize these developmental networks will shape individuals' development over time, and how individuals' developmental networks evolve over time.

Recent works on leadership competences and leadership development strongly indicate that individuals vary in their capacities to cultivate and sustain mentoring and other developmental relationships. Dan Goleman, and his colleagues in the Consortium for Research on Emotional Intelligence, have delineated a range of emotional competences including self-awareness, self-regulation, empathy and a range of social skills that facilitate relationship-building. We are just beginning to understand under what conditions individuals can develop these critical competences through one-on-one coaching, classroom training, 360° feedback and/or on-the-job experiences. As the design and impact of these educational practices are better understood, it will be possible to better prepare individuals to mentor and be mentored.

Of equal importance is the need to acknowledge and understand the causes, nature and consequences of dysfunctional relationships that sometimes eventuate. There is an underside to what is otherwise considered an invaluable developmental tool: mentors can be too controlling, unaware of how their own values, stereotypes and limitations may undermine the development of their mentees; personal insecurity and organizational politics can infuse relationships with hidden agenda and destructive dynamics; and excessive dependency needs can contribute to unproductive attachments that thwart growth as well as productivity.

We enter this decade with a clearer understanding of the nature of mentoring, and with a substantial list of unanswered questions. Hence the need for this book. Here, scholars and human resources practitioners from around the world have contributed their current thinking about mentoring. Each brings a unique lens to the phenomenon and offers new insights that will undoubtedly enhance the value of mentoring to those seeking to find mentors, to be mentors or to facilitate such developmental relationships for others. In addition, the work reported here will undoubtedly stimulate the next steps in research that will refine our current understanding of mentoring even further.

David Clutterbuck and Gill Lane have amassed an unusually diverse and capable list of authors who from their varied perspectives have addressed some of the critical questions that still remain about mentoring. For example, Gill Lane, David Clutterbuck, Ann Darwin, Anthony Grant, Margaret Parkin, Terri Scandura, Ekin Pellegrini, Truls Engstrom and Melanie Lankau offer systematic frameworks for defining the competences that mentors possess, suggesting that some of these are generic and others are situation-specific. Each chapter offers a unique lens with which to view mentor and mentee competences. Together, these authors' works consider personality factors, situational factors, and both mentor and mentee competences, thus providing the reader with a complex array of the factors that shape mentoring competences. Some consider whether and how these competences can be developed.

Several authors including Bob Garvey, David Clutterbuck and David Megginson consider the phases of mentoring relationships, and the factors that shape their ending, resolution and evolution over time. The methods by which mentoring relationships can be facilitated in organizations are addressed in unique ways by Liz Borredon, Marc Ingham, David Megginson and Paul Stokes. Bob Garvey, Terri Scandura and Ekin Pelligrini consider the important issue of when and why dysfunctions occur in mentoring relationships, whereas Stephen Gibb explores moral issues surrounding mentoring. And, consistent with the dramatically new context in which mentoring is embedded, Ellen Fagenson-Eland and Rachel Lu consider the capabilities required to benefit from e-mentoring.

This volume is unique in bringing together scholars and practitioners from different parts of the world. It is not dominated by North American, European or Australian views of mentoring, but rather embodies the similarities and differences that reside among these varied cultural perspectives. My review of the manuscript left me with new wisdom, and with a sense of excitement and increased clarity about the work that remains to be done. I trust that you will be equally inspired as you read what follows.

Kathy E Kram
Boston, Massachusetts
March, 2004

Introduction

DAVID CLUTTERBUCK

The rise of mentoring as a major force in society, particularly in Anglo-Saxon and European countries, has been one of the significant factors in redefining relationships at work and in the community. There are many reasons for this phenomenon, including the following:

- the collapse of the extended family as the core source of support and advice in the developed economies has left a substantial gap, which has been partly filled by an assortment of counsellors, therapists and advisers – mentoring provides a less threatening resource, based on ties of friendship, compared with these other sources of support, where an element of detachment is expected or even mandatory
- the recognition in business and government that equal opportunity objectives cannot be fulfilled, unless those people at a relative disadvantage have equal access to the informal networks of information and influence
- the increasing complexity and stress of working life, which makes it more and more important to have some form of 'safety valve'
- the expectation, among many talented young people joining organizations, that they will have access to the experience of older, generally more senior employees
- the increasing emphasis on retaining talent and the clear evidence that mentoring contributes significantly to managing this issue
- the need, particularly at senior levels in organizations, for just-in-time support in learning and reflection, rather than just-in-case methods, such as classroom training.

Yet only 30 years ago, the concept of mentoring was confined to a very narrow set of circumstances. Although the process had its origins in the medieval concept of apprenticeship, mentors were for the most part a benefit for the privileged few. Princes, statesmen and military officers might be taken under the wing of a more experienced, more powerful patron, but ploughmen and ostlers were not normally in the picture. Mentoring had a strong association with the development of leadership skills that persists till this day. Daniel Levinson's groundbreaking book *Seasons of a Man's Life* painted a picture of young men constructing their careers with the aid of an older, more senior person, who would act as sponsor, guru, role model and adviser.

Since then, mentoring has expanded into almost every aspect of life, from helping young offenders back to the straight and narrow, to helping people at the end of their main careers phase into a healthy and rewarding retirement. Inherent in the concept is the notion of a transition – a movement from one state of being to another, whether that be in personal capability, position or some other area of achievement. In sport, mentoring has become the route to performance that transcends the merely good – while coaches work on the mechanical skills, mentors work on the bigger contextual picture, helping the individual build and draw on inner strengths they often do not realize they have. In the world of work, mentoring has become the pathway to wisdom – an opportunity to reflect and review in tranquility and an atmosphere of honesty with oneself.

The model of mentoring has changed radically in the non-US world. The sponsoring and hands-on career management elements of the mentor–protégé relationship have been replaced by a learning alliance, where the mentor often acquires as much insight as the mentee (not an attractive word, but it emphasizes that this is not a protection relationship) and where the focus is on helping the learner achieve independence and self-reliance.

Along with this rapid expansion has come a mass (some would say a morass) of definitions and applications of mentoring. To some extent, definitions do not matter greatly, if those in the roles of mentor and mentee have a clear and mutual understanding of what is expected of them and what they should in turn expect of their mentoring partner. But some kind of definitional standard is important in bringing order to the chaos of academic study, where so much of the literature is invalidated, in whole or part, because it is not clear what kind of relationships are being measured, nor whether the expectations of different dyads (or even participants in the same dyad) are similar. Equally, those designing and managing structured mentoring programmes need guidance in how best to prepare mentors and mentees for the role. Lack of clarity about what effective mentors do frequently leads to training that is inadequate in both content and quantity. It is very common for senior managers and even some senior human resource professionals to assume, for example, that executives can simply pick up the skills of mentoring with only the briefest of briefings, on the grounds that these are no more than the leadership skills they should already have. In reality, most executives have a significant amount of unlearning to do before they become truly effective as mentors.

Mentoring practice is made even more complex by the need to adapt it to the cultural norms around the world. People who have grown up in a high power-distance culture (one where respect for authority is deeply ingrained) such as Malaysia or Indonesia may find challenging and confronting much more difficult than their counterparts in, say, northern Europe. Those organizations that have attempted to impose one style of mentoring across all their international operations, have typically not met with great success. It is very easy to dismiss an approach as 'not right', without recognizing that within its cultural context it may be appropriate. I recall being horrified at a US company that issued mentors and mentees with a discussion sheet each month, telling them what to talk about in their regular meetings. How could such relationships generate spontaneity and depth? It took some while for me to recognize that the aim here was a very narrow, educational agenda and that the culture of the organization was prescriptive and bureaucratic. In all probability, the mentors would have struggled to cope with a more holistic agenda, and perhaps felt too lacking in confidence to participate in the programme. (I still think this was a missed opportunity to *change* the culture, however!)

Given these factors, it is perhaps not surprising that, in recent years, the perception of mentor competences has evolved, from an assumption that all or most of the skills required are generic, to a recognition that they are, in large part, situational. The skills required of an adult assisting an underachieving schoolchild are not the same as those needed by the mentor working with a senior corporate executive, for example.

The rationale for this particular collection of writings, therefore, begins with a need for both greater clarity and greater acceptance of different perspectives and approaches. Behind this rationale are a number of other reasons. In particular:

- *Most mentors want to do it right.* Whenever we conduct review sessions with mentors who have been doing the role for a few months – and sometimes with people who have been doing it for many years – I am struck by the humility so many of them have about their competence for the task. Delivering value for the mentee and for the organization is important to them. An observation, which I believe to be accurate, is that the more effective they have been as mentors, the greater their feeling that they still have a lot to learn (and vice versa). It is the ineffective mentor who thinks he has the role sussed!
- *The high rate of relationship failure* in some schemes appears to be directly related to inadequate attention to preparing mentors and mentees for the role and, once a relationship has been created, to supporting the pair with further opportunities to reflect upon good practice. While relationship failure can be the result of personality clashes, mentor competence is a more frequent antecedent, from our field observation.
- *Having a mentoring programme is no longer enough.* On the student milk round, prospective recruits are no longer just asking whether there is a mentoring programme. They also want to know how good it is. Many graduate mentoring programmes have been allowed to drift along, with little measurement of impact, and minimal commitment from middle and senior managers, because they have generally been seen as a good thing. Suddenly, there is an expectation that these programmes should deliver real value to those who participate in them. In the same way, more and more organizations are tying their programmes in general to business objectives, and are wanting real results.

THE BROADER ISSUE OF STANDARDS

The issue of standards in mentoring has arisen for two reasons. Firstly, the rapid spread of mentoring programmes aimed at young and vulnerable people requires close attention to risk management, and government-supported programmes require standards as an element of impact measurement. Secondly, the rapid growth of executive coaching and mentoring inevitably gives rise to calls for regulation, given that anyone can claim to have the necessary skills and experience. The increasing volume of qualifications offered in coaching and mentoring does not necessarily help, as they tend not to be specific about the level of competence required (length of experience does not equate to quality of performance!), nor about the audience-specific factors that may demand additional competences (for example, knowledge of cognitive development and skills in behaviour management for mentors of children and persons with special needs.)

There does, however, seem to be room for a generic or core set of mentoring standards, which will apply with minimal adaptation to most or all situations and to which situation-specific competences can be added as appropriate. One valiant attempt to do this is the *Draft Occupational Standards on Mentoring*, produced by the University of North London, in association with a variety of other academic and practitioner bodies. This was evaluated in over 300 mentoring schemes in all sectors of education, government and business.

More recently, a set of standards for mentoring programmes has been generated and subjected to public consultation with the assistance of the European Mentoring and Coaching Council.

Standards codify competences into a framework that can be used to assess how well an individual performs against them. The virtue of such a framework is that it provides a structure upon which evidence of competence can be gathered, in terms of both knowledge and effective practice. Unlike most qualification-based programmes, they provide an objective, independent measure. How useful that measure is depends on how credible the standards are perceived to be by programme participants and organizations using mentoring. It is probably fair to say that the jury is still out on this issue.

The Situational Mentor does not attempt to predict or establish standards for mentoring, even in specific contexts. The fact that there are so many behaviours identified, by so many eminent scholars and practitioners, suggests that a prescriptive approach to standard-setting would not easily encompass the wide church of applications and cultural adaptations. Our goal is rather to explore the rich tapestry of mentor behaviours and to attempt to extract those that contribute to the initiation, maintenance and eventual dissolution of successful learning relationships. From these, we hope, the informed reader will be able to make his or her own decisions about what constitutes a relevant and valuable competence in the context of their scheme or relationship.

WHAT YOU CAN EXPECT TO FIND IN *THE SITUATIONAL MENTOR*

In this book, we bring together in one volume the perspectives of most of the leading thinkers in mentoring, both academics and practitioners, from around the world. *The Situational Mentor* is aimed at the hundreds of thousands of people in all walks of life who take on the role of mentor, at co-ordinators of mentoring programmes and at HR professionals in general, who may, for example, need to oversee the use of external mentors, or who simply want to improve their understanding of the mentoring phenomenon.

Chapter 1, *Key themes*, is a literature review, by Gill Lane, who explores the dominant themes about what mentors do, which emerge from the thousands of articles and dissertations written about mentoring in the past two decades. The word 'competence' occurs but rarely in this mass of literature; most behavioural checklists seem to be drawn from a mixture of post-event reported behaviours and anecdote, rather than from observation. There also seems to be a multitude of approaches to defining what good mentors do. It is also clear that mentoring is a *situational* competence – one where the context affects the required skill set considerably – and this is a theme both editors explore in their respective subsequent chapters.

Chapter 2, *The moral dimension of mentoring*, explores the different theories of morality and how they are applied in the business context. The extent to which moral values are required for effective mentoring is investigated, and there is a test at the end of the chapter designed to help readers view their own opinions of the extent to which morals are involved in good mentoring practice.

Chapter 3, *Characteristics ascribed to mentors by their protégés* is the report of an Australian study, in which data from almost 2000 people was factor-analysed and yielded eight factors, each of which describe a cluster of mentor characteristics – Authenticity, Volatility, Nurturance, Approachability, Competence, Inspiration, Conscientiousness and Hard-working. Standardized scale scores were developed from factors and used to examine the extent various people differed with respect to the characteristics ascribed to their significant mentor.

In Chapter 4, *Mentor competences: a field perspective*, David Clutterbuck pulls together the strands of observation from mentors and mentees both before and during mentoring relationships. The chapter offers two structures for defining mentor competences: one based on the five evolutionary stages of a successful mentoring relationship; the other a more generic portfolio of pairs of competences.

In Chapter 5, *A quantitative view of mentor competence*, Gill Lane gives details of a quantitative study undertaken with a range of organizations, with mentors, mentees and academics interested in mentoring, to consider the core skills and competences – both behavioural and personal competences – that make effective mentors.

Chapter 6, *What about mentee competences?*, starts from the assumption that the mentee has a considerable potential to influence the receipt of mentoring, the way the relationship is managed and its outcomes. David Clutterbuck explores how mentees can make it harder or easier for the mentor and suggests a progressive framework of competences that parallel the development of the relationship.

In Chapter 7, *Competences of building the developmental relationship*, Terri Scandura and Ekin Pellegrini delve into attachment theory and the issues of dependency and counter-dependency, from both mentor and mentee perspectives.

In Chapter 8, *Development and supervision for mentors*, David Megginson and Paul Stokes provide practical approaches to developing mentor competences within structured programmes.

In Chapter 9, *Insights from the psychology of executive and life coaching*, Anthony Grant discusses how the competences of mentoring fit within the broader framework of psychology.

In Chapter 10, *Developmental relationships: a mentoring approach to organizational learning and knowledge creation*, Liz Borredon and Marc Ingham explore competences in building the mentoring relationship. Using a case study as illustration, they consider how the mentor stimulates a network of learning relationships within an organization.

In Chapter 11, *The mentor as storyteller*, Margaret Parkin looks at the roles of storytellers throughout history, and gives an insight into the various ways in which the skills of the storyteller aid the learning and development of the individual. Examples of how the storyteller's skills are appropriate for the effective mentor are also featured.

In Chapter 12, *Variation in mentoring outcomes: an effect of personality factors?*, Truls Engstrom explores the outcomes of mentoring relationships against the background of personality measurements of the participants – both mentor and mentee. Concluding that some personality factors are more conducive to relationship success than others; and that the personality mix between mentor and mentee is an important contributory factor.

Chapter 13, *Virtual mentoring*, investigates the capabilities required when mentoring at a distance, by e-mail (e-mentoring). Ellen Fagenson-Eland and Rachel Lu recognize the difficulties and the advantages of relationships, where face-to-face meetings are rare or non-existent.

Intriguingly, their collaboration in writing the chapter involved considerable e-mentoring and enriched their conclusions.

In Chapter 14, *When mentoring goes wrong...*, Bob Garvey explores the competence issue from the perspective of schemes and relationships that fail. In particular, he discusses the importance of early dialogue within the mentoring pair to establish a mutual understanding of the context and the expectations each party brings.

Chapter 15, *All good things must come to an end: winding up and winding down a mentoring relationship*, looks at the behaviours necessary to achieve a successful conclusion to a mentoring relationship. David Clutterbuck and David Megginson compare the experiences of winding up (a planned, clear transition) and winding down (a gradual dissolution), and find that the former is more closely associated with relationship satisfaction.

Finally, in Chapter 16, *What have we learned from this book?*, we attempt to pull together the threads from the various chapters to extract lessons for practitioners and to provide a research agenda for academics. In some ways, this is the most difficult task we as editors faced, because the various approaches described all depict mentoring from a different perspective. Indeed, the breadth of ways of understanding mentoring and what makes it work in different circumstances is perhaps the dominant theme of this collection. Mentoring is a powerful intervention precisely because it is so complex a phenomenon.

Among the many metaphors for mentoring, one in particular appeals to us in compiling the chapters for *The Situational Mentor* – that of poetry. Poetry is communication at a deeper level of meaning than normal discourse. Each reader or hearer extracts their own meaning. And the beauty and strength of mentoring can be so easily destroyed by being too analytical, too bureaucratic, too measured and evaluated. As the poet John Keats wrote in his poem *Lamia* (1884):

> *'There was an awful rainbow once in heaven:*
>
> *We know her woof, her texture; she is given*
>
> *In the dull catalogue of common things.'*

What we have tried to do in this book is reflect the richness and diversity of mentoring without reducing it to the mechanical or lowest common denominator. Mentoring should never be dull – indeed, it cannot be if it is to succeed – and its purpose is to rise above the commonplace, enabling people to achieve beyond their expectations. Perhaps the greatest skill for a mentor is to preserve that small sense of wonder both during the formal relationship and long after it has ended.

Several chapters in this book begin with the author introducing and defining the concept of mentoring. Due to the complexity of this concept, as explored above, each author has referred to what mentoring means to him or her, therefore defining their own perspective on their research.

Further, the use of the different terms 'protégé' and 'mentee' appear frequently through the text and can be explained in that 'protégé' tends to be used in a sponsorship type of mentoring relationship. 'Mentee' is more common in the developmental style of mentoring.

1 Key themes: a literature review

GILL LANE

The elder penguins would take the younger penguins under their wings and coach them on how to be successful

Hateley and Schmidt, 1995

Mentors have a diverse range of roles and thus an equally diverse and complex range of associated activities and underlying competences. Roles and activities of mentors are the first step to uncovering the variety of competences that underlie effectiveness, and much has been written in the literature about roles and activities. It is only more recently that we begin to see attempts at detailing competence. As such this chapter explores:

- the roles and activities of mentors from various literature sources
- some considered critical success factors through the literature that make for effectiveness as a mentor
- suggestions for ways that mentor competence could be measured
- the use of different roles and activities (and therefore presumably different competences) for different mentor situations.

ROLES AND ACTIVITIES

Examining the literature, one is struck by the number and variety of roles and activities that mentors perform – the list at first seems endless. Then as you read more it is clear, and not surprising, that the list predominantly includes many helping-type functions together with supporting roles. It is a mixture of functional approaches and characteristics. It includes some organizational knowledge and considerable ability at handling people. All writers on what mentors actually do list a host of activities undertaken and, whilst it is hard to see any key themes emerging within the activities, some do give attempts at a breakdown of key areas of focus.

Julie Hay, in her text *Transformational Mentoring* (1995), refers to the complex range of activities that mentors may undertake – guiding, being a role model, utilizing experience and knowledge, listening to mentees' ideas, talking through career issues, together with coaching and counselling. Similar activities are acknowledged by Leeds Metropolitan University (1995)

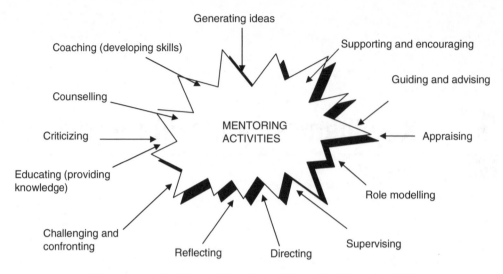

Figure 1.1 Mentoring activities (Leeds Metropolitan University, 1995)

from their research work published in their report *Mentoring: the 'Working for a Degree' project*: Final project report Vol 1, Jan 1995 and shown in Figure 1.1.

Clutterbuck (2001) comments that the more recent origins of mentoring lie in the concept of apprenticeship where the mentor is deemed to be the older, more experienced person who passes down his or her knowledge to a more junior person, not necessarily in a direct line relationship. As a role model the mentor acts as a:

- guide
- tutor
- coach
- confidant.

Clutterbuck (1998) tells us more about the role model, that in practice this always takes place in any one-to-one learning relationship with the possibility of 'transference' from one person to the other.

A survey on women mentors (Vincent and Seymour, 1995) indicates female mentors are a role model for other women. Gender role models are endorsed by Gladstone (1988) with reference to the way that women as mentors can act as a role model for women in business careers. The Arnold and Davidson (1990) study of 30 UK managers indicated that the mentor acting as a role model was important with 'same gender' mentors.

Functional activities alone do not constitute the full range of role requirements of a mentor, and personal characteristics are equally important. Hay (1995) indicates such characteristics as trust, respect, ethical approach, coupled with qualities such as self-awareness and self-development, and that attitude is important.

Distinct aspects of the role in both functional approaches and personal characteristics of the mentor are highlighted by Caruso (1992). (This provides a strong link with the competence aspects covered later in this chapter when one talks of functional and behavioural competence as the 'doing' and 'being' type competence essential for the mentor.) Caruso provides detail of major research undertaken by PA Associates in 1986 at Motorola on a survey of senior managers across eight countries. From a sample size of 2000 with a response rate of 19 per cent, Caruso shows the study highlights the importance of mentoring in terms of career development. In addition, he draws from studies analysed by the International Centre for Mentoring, based in Vancouver, which in turn drew data from 500 published articles, 225 conference papers, 150 doctoral dissertations, 65 books and 150 mentoring programme descriptions. Caruso was thus able to define a mentor as having:

- attributes (such as knowledge, experience, power)
- roles (coach, counsellor, teacher, guide, sponsor)
- functions (teaching, career assistance, counselling).

Clutterbuck (1985), Parsloe (1992), Caruso (1992) and Baird (1993) have drawn similar conclusions on the role of a mentor being that of giving advice and direction, providing support and encouragement, and acting as a critical friend and confidant.

Clutterbuck (2001) defines the role as having three distinct areas, these being:

- to encourage and motivate the mentee
- to nurture the mentee to develop
- to teach the mentee relevant skills and promote their learning potential.

He also places mutual respect as a key ingredient.

The Open University study (Open University Quality Support Centre, 1995) outlined the mentor roles as being befriending; role modelling; coaching; career guidance; supervising; counselling; facilitating; assessing, designing and managing learning; and playing a liaison role. In an article entitled 'Are you mentor material?', Dianne Molvig (1995) suggests that a mentor combines the roles of coach, advisor, counsellor, advocate, teacher and friend. She suggests that the exact mix of roles varies from one person to another and that this is dependent on individual style and the situation. She does state that a crucial point is that 'true' mentoring should be more than any one of these roles. A 'true' mentor is also referred to by Kalpna Parag (1995), who said that 'a true mentor is an advisor, guide and friend'.

Hoschette (1995) reminds us that the dictionary defines a mentor as a 'wise and trusted counsellor or teacher'. He considers that one should consult a mentor in 'difficult times' in addition to utilizing mentors as sounding boards for new ideas and new approaches to problems that may arise.

Parsloe (1992) agreed with Clutterbuck's reference (1985, 2001) to the mentor being a guide in addition to other activities, but added activities of advising and counselling. Clutterbuck (1985, 2001) included activities of encouraging, motivating, nurturing and teaching, and in terms of these being 'helping' type functions Caruso (1992) refers to activities highlighted by Kram (1988) and Noe (1988), who mention 'help functions' being in two district categories of career development activities and personal help activities. In addition, he refers to a third category raised by Alleman (1982) – the 'teaching help function'. From Caruso's own review of mentoring literature, the activities or functions that mentors repeatedly performed fell into the three same categories, that is:

- teaching
- career development
- personal help.

He outlined the key activities as being those of coaching, counselling, teaching, guiding and being a sponsor in addition to offering experience and knowledge, and giving career assistance. Mumford (1989) also talks of the sponsor role with his reference to the 'door opener' approach providing opportunities for the mentee.

Being a 'friend', 'supportive friend', 'critical friend', 'wise and trusted friend' and 'confidante' are activities mentioned by Baird (1993), Clutterbuck (1985) and Simosko (1991). Collaboration and acting as a 'critical friend' are roles introduced by John Baird in Caldwell and Carter's text (1993), who see the role as being applied in three ways: that of consultant, co-researcher and friend. Gardner (1997) in her study into 'professional friendship' suggests objectivity and safety within the mentoring relationship, with trust and confidentiality being central.

Advisory- and assessing-type activities came forward from Simosko (1991) and Parsloe (1992) with advisory added by Clutterbuck (1985). The counselling activity is endorsed by Clutterbuck (1985), Caruso (1992) and Parsloe (1992), but Simosko (1991) considers counselling to be an inappropriate activity, preferring to keep the relationship on a more professional level, as she considers there may be a tendency for a mentor to become too involved in the mentee's life. Thus she places emphasis on the mentor as a resource rather than a counsellor. This view is shared by Levinson *et al.* (1978).

A study of 30 UK managers by Arnold and Davidson (1990) showed that the most important mentor activity was that of encouragement. Within the 30, a total of 20 female managers referred to their lack of confidence, and the help and support provided by their mentor.

The vast range of mentor activities is acknowledged by Shea (1995), who states that the core of mentoring is a developmental, caring, sharing, helping relationship where one person invests their time, knowledge, experience and energy in increasing and improving another person's growth, knowledge and skills.

The need to draw from one's own experience as a mentor is endorsed by William Barry (1995). He suggests that the more experienced should be willing to teach or become a mentor to inexperienced colleagues. Utilizing coaching techniques a mentor can help a mentee to develop reflective and problem-solving expertise whilst being able to clarify and probe responses and remain non-judgemental (Barnett, 1995). Marilyn Kennedy (1994) also talks of the coaching approach of the mentor in her paper 'Good coach, bad coach' and in particular of the need for 'objective' feedback, something that she recognizes a mentor can provide.

With such an exhaustive list of roles and activities, and with the advent of the competence debate across many organizations, it is natural that a number of writers have started to consider the underlying skills, knowledge, functional and personal behaviours that make up competences for mentors.

EFFECTIVENESS

Whether we look at roles and activities or at competence, perhaps what really matters is the list of activities, functions and characteristics that make for an effective mentor.

Clutterbuck (1985, 2001) suggests that a good mentoring relationship is one where *mentor and mentee have mutual respect*, recognize their need for personal development and have at least some idea of where they want the relationship to go. The mentor should manage the balance between his normal job function and that of being a mentor, must encourage and motivate the mentee, nurture the mentee to help their development, teach them relevant skills and promote their learning potential.

Allen Walker and Ken Stott (Caldwell and Carter, 1993) suggest that the key to successful mentoring is in the establishment of a good relationship between mentor and mentee. In terms of activities, this puts an onus on the mentor to work at establishing rapport from the outset. (For stages of a mentoring relationship, see Clutterbuck elsewhere in this text plus Gray's model (1988) at the end of this chapter.) Baird (Caldwell and Carter, 1993) referred to 'collaboration' and the 'shared adventure'. Clutterbuck (1985) suggests that both mentor and mentee need some idea of where they 'want to go'. Promotional literature by Roffey Park (1994) refers to the need for the mentor to avoid time-wasting meetings. Mumford (1989) suggests that caution is needed in the relationship whilst Levinson *et al.* (1978) suggested the need for an alliance. Parsloe (1992) considered that the relationship should be kept on a professional level, particularly where cross-gender mentoring was taking place. Caruso (1992) felt that the different approach in a closed mentoring arrangement (one assigned mentor) compared to an open mentoring arrangement (many self-chosen mentors depending on the various needs of the mentee) would have differing impacts on the relationship. Zey (1984) studied the relationship between mentoring and career mobility through interviews with over 100 executives, and concluded that mentoring is a powerful factor in career advancement.

Knippen and Green (1991) consider it essential that the mentor understands the mentoring process, initiates mentoring opportunities, makes the most of mentoring situations and formalizes the mentoring relationship.

Qualities an effective mentor possesses are that they should be:

- good teachers
- good coaches
- compatible with their trainees
- patient
- available.

These five qualities come from Kalpna Parag (1995), who also considers that mentors should not tell trainees what to do or rescue them every time they make a mistake.

Howe (1995) considers that to be effective a mentor must want to 'give of themselves' in order to advance the interests of someone else. She suggests that the relationship therefore calls for a bond which cannot be artificially forged. In addition the underlying philosophy of the mentor is often a determinant in how successful the mentor might be in providing valuable guidance.

Mentoring helps individuals to take charge of their own development. Barnett (1995) considers that an important function of mentoring is to assist the 'protégés' in becoming autonomous professionals who are able to reflect and to solve problems presented to them from an expert viewpoint. He considers that the mentor helps the mentee to become 'expert' and is an essential component in helping the individual mentee as a learner to grasp the 'higher-order' conceptual skills. To help the mentees to help themselves would seem to be at the core of mentor effectiveness. Scott Ambler (1994) also considers that the 'good mentor' only helps in the development, the majority of the effort being performed by the mentees, with the mentor providing expertise and advice.

The aspect of the mentor being more effective in a supporting role is further endorsed by Hagenow and McCrea (1994) who say that a mentor should not provide answers, but should ask the right questions together with listening rather than talking, and be strong enough to expose one's vulnerability.

The action of challenging the mentee as a way of encouraging their interest in themselves and stimulating self-development comes through from Baird (Caldwell and Carter, 1993) in his model 'A conceptualization of effective mentoring', shown in Figure 1.2 below. With such a challenge, the mentor needs to stimulate, motivate and build interest within the mentee, all factors promoted by Simosko (1991) in her reference to empowerment. Engendering confidence might be part of such an activity.

The effectiveness of the mentor is brought out by Baird (1993) in his model, where the mentor activities and the process lead to effective change and effective development. Caldwell and Carter (1993) refer to the mentor as requiring a personal repertoire of skills to be effective and Zey (1984) draws effectiveness through the strength of the individualized relationship between mentor and mentee. Effectiveness is an issue mentioned by Development Processes (1994), where they consider the effectiveness of the mentoring relationship depends on the mentor being able to establish a rapport, offer respect, be empathetic and show a genuine interest in the development of the mentee.

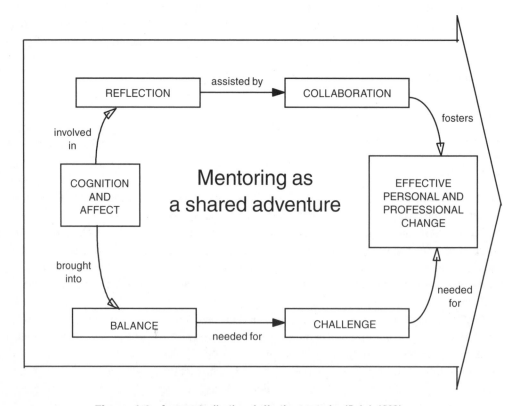

Figure 1.2 A conceptualization of effective mentoring (Baird, 1993)

The Open University study (Open University Quality Support Centre, 1995) suggested that not all people possess the skills necessary to perform effectively as a mentor. The researchers considered that an expert mentor might be expected to possess and demonstrate that they had strong interpersonal skills, including negotiating, listening, feedback skills, intervention skills, questioning, motivation and self-awareness, and be able to both coach and teach. In addition, the expert mentor should have organizational skills, including contracting, recording, structuring of sessions, time management, evaluating, assessing, report-writing, maintaining boundaries plus working with learning contracts and action plans. The mentor should show organizational knowledge, have 'exemplary' supervisory skills, possess personal power and charisma as well as having status and prestige. With a willingness to be responsible for another person's development they should be able to share credit, be patient but also willing to take risks and have appropriate technical competence.

CONSIDERATION OF MENTOR COMPETENCE

With so many roles and activities outlined irrespective of the effectiveness of mentors, the attempts at demonstrating potential mentor competence have been limited. Research started to emerge in recent years with people such as Carter (1994), Carter and Lewis (1994), the Open University Quality Support Centre (1995), Lane (1996) and Clutterbuck (2001). When one looks, however, at text and articles on mentoring arrangements, one begins to amass information on roles, activities and practices of a mentor, thus leading to a picture of the underlying requirements of a competent mentor. It is from such generalities that a more comprehensive list of competence requirements can be established.

In addition to the roles of a mentor, plus general activities and issues surrounding the building and maintaining of a good workable relationship between mentor and mentee, the text references indicate various skill approaches such as counselling and coaching. These skill areas can themselves be dissected to differentiate the various competence components that make up, for example, a competent coach. It is possible therefore, to add further dimensions of competence, given that each mentor activity may in itself contain a number of competences; for example, a competent coach would need to be a good listener in addition to possessing many other skills and abilities. By considering the activities of a mentor in this way, one can begin to understand the diverse nature of the underlying competence required of the role holder.

Carter (1994) and Carter and Lewis (1994) asked: what do mentors do? They came up with seven elements of competence including: knowledge of the organization to facilitate learning; communication; establishing support; giving feedback; overseeing learning; recording; and creating interaction. From these results they outline four areas of focus, which they refer to as 'bases' of mentoring, these being:

- organizational
- interpersonal
- development
- context.

With the Open University study (Open University Quality Support Centre, 1995) the researchers undertook a functional analysis approach to break down the component functions associated with mentor roles to show that mentors were required to undertake a variety of functions – a variety of competences (Table 1.1).

Research into the competence set for senior management by Lane and Robinson (1992) led Lane (1996) to explore the potential for initially developing a suite of competences essential for senior managers to be effective mentors. What emerged showed that the competence set was the same irrespective of level of seniority but that personal competence by way of characteristics of mentors rated more highly than the functional/behavioural competence set (further details can be found in Chapter 5).

Clutterbuck (2001) outlines ten mentor competences:

- self-awareness (understanding self)
- behavioural awareness (understanding others)
- business or professional savvy
- sense of proportion/good humour

Table 1.1   Open University study: development of workplace mentors – functional analysis

Mentor roles	Component functions
Core	• Contribute to quality of learning
	• Promote equality for all
	• Contribute to health and safety of learners in the workplace
Befriending/role model	• Show sensitivity to others' needs
	• Relate to others
	• Present oneself positively
	• Show self-confidence and drive
	• Manage emotions and stress
Coaching	• Facilitate opportunities for learning for individual groups
Career guidance	• Provide information and materials
Supervising	• Carry out work-based advice and guidance on a one-to-one basis
Counselling	• Provide learning opportunities and support
Facilitating	• Provide workplace induction
Assessing	• Supervise work placement performance
Designing and managing learning	• Assist learners in clarifying aims and objectives
	• Enable learners to decide on a course of action
	• Assist learners to plan the implementation of the course of action
	• Identify and structure individual and group learning requirements and opportunities
Liaison	• Provide information on the effectiveness and efficiency of work placement learning
	• Contribute to new developments in workplace learning

- communication competence
- conceptual modelling
- commitment to their own continued learning
- strong interest in developing others
- building and maintaining rapport/relationship management
- goal clarity.

A further development of this was presented by Clutterbuck and Ragins (2002) where they considered five pairs of competences to be needed by mentors in a business context. Here they linked self-awareness with behavioural awareness; business or professional shrewdness with a good sense of proportion; communication ability with conceptual modelling; commitment to their own learning with a strong interest in developing others; and relationship management skills with ability to set and pursue goals. The overall text is about diversity and as such they suggest that an additional competence is one of being willing to accept and value alternative cultures and perspectives, and then translate those experiences from one background to another.

SITUATION-SPECIFIC SKILLS

Whilst the vast range of activities can be viewed as generic there are particular situations in which writers suggest that certain mentor skills apply more than others. Given that different competences underpin the differing roles and activities and different parts of the mentoring process, then it could be presumed that different situations may require different competences from mentors. The situations mentioned here are merely examples and mentors may have others to draw upon. We can view the situations in a number of ways, and here we have:

- situation by extent of mentor interaction, such as personal development, career development or current role focus
- situation by type of mentee, be it by sector, by profession or by level within the organization (the latter affecting power distance)
- situation by how far into the phases of the mentoring relationship the mentoring has progressed.

SITUATION BY MENTOR INTERACTION

Here we have three scenarios of the mentor taking a career development role, helping the mentee with their current role focus, and adopting a personal development role.

Career development

Looking first at career development, Farren, Grey and Kaye (1984) suggest that mentoring is a 'boon to career development' and that career development programmes benefit by the addition of a mentor. This is further strengthened by Mumford (1989) who talks of a 'door opener' role in which the mentor provides opportunities for the mentee, in other words, acting as a sponsor to help the mentee.

A mentor scheme run by the National Mentoring Consortium aims to bridge the gap between university and employment. Both mentors and mentees are from ethnic minority backgrounds as a way of helping mentees gain skills and move into the working world. One of the aims of the mentor scheme is to help the mentee increase their own awareness of the different types of career and preparation needed to be able to apply for those careers (Equal Opportunities Review, 1995).

The career developer activities are raised by Caruso (1992) and Schein (1978), with Parsloe (1992) talking of the guiding activities in relation to professional development, and again Parsloe (1992), Caruso (1992) and Clutterbuck (1985) plus Schein (1978) referring to the activities of coaching in relation to career development and enhancement.

Supporting the mentee in career aspects is an activity mentioned by Baird (1993), whilst and Parsloe (1992) and Lane and Robinson (1992) mention the importance of the supporting function.

Kram and Isabella (1985) talk of the career-enhancing function of the mentor. Arnold (1997) considers the management of careers into the twenty-first century, conceding that mentoring is currently a popular career management approach. He considers mentoring to consist of a more and a less experienced person forming a relationship for the more experienced to help the less. The mentor role of being an advocate, protector and counsellor Arnold sees as possible career management interventions.

The activities of being the 'opener of doors' and taking a networking approach together with the political activities in helping a mentee to understand the organizational dynamics would also go with the activities of the sponsor, helping and supporting the mentee, particularly in relation to career development. Both Mumford (1989) and Schein (1978) talk of the mentor acting as sponsor and as 'opener of doors'. Caruso (1992) mentions the sponsor activities and refers to the mentor being in a position of power in helping the mentee in the organization.

A study of 10 male and 20 female managers in the UK (Arnold and Davidson, 1990) showed that the majority of both male and female managers found their mentors to be important for introducing them to the formal network of organizational politics, helping to enhance their career opportunities in addition to providing support in their current role.

Kram and Isabella, (1985) described the career-enhancing developmental functions of the mentor as being the activities of sponsorship; coaching; exposure and visibility; protection and challenging work assignments.

Where an individual has been attending a formal external development or qualification programme, they may have been allocated an academic tutor who might provide an 'academic mentor' role. Parsloe (1992) considers there are three distinct roles, including the professional qualification mentor required by a professional body to guide a student through a course of study and the vocational qualification mentor appointed to guide a candidate through a programme of competence development (his third role being that of the mainstream mentor who acts as guide, adviser and counsellor).

Current role focus

Similar activities are found when one looks at the actions of a mentor concentrating on developing the mentee in their current role within an organization. Coaching remains a key activity, as already credited to Clutterbuck (1985), Parsloe (1992), Caruso (1992) and Schein (1978). To this one might add such elements as teaching job-related skills (Caruso, 1992; Schein, 1978) and training the mentee in on-the-job activities (Clutterbuck, 1985; Parsloe, 1992; Caruso, 1992; Schein, 1978).

Supporting again is a key activity with regard to mentoring for a focus on the mentee's current role, as outlined by Baird (1993), Parsloe (1992) and Lane and Robinson (1992). The directing activity comes through from Simosko (1991), with the need for the mentor to provide information, advice and guidance whilst not being overprotective.

Simosko (1991) also talks of the mentor developing the mentee's on-the-job talent and providing learning potential. This is endorsed by Clutterbuck (1985), Parsloe (1992), Mumford (1989) – with his references to the mentor understanding the learning processes and styles – and Schein (1978), plus the educative approaches outlined in the Leeds Metropolitan University report (1995).

Clarifying and agreeing action with the mentee is mentioned by Parsloe (1992). He talks particularly in respect of developing competence in relation to the mentee's current role. Baird (1993) talks of collaboration between mentor and mentee and this would be needed to agree appropriate action.

The activity of stimulating the mentee to want to undertake learning in relation to work-based activities, and the resultant building of confidence, are referred to by Lane and Robinson (1992). Again, the mentor draws from their own experiences to help the mentee in aspects of developing within their current job. These actions are highlighted by Clutterbuck (1985) and Caruso (1992), with Caruso adding the aspect of drawing from knowledge in addition to experience.

An important function of the mentor through the mentee's learning process is to provide the mentee with adequate and appropriate feedback, a view endorsed by Ribeaux and Poppleton (1978) and by Bennett (1992).

During 1994 Mainframe Consultancy (later to become part of Middlesex University Business School) undertook a Department for Education and Employment-funded project which, in conjunction with the Open University Quality Support Centre resulted in the document *Signposts for Staff Development (2): Workplace mentors* (1995). The project looked at developing guidance for supporting learners in the workplace, and the document on workplace mentors was part of a three-part series. The document is intended as a guide for developing mentors and provides a basis for analysing the function of work-based learning within a programme of learning, and the role of mentoring in support of such learning.

Here we could also consider the assessor role as a newer breed of mentor, particularly for work-based learning programmes, for example National Vocational Qualifications (NVQs), where assessment of the individual is a specific requirement of the mentor role. Where such emphasis is on work-based experiential competence development, then unless the mentor is conversant with the competence needed at that specific work base, they will be less effective and thus less able to assess the relevance of development to the work-based situation. The growth of interest in continuing professional development (CPD) by professional bodies and the need for a portfolio approach for assessment combine to place greater emphasis on the mentor as both supportive and grade assessor.

Perry (1991) endorses the assessor role and stresses the importance of support from the mentor, the confidentiality of mentor–mentee discussions and the need for accuracy by the mentee in submitting work-based evidence for the mentor to assess. Parsloe (1992) and Lane (1996) also talk of the assessor role.

Support to both the mentee and the organization across a range of management development areas is an important role for the mentor to play (Conway, 1995), with involvement in management development, communication improvement, succession planning, culture change, plus identification of key competences. Conway (1995) sees the involvement of the mentor as 'allowing an organization to keep pace with change and unleash individual potential and talent'.

Personal development

Kram in Torrington and Hall (1987) says that the mentor is involved in psychosocial functions, helping the mentee to enhance their competence, identity and managerial effectiveness.

Feedback, support and coaching are also important when working with the mentee in terms of their personal development. These, together with the activities of the mentor in helping build confidence within the mentee, are endorsed by Baird (1993), Parsloe (1992), Lane and Robinson (1992) Leeds Metropolitan University (1995) and Roffey Park (1994).

Counselling seems to play a strong part in helping the mentee with specific personal development, and Parsloe (1992) talks of this together with guiding and advising. Caruso (1992) refers to the counselling role and the need that the mentee has to obtain counselling for what he terms the 'personal help functions'. Simosko (1991), however, considers the counselling role too close and suggests a professional distancing.

Helping the mentee to decide appropriate action for enhancing personal development is suggested by Baird (1993) in his model (see Figure 1.2), where he shows both a reflective and a collaborative approach for effective personal change. Agreeing action is mentioned by Baird (1993) and Simosko (1991). Stimulating and encouraging the mentee are activities mentioned by Clutterbuck (1985), Simosko (1991) – in terms of encouraging but not being 'over-protective' – and Lane and Robinson (1992).

SITUATION BY TYPE OF MENTEE

There are a number of examples where writers suggest specific mentor activities – and thus competence – to help mentees in specific sectors, professions or occupations. A few of these are given below.

In the American legal profession (Templeton, 1996), experienced paralegals coach and mentor new paralegals in the early days of their careers. In addition, experienced paralegals use their own mentor insight to guide their rise in career steps and options. The mentor is often the key contact person to talk through various career aspects (Samborn, 1994).

Hoschette (1995) suggests that engineers have at least one technical mentor, plus others with business and political acumen. As assessor the mentor provides feedback on performance to the mentee both informally at meetings and formally through the Institute of Mechanical Engineering's Professional Development Scheme as outlined in the document *A Guide to Mentoring* (Institute of Mechanical Engineering, 1990).

The supportive role of the mentor is endorsed within the education of teachers. Findings of a research project on mentoring and teacher education in England and Wales (Bush and Coleman 1995) outline the importance of a mentor providing 'peer support' to a new headteacher to help adaptation to the new role.

Detailed data from a survey of public accounting employees (Scandura and Viator, 1994) was used to identify mentoring functions within public accounting. It was found that mentors in this sector had three separate roles of:

- social support
- career development
- role model.

Scandura and Viator (1994) again refer to support from the mentor plus the mentor acting as a 'partner'.

The Open University study (Open University Quality Support Centre, 1995) identified four models for mentoring of students:

- an apprenticeship model where the mentor acts as 'master'
- a competence model where the mentor acts as both supervisor and assessor
- a reflective model where the mentor becomes a reflective practitioner
- an informal model where the mentor acts as a sponsor or friend.

The activity of encouraging another is cited by Victoria Pasher (1995) when writing about women overcoming obstacles. She states that, according to a survey by the National Association of Insurance Women amongst its members, where women have opened their own agencies a key factor has been that of encouragement from a mentor. Gardner (1997) suggests that for women to gain empowerment at work it would be useful for them to adopt a friendship model in their professional relationships. Ragins and McFarlin (1990) express concern about the cross-gender mentoring role and suggest that care is needed in the mentor acting as a role model and in out-of-hours networking where cross-gender mentoring is taking place.

Supporting those on company graduate training schemes has been acknowledged as a mentor activity where the two, namely the mentor and graduate trainee, have been brought together. Mentors also work with undergraduates, as is the case with schemes organized through the National Mentoring Consortium. A national mentoring scheme was launched in 1994 for those from ethnic minorities and includes aims such as support to undergraduates through their studies, together with encouraging and preparing them for graduate training schemes. The mentors also become involved in helping employers recruit graduates (Equal Opportunities Review, 1995).

Female students are seen to enhance their professional business skills by having female role models who represent levels of high achievement in working situations, as shown by Williams (1982). Gladstone (1988) refers also to the role model gender mentoring of women mentors working with those women in nursing careers.

The University of East London in 1992 set up a pilot mentor scheme (Equal Opportunities Review, 1995) to address some of the barriers facing ethnic minority graduates in employment. One objective of their mentoring programmes is to provide role models who will encourage the mentees to maximize their potential.

Academic activities associated with mentoring can be found in details from academic institutions such as Henley Management College, where the mentor on its Doctor in Business Administration Programme serves as an 'editorial commentator' in addition to guiding the doctoral associates through the early parts of their programme of study. Lancaster University Management School refers to the mentor providing witness statements as part of the academic process. A similar view is adopted by Huddersfield Polytechnic, where the mentor undertakes academic assessment and guides the student into self-assessment of work-based learning projects.

SITUATION BY PHASE OF MENTORING RELATIONSHIP

The final part of the situational examples is that different mentoring approaches, and thus underlying competence, apply at differing stages of the mentoring relationship.

The natural life cycle of the mentoring relationship is described by Leeds Metropolitan University (1995) as having four definable stages these being initial orientation, getting established ('adolescent' stage), performing ('mature' stage) and ending.

The Leeds study found that more experienced mentors acknowledged that the mentor–mentee relationship adjusts as it continues through these four stages, and the mentor activities adjust accordingly. At the outset the mentor is more proactive, supporting and encouraging but as the learner develops independence, confidence and autonomy, the mentor needs to be more critical, challenging and confrontational, encouraging reflection. It is important for mentors to strike a balance between providing support and being confrontational.

Gray (1988) gives us a different model of the 'Five-phase mentoring model for career development', the phases, themes and activities of which are reproduced as Table 1.2 below. We can see from this Gray's suggestions as to the mentor interventions at each stage.

Table 1.2 Gray's (1988) five-phase mentoring model (taken from Caruso, 1992)

Phase	I	II	III	IV	V
Main theme	Prescriptive	Persuasive	Collaborative	Conformative	Independent
Type of activity	Mentor directs protégé	Mentor leads and guides protégé	Mentor participates jointly with protégé	Mentor delegates to protégé	Protégé achieves functional independence

SUMMARY

This chapter has attempted to give only some examples of the roles and activities of mentors, drawn from the variety of literature on the subject, and concludes that a vast array of such roles and activities are suggested. It then draws from those writers the idea of effectiveness in mentoring.

Underlying competence is still a new area in respect of literature on mentoring but continues to develop as writers outline the underpinning skills, knowledge and abilities required. There is further scope for capturing competence in detail by those who appreciate the underlying complexity.

Context is relevant too. The situational examples demonstrate the variety of mentor interventions that apply to different applications, be they the focus of mentoring by extent of coverage, the type of mentoring by profession, or specific skills at specific stages of the mentoring process.

The literature already provides us with many examples of roles, activities and the effectiveness of mentors from various practical experiences of the writers. There is scope for extending the literature on competence as this is further developed. There is also scope for considering the vast range of situation-specific skills of the mentor in context. Both of these would be valuable to many developing their mentoring ability.

2 The moral dimension of mentoring

STEPHEN GIBB

Mentoring is a simple relationship in a complicated world. For those who see the simplicity it is best to define the parts, the capabilities and conditions which inform effective mentoring, and seek to disseminate these as widely as possible. But for those who see the complications there is more to mentoring than this. It is then necessary to elaborate frameworks and seek to explore mentoring as sensibly and as fully as these frameworks allow. Such frameworks from psychoanalysis, gender relations, network theory, power relations and organizational culture have all been used to this end, to explain mentoring and its significance as part of a more complicated world.

NOW IMAGINE THIS...

It's a cold, dark November morning, and there are three managers in a company, Jim, Sarah and John, who have gathered in the conference room for a meeting. There has been a decline in sales for their once dominant product line. They are discussing heatedly how to deal with this. The inquest on why events have reached this state has abated, and the focus is now the detail of a possible organizational restructuring. As they discuss this, each has a different set of concerns at the back of their mind.

Jim has in his mind the problems that will ensue if things cannot be turned around, for the whole organization will go bankrupt. Some jobs will have to be sacrificed, but that has to be minimized. He can sense Sarah's resistance to this, but is finding it hard to make much sense of what John is arguing.

Sarah is mulling over what ought to be done to minimize any job losses; perhaps new products could be launched quickly, to avoid making anyone redundant. She has been made redundant before and would not want anyone to go through that if it could be avoided. She is surprised that John is supporting her ideas on the one hand, because she had heard from another source that he had ridiculed these suggestions in meetings with his own staff. And he is also supporting Jim's suggestions. It does not really make sense.

John, meanwhile, is busily calculating how his department may be exposed by any restructuring or quick new product launches, and figuring out what he can do to avoid that. He has been condoning false accounting for years, in order to keep things looking good in his department. He is figuring out how to play things so that his department is not subject to any hard scrutiny. He is also thinking about being able to put enough spin on the story of this company's failure (he has decided the game is over here) so that when he moves to his next job (and he will move as soon as he can) he will come up smelling of roses. He can tell that Jim and Sarah have opposing ideas, and he hopes to play them off against each other enough to paralyse any analysis until he has gone.

Which one of these managers has had the best mentor?

WHY MORALITY?

I believe that most readers would pick Jim as having had the best mentor. This is the 'right' managerial approach after all, taking the big picture into account and seeking to act in the interests of the company as a whole. Whoever has helped him develop that mindset would have been a good mentor, and would have been made that way through much experience. Some may have sympathy, and respect, for Sarah. She is concerned with people as people, not just the business. Whoever helped her develop that mindset would have been a good mentor, and would have been made that way by being a person of great integrity whom she admired. But this can be seen as soft-headed, wishful thinking. I would doubt that many, if any, would suggest that John had been well mentored. His behaviour has been corrupt, and his concerns are entirely selfish. Whoever influenced his development along those lines would be judged to have failed as a mentor. But then, on the other hand, setting moral judgements aside, which person do you think will come out of this situation best?

Deciding which of these people has been well mentored, and by implication endorsing a kind of mentoring as the best, is then a matter of moral judgement. The three different positions exemplified above with Jim, Sarah and John can be investigated as moral positions in more detail. But first we must make an initial analysis, of why morality matters in the first place when thinking about judging what makes someone a good mentor.

While many different approaches to the issue of moral identity are available (Thompson, 2000), two opposing views of the place of moral analysis in thinking about management in general can be identified. There are those who argue that a moral perspective is inappropriate for judging the actions and behaviours of managers (Stark, 1993; Nash, 1994). The nature of business is such that decisions and behaviour have to be free from the constraints of morality. There are no moral dilemmas in business, just the rule of competition. They are opposed by those who advocate a moral perspective as a necessary part of the analysis of all human action and behaviour (Velasquez, 1982; Vallance, 1993). That must include management.

The debate on the place and role of morality in management has generated many studies. Two contemporary studies and interpretations of the general cases, the one against moral identity influencing management behaviour and the other for greater moral analysis, are available. First Schrijvers (2002) represents the view that morality has no place in management. His text 'How to be a rat' argues, and advises, that to succeed as a manager it is necessary to be at least amoral, and if circumstances justify it, to be what others would define as immoral. It is justifiable to lie, to bribe, to cheat, to cause fear and to intimidate. Getting down into the sewer, becoming a 'rat', involves a range of activities that are, in themselves, not controversial or offensive. First, people, including managers, need to identify and be committed to their own interests and aims. They should have goals. Second, they need to accept that political battles will happen, and be prepared to engage in them. They need to be realistic. Third, they need to work on their own sources of power. They should be savvy. Finally, they have to play to win; not be a victim. They need to be active.

These kinds of prescriptions are not unusual. What is different with Schrijvers' analysis, and is controversial in many regards, is how these general concerns are translated into specific tactics. He prescribes, for example, deliberately feeding people's fears; in order to distract them from properly and rationally evaluating situations and to make them malleable. He advises that humiliating people where necessary to achieve one's goals is appropriate. And he counsels that knowing one's own vanities is important in order to avoid having others manipulate them. The idea is not to be self-enlightened, or even cunning, but to be sneaky and verminous. Such a view is not unique, and has been celebrated in other contexts as being liberating (Young, 2001) and desirable.

Schrijvers is consciously and explicitly updating the well-known and classic counsels of Machiavelli, originating in an era of medieval principalities; a context which is taken to provide parallels with contemporary business. He is also updating the lesser-known analyses of Nietzsche, originating in an era of declining belief in Christian values and proposing the legitimation of the 'superman'. Schrijvers' arguments replicate Nietzsche's in particular. Nietszche concluded that morality, embodied at the time he wrote in the west as conformity with Christian values, was based on what he saw as a slave mentality; lacking pride, arrogance, assertiveness were good qualities, and to be aspired to. The 'masters' had been seduced by this, and so had to constrain their real nature, their 'will to power'. The qualities of pride, arrogance and assertiveness had to be repressed. However, as commitment to these Christian values eroded and their influence declined, an alternative was required. That alternative, for Nietzsche, was a rebirth of the old master's morality, the will to power. To be arrogant, assertive and self-serving was again respectable. The liberation of the 'will to power' from the restraints of slave morality would allow new supermen to flourish.

This is a legitimation of self-creating and striving individuals as the foundation of the modern order, rather than adherence to conventional values in a community. Such legitimation has been interpreted as one wellspring for the development of a more individualistic rather than collective and communitarian culture and society. In that form the influence of the core ideas has been accepted in diffuse but widespread ways. They have also been associated with the legitimation of fascism; where a race or nation, rather than an individual, could be deemed to be superior, with a will to power that ought to be expressed assertively. In that form the influence of the core ideas has been opposed and contested.

Schrijvers is not a contemporary apologist for fascism, rather he is an advocate of continuing and expanding the idea of the 'will to power' as a natural and healthy force, producing self-creating and striving individuals. For him it is the contemporary morality of 'professionalism' in management which has played, and is playing, a similar role to the 'slave' morality of Christianity. Intellectualization about how to manage change and act as a professional manager in a moral way, of the kind that he argues is 'taught in business schools', represents such a contemporary slave morality. This professional morality, which denies the realities of how management really works, hinders rather than helps the manager. When managers and professionals use their 'at home' language to talk about these realities they talk about learning about and from the villains, about how the opportunistic and power-seeking, those with an unabashed will to power, are those who succeed. That, he concludes, is the norm. Schrijvers then seeks to displace the rhetoric of a sanitized view of what is morally 'right' with an analysis of the realities of how managers actually succeed. And success goes to rats, because rats make things happen.

Glover (2001) represents the opposite view; that morality matters, and matters more urgently, in all areas of human action and behaviour. This is because a 'moral gap' has grown throughout the twentieth century, becoming the Achilles heel of our otherwise invulnerably ordered and civilized societies. People approach some situations and relations morally, but then approach other situations or relations amorally. There is a gap between having morals and applying them; that gap has always existed, whichever definition of morals is used. Glover argues that this gap has been increasing. Rather than people becoming less moral, they seek to maintain a moral identity, but in practice they use it less often. This is a situation fraught with problems.

Glover does not deal with management directly; his subjects are people at war, the cruelty of torturers and the origins of genocidal behaviour. In these situations it is the existence of a moral gap more often than a complete absence of morality which allows the worst to happen. The problem of the 'moral gap', he argues, has increased in all cultures throughout the twentieth century, and it now permeates all aspects of society. Management in organizations is as prone to the problems of the moral gap as other areas of life where contest and conflict are present, and where power is being exercised. Management is likely to go awry when natural human responses and moral identity are compromised or absent. For Glover, natural human responses include respecting others' dignity or status, and feeling sympathy and caring about others' misery or happiness. For Glover, having a moral identity entails commitments to being a certain kind of person, to having integrity. Such a moral identity and moral responses are active for those in a community, but not to those outside; for them there will be indifference or hostility.

The imperative is to try to close this moral gap, not to accept it. There is a need to reinvent morality, and better apply it, in all kinds of circumstances. That would mean seeking to activate the moral identity and moral resources in more situations and relations, not fewer. At the very least, even if such a moral gap cannot be eradicated, it can be better contained. People can become more sensitive to the possibilities that their actions and behaviour are subject to being influenced by being in the moral gap.

WHAT MORALITY, WHAT AMORALITY?

The questions then are which argument is right, and what implications does that have for mentoring. Is there a need to free people from the illusions of management rhetoric, which include contemporary versions of the 'slave morality'? Or is there a need to reinvent and reapply a moral identity and responses among managers? A simple choice of one or the other is of course possible. But there are then complications, whichever choice is made. The first complication encountered is that people are talking about different things when they talk about morality and amorality. Take the cameo that introduced this chapter. It is an example of a generic situation, where there may be a moral element to the situation and the relations people have. Table 2.1 illustrates how these three characters represent three different interpretations of morality.

Table 2.1 Three approaches to morality

	Sarah	John	Jim
	Kantian Apply general principles	Machiavellian Sceptical about applying general principles	Utilitarian Avoid suffering, give happiness
Imperatives	There are categorical imperatives; things you ought to do to maintain your own integrity and values. Identify these values and always abide by them.	Imperatives are only hypothetical. What matters is doing what is necessary in the exercise of power. Set aside traditional virtues if needed.	Balances of happiness among communities of people in the short and long term.
Relations	People are always to be seen as ends, never as means. Conflicts arise from different people have differing values.	Princes have responsibilities, which mean that inflicting 'injury' and acting in ways that may seem cruel can be necessary. Conflicts arise where people object to being seen as means to an end.	Happiness is the end, logical analysis is the means. Conflicts arise in determining what is the greatest happiness for the greatest number.
Moral identity	People are inherently good; they have a moral nature and can make good choices.	If all other people were good then leaders could be too. But people are inherently self-interested and may act badly.	People are rational and calculating, they can logically figure out what the right thing to do is.
The manager's moral aim	Be loved and respected for having and abiding by values that others endorse.	To be feared by those who might upset good order is better than to be loved.	Attain the greatest happiness of the greatest number.

IMPLICATIONS FOR MENTORS

The dominant impression in discussions of mentoring, and in the prescriptions which accompany training for mentors, is that morality does matter. Schrijvers' position would be opposed, Glover's position would be endorsed. Moral identity and moral responses matter, in the senses which Jim and Sarah would use to describe their concerns. John's position would be opposed. There is an implicit assumption and often an explicit expression of mentoring as involving and requiring morality in one of these guises. But helping people through psychosocial development, and being in a position to take on the responsibilities that come with career progression, may require elements of any of these positions on morality; with elements of considering the bigger picture, of having and abiding by certain values, and of being able to be flexible being relevant.

Indeed for the 'princes' and 'princesses' of management, the participants in the power struggles that permeate the contemporary workplace and the change projects they involve, John's perspective makes a lot of sense. They, like Schrijvers, take the view that winning means success in managing these changes, as that is what makes people happy; and to win it is necessary to be amoral. Schrijvers argues, based on personal anecdotal evidence, that those who have achieved success as managers have done so by being amoral. They then need to, and have to, encourage the new generation to follow in those footsteps; but they have to do so quietly. For the best rats are always well hidden; people do not realize they are rats. What they have to avoid is getting a reputation for being sly or sneaky. Carefully concealing their sneakiness under a cloak of integrity or cunning is what they do. Mentoring for verminicity, how to be a rat, is the reality. Only this ensures that managers will understand what is happening in power plays in organizations and be able to deal with them.

The power of Schrijvers' analysis is partly in its expression of this argument, in the deft integration of a number of common themes and concerns which in themselves are not controversial. Is it always right to tell the truth? Is it not naïve to fail to use what power you have to achieve goals where others are being obstructive? But put together they become something more. Schrijvers' account of the sense and relevance of an anti-moral perspective in the modern world of management and organization needs to be answered.

It could be answered with evidence, but that is not widely available; how would the 'verminicity', or otherwise, of managers be operationalized and explored quantitatively? Schrijvers himself cites stories and anecdotes from his experience, eschewing even the more widely known cases in the public arena, such as the recent Enron scandals and their equivalents. It can, however, also be answered intellectually. That there is a need for a greater commitment to recreating morality, not hastening its demise, can be argued.

The primary problem can be redefined. Schrijvers assumes that the primary problem is that individual managers labour under illusions, obfuscations of reality induced by their education and development, due to the baleful influence of ideologists of morality creating a false consciousness. But the primary problem can be seen to be the encroachment of a moral gap, and the struggle to cope with that.

The case for taking this moral gap as the primary gap is simple. On the one hand there is an evident espousing of, and attainment of, sympathy, respect, dignity and care with respect to some situations and relations. On the other hand there is indifference and hostility instead of sympathy, respect, dignity and care with respect to other situations and relations. In the management context this can be argued to be inherent in the nature of relations in capitalism, with relations within and between organizations determined only by the need to compete and survive. This gap between having a moral identity in some relations and conditions but not in others is, however, a universal human problem, not one created by a particular set of economic relations. It may be universal, but the moral gap should not be accepted. The risk that the worse aspects of human nature can come to the fore is ever present, and needs to be managed. For otherwise, the consequences are the erosion of the moral identity that people do have, with further and greater problems being caused.

SOME COMMON GROUND

While their positions are antithetical, Schrijvers and Glover would both agree on one thing: that there is a need to insist upon an understanding of human nature with all its elements, including its darker elements. This, rather than more loudly prescribing and espousing an enlightenment and humanistic belief in the essential goodness of people, is needed. Schrijvers would shift from that premise to the tactics of the rat; Glover would shift from that premise to seeking to close the moral gap. But recognizing and acknowledging that human nature does include a capacity for cruelty, various kinds and degrees of emotional inadequacy, and that moral resources and identity are fragile, is the foundation of both views.

This acknowledgement, rather than denial, can best help to avoid repeating past failures and disasters. For Schrijvers these are failures and disasters for individuals in the management of change in organizations. For Glover they are failures and disasters of the kind associated with discrimination and harassment, which become victimization and genocide. While these failures are in some respects worlds apart, they are also joined. An awareness of and alertness to how and why people may come to have their best aspirations overwhelmed and their baser, cruel, tendencies given rein is common ground. Even rats do not want to be seen to be rats. And even being a rat is not the worst that is possible.

DIFFERENCES

Schrijvers and Glover differ on what to do with this awareness of human nature. Schrijvers follows Machiavelli and Nietzsche, and provides his guide to being a rat; putting practical questions of morals that are important to managers upfront, and advising amoral behaviour. This will make people happy; it will make managers happy, it will achieve change and therefore make those who sought the change happy. Above all, it is consistent with the way people are, it is natural; and acting naturally is the best strategy for happiness and success.

Glover, in contrast, follows Socrates in arguing that such 'natural' amorality does not lead to happiness. It is self-knowledge which enables happiness, including self-knowledge of the darker elements. This is because self-knowledge enables people to be at harmony with themselves, their complex human nature, and therefore with other people. Most importantly, Glover argues, in practice, amoralists will tend to be subject to conflicts which will disturb and upset them as they trample over others to get what they want. Aside from exceptional cases, amoralists invariably have some vestiges of human response, some moral resources and a moral identity. And, as the experience and consequence of such conflicts will be unacceptably great – in Glover's phrase, 'often but not always' – people will not trample over each other to get what they want.

For Schrijvers this is just a version of enlightenment optimism, with what he deems its naïve humanitarianism; this permeates the language of professionals involved in management and managing change. Replacing the 'thin' psychology of the enlightenment with something more complex and closer to reality does demand a darker account of human nature. But for Glover enlightenment optimism is thin and mechanical, and should be replaced with something more complex and closer to reality; a darker account of human nature. What is needed is a dialogue; applying moral principles, but also modifying them; being pragmatic not Procrustean.

CONCLUSION

While a proliferation of frameworks for understanding mentoring in a more sophisticated way brings some benefits, insights and reflections that can help in theory and in practice, it also has a disadvantage. If mentoring is as complicated as these many frameworks suggest, then many will be wary of it, or reject it. They will seek other simplicities instead, to manage elements of psychosocial development or career development with tools and techniques they find more amenable. That would be unfortunate. Of course there are several different versions of what kind of complexity it is that mentoring embodies, all competing to be the best explanation of mentoring. Each has its own conceptual complex. To be concerned with mentoring is then to be concerned with shrouds of conceptual complexes, and as well as seeking to disseminate good practice there is also a need to explore these conceptual complexes.

The issue here has been whether the people who reach the farthest and highest points of success do so because they have been the most moral people, or because they have been the least moral people. To answer that requires us to consider different perspectives on what being moral or amoral means. For the utilitarian it is doing the greatest good for the greatest number, and amorality is irrationally doing the greatest harm to the greatest number, or great good for the few. For the Kantian it is about maintaining an integrity with one's values, or categorical imperatives, doing what they ought to do given their values. This is to be based on doing unto others what you would have done to you. The opposite of this is to act for reasons other than core values, and in so doing act in ways that would be objected to if they were applied to you. For the Machiavellian the issue is to be flexible, with higher purposes in mind, given the flaws that people have and the threats they may present to achieving these higher purposes. To be amoral would be to behave 'flexibly' without justification in relation to higher purposes.

So is effective mentoring, and are effective mentors, to be described in the context of producing good utilitarians, people who take the general interest of the business or organization into account? Or is it about producing good Kantians, people able to define and act consistently with what one 'ought' to? Or is it about the creation of new generations of 'princes', able to discharge the responsibilities that go with power with a clear conscience? Most often the first two are taken as the right options, and are taken to represent the real dilemmas of morality in management and therefore in mentoring. But the third way is perhaps the one that presents the greatest challenges.

Again, the question of evidence can be raised. In the absence of evidence it is reasonable to conclude that those who have negotiated the path to success as far is it goes know one thing for sure; that it is strewn with 'failures', with people who did not make the stages that they have themselves negotiated. For each person that makes it, there are many who do not. Are these people failed utilitarians, failed Kantians or failed Machiavellians?

Mentoring functions, discussed in relation to psychosocial and career functions, can also be reinterpreted in relation to these moral positions. There may be psychosocial functions in any of these senses, with mentor support to meet the demands and pressures of development as an effective utilitarian or Kantian or Machiavellian. Or there may be career development issues, where people face choices that test their practice as a utilitarian or Kantian or Machiavellian type. Whether it is put in psychosocial or career development terms, did those who had mentors succeed with moral and ethical guidance, and if they did, what kind of moral support and guidance was that?

These psychosocial and career issues blend individual actions and organizational cultures together. The moral dimension of the mentoring relationship between individuals is seeking to do the right thing by each other. Here the morality of mentoring is an instance of people making choices and acting with consequences for their interpersonal relations. There is also the moral dimension of the organizational context for mentoring. Mentoring is always part of an organizational or institutional culture, and will both be influenced by that and be one of the contributors to it. Does a culture favour utilitarian, Kantian or Machiavellian behaviour? Are individuals in these cultures experiencing greater moral gaps as structures and strategies change to achieve high performance? Does mentoring in these contexts provide a bulwark against the erosion of moral identity and the encroachment of a moral gap?

These questions suggest that the making of mentors cannot be reduced to lists of competences. Returning to the case of Jim, Sarah and John, there are apparently many successful managers in positions of power who are like John. I have known many, and so do most of the people I have worked with throughout the time I have been studying human relations at work. Perhaps not as extreme as him, but in the same territory. Is this indeed a failure of mentoring, or is it in fact a predictable and justifiable product of mentoring? The same question can be asked of Sarah, and her concern with maintaining personal integrity, which is an issue facing many. And, what about the approach of Jim? On reflection, is there not something redolent of a bygone era in his concerns, a response that seems old-fashioned? The modern manager is no longer meant to be shackled to old commitments in an era of change, but open to moving on. Who can say who of these has had the best mentor? And who would confidently predict which of these would make the best mentor to the next generation?

FINALLY, TAKE A TEST

If good mentors are people who have themselves succeeded then it is possible to consider the generic preconditions for success, and in so doing explore some of the moral dimensions of what makes a mentor. Schrijvers suggests there are several things that can be audited. His aim is to let people 'test' for their level of verminicity.

The following test (Table 2.2) is an amended version of Schrijvers' 'rat audit'. Taking this test provides you with a way of reflecting on specific matters of morality in regard to being a

Table 2.2 A morality test for mentors

	A: Yes	B: No
Good mentors really enjoy participating in political games in the company	2	0
Good mentors always carefully assess the interests involved in and around their work	2	1
Good mentors understand how their company's 'court' works	2	1
Good mentors are able to interrogate and get information	3	1
Good mentors always know where they are going. They know their aims.	2	0
Good mentors always plan three steps ahead	3	1
Good mentors know exactly which power sources they can tap	2	1
Good mentors frequently reveal everything they know and feel	0	3
Good mentors always look for the other person's weak spot	4	1
Good mentors are scared of 'losing'	1	3
Good mentors object to office politics	1	3
Good mentors hate creating victims	0	2
Good mentors think the end justifies the means	2	1
Total	A:	B:
Total: A + B		

good mentor. It offers an opportunity to clarify what you really think about success, and what that tells you about the moral dimensions of 'what makes a good mentor'.

- Read the statements carefully.
- Respond quickly with an intuitive 'yes' or 'no'.
- Add up the figures for each question.
- Determine your score.
- Read the reflections on statements.
- Finally, check what your score means.

REFLECTIONS ON THE STATEMENTS

Good mentors really enjoy participating in political games in the company: It is common for politics to be considered a dysfunctional aspect of organizational life. It is, nonetheless, endemic. People who realize that the political stuff is part of life, and can actually be enjoyable, sharpen their eyes, experiment and develop the sensitivity that is so vital to be a good mentor. Successful people know this. Good mentors do this; good protégés learn it.

Good mentors always carefully assess the interests involved in and around their work: There are certain areas where people may talk in terms of interests, and others where this is off limits. This requires some consideration, both in the cause and the consequences it has for the good mentor. In many companies, interventions aimed at strengthening the 'united' and 'shared' feelings and stamping out internecine conflict are common. 'We are this type of company.' 'This is our mission.' All the unifying rhetoric and drama can be seen as little more than calculated 'polite' language that blurs a clear view of the differences and similarities between 'thine' and 'mine'. Successful people do this. Good mentors know this; good protégés learn it.

Good mentors understand how their company's 'court' works: Any company has a clique that discusses strategy, fights the fight and shares out the spoils. Every company has its own 'court'. They are the people who cluster around the centre of power. They are the courtiers with whom the powerful share some, if not all, of their problems. Good mentors have to be part of the court. They are then the bosses' senses. The courtiers are expected to observe what is going on amongst the employees and the outside world. In informal conversations, when they 'spar' with their boss, when they 'catch up' on things and 'co-create' ideas, they warn, confirm and encourage their sires and, on the odd occasion, carefully and politely contradict them. Second, good mentors are sparring partners. Ideas are first launched for them, so that they can either shoot them down or wish them Godspeed. Successful people know this. Good mentors do this; good protégés learn it.

Good mentors are able to interogate and get information: Some people always seem to manage to get you to tell them more than you were planning to do. People who, with a sincere or assumed innocence, approach you, break down all your defences and let you talk, occasionally making an encouraging remark, or nodding understandingly as a reward for your openness. And documents, snippets of gossip, e-mails, back corridors and confidentialities – the good mentor uses them all to formulate their ideas, their queries, their suspicions, and then uses these methods to innocently verify and falsify any ambiguities. They know what they are looking for, and where to find it. This is something that talented consultants, diplomats, ambassadors and leaders have always done, and will certainly continue doing. Successful people do this. Good mentors do this; good protégés learn it.

Good mentors always know where they are going. They know their aims: This is an obvious statement. And yet it is essential to stress that good mentors should set their own goals. But do you really know your aims, other than getting through the week? Could you list your aims without having to think about them? Probably not. The good mentor needs aims, because they give them an instrument for determining their strategy and planning their tactics. Talk about them as little as possible, unless that suits your plans. Successful people do this. Good mentors do this, good protégés learn it.

Good mentors always plan three steps ahead: Many mentors, as with most professionals, have undergone much training in long-term strategy and have learnt many models. Yet most of them can't think farther than today's lunch appointment. They have plans; but they are seldom able to explain how those plans relate to the current climate or to the present-day situation in the company. Yet this is something a good politician within a company can easily master: determine now what the next three steps could be. What will happen if I do this? And what will I do if somebody else does that? And what...? Successful people do this. Good mentors do this; good protégés learn to do it.

Good mentors know exactly which power sources they can tap: It is rare that somebody is apathetic and paralysed, trapped without any room for movement. Every single person possesses sources of power that can help them make their work, their department and even their boss dance to their tune. There are examples of companies where employees, thanks to ingenious manoeuvrings and understanding their sources of power, have been able to topple seemingly impregnable top managements by exposing their words, actions and emotional tyranny. Successful people know these. Good mentors know these; good protégés learn them.

Good mentors frequently reveal everything they know and feel: In our culture that preaches unconditional openness and honesty, and tries to persuade us that every business and personal success depends on them, developing an acute understanding of what we should and should not say is something that belongs to the past. In most books about power and politics, silence is praised as a noble virtue.

People learn from bitter experience that it is better to remain silent on crucial issues. And the result can be seen in so many organizations: the comedy of open communications. People who follow their emotions, who promote their interests, who air their displeasure about the way things go on and issue warnings in the corridors, canteens and even at home, are unsuccessful. Successful people know this. Good mentors know this; good protégés learn it.

Good mentors always look for the other person's weak spot: Good mentors should pay particular attention, as does a psychotherapist, to the aberrations and distortions in people's character. It is these characteristics that make the other weak, threaten their autonomy and promote dependency on others. And it is exactly this dependency that interests us since it affords us the chance of taking control. Everybody has a weak spot, a bad habit, a vice, or a blemish in their character. Expose them and use them to our advantage. Managers have made use of the fears, the pride, the ambitions, the childish desires and lusts of others; they have, until now, called this 'motivating', 'inspiring', 'committing' and 'challenging'. Successful people know this. Good mentors know this; protégés learn it.

Good mentors are scared of 'losing': Anybody who plays the game of power and doesn't like losing has taken on an additional burden. Not only do they have to think about aims, strategy, moves, surveying the arena and revealing the weaknesses of the opponent; they also have to consider the possibly damaging consequences of the game. Anybody who is scared of the consequences places themself at a disadvantage; if you're scared of losing, then you've already lost. Successful people know this. Good mentors know this; protégés learn it.

Good mentors object to office politics: Many are scornful about political manoeuvring. They are really concerned about any negative consequences to the business. In a company where political games are played, people are constantly on their guard, whether in their offices, their meeting rooms or during 'bilateral' discussions. Anything they say or do is coloured by suspicion. Because of this, real issues that can provide essential information to management are never discussed. Everybody is on guard against saying anything that can be used against them. Politicizing business, they say, erodes the very structure and foundation of individual relationships. But there will always be political machinations in a company, either out in the open or underground, and the only influence they have is whether to accept it gracefully or allow it to work as a red cloth in front of a bull. Successful people know this. Good mentors know this; protégés learn it.

Good mentors hate creating victims: Most people will tend to agree with this statement: yes, good mentors really hate creating victims. But decide exactly who deserves the label 'victim' and who doesn't. People who suffer the consequences of avalanches, floods, volcanic eruptions and extremes of cold and heat are victims. And the same is true of those people who suffer the consequences when a factory, oil refinery or aeroplane through technical or human error explodes, burns down or crashes. But then there is a third category: people who, because of the deliberate decisions of others and the consequences of such decisions, see their ambitions, aims and interests come under threat. Are these victims? It depends. In day-to-day conversation, we often talk about 'innocent' victims, and 'losers'. The label of victim entitles people to sympathy and generosity from people around them. But should bosses, colleagues and employees in companies hijack this label? In organizations, people can win or lose. And if, in their desire to win, they have to hinder others, crush ambitions, shatter dreams, thwart plans, wreck careers, eliminate people and prevent people reaching the market, then that's the way it is. Successful people accept this. Good mentors accept it; protégés need to accept it.

THE END JUSTIFIES THE MEANS

If you agree, then you are prepared to reach for unaccepted means. If not, then you have to live with the knowledge that ethics may condemn you to losing. Look after your own interests with clever, smart and devious methods or, for a high-minded principle, allow yourself to be beaten. The former accept responsibility and don't mind dirtying their hands, even if they find that distasteful. They know just how far they can go and where the border between acceptable and unacceptable behaviour lies. That they nevertheless make tough and well-considered decisions required by circumstances demands respect and our admiration. Successful people respect that. Good mentors respect that; protégés need to respect it.

SCORES

Up to 12 points: *Good mentors are definitely not rats.* Mentors are at the opposite end of the spectrum from Schrijvers' rats. They are moral. Schrijvers would argue that this means they are 'good' but naive. They resist politics and all that goes with it. Schrijvers would argue that in practice they will also be losers. Successful people are not like this.

13 to 20 points: *Good mentors share some characteristics of clever rats.* Good mentors possess quite a bit of verminicity. Their moral identity includes a capacity to do what is necessary to operate in the political arenas which constitute organizational reality. Successful people are like this.

21 and more points: *Good mentors are filthy rats.* Good mentors are like true rats. They know about winning and losing. They understand the game. They have a lust for power, and the threats to integrity that go with it.

Reflecting on what makes people successful, from a moral perspective, provides one way of seeing how the moral dimension matters when it comes to defining what makes a mentor. Or maybe mentoring is a complicated relationship in a simple world.

3 Characteristics ascribed to mentors by their protégés

ANN DARWIN

The stereotype of a mentor as a wiser, older man who sits on the mountain top dispersing pearls of wisdom was debunked in a Australian study that asked people to describe the personal characteristics of their mentors. Data from nearly 2000 people was surveyed for their views and descriptions of mentoring. More structured information from 555 of them was factor- analysed, yielding eight factors, each of which describes a cluster of mentor characteristics. Standardized scale scores were developed from factors and used to examine how these various protégés differed with respect to the characteristics they ascribed to their mentors. Later, one-on-one interviews were conducted with selected protégés to explore how such mentoring characteristics manifested themselves in their relationships with these mentors and in day-to-day work settings.

BACKGROUND

When researchers first reported their findings on mentoring in the 1970s, there was an 'aha' phenomenon. Most adults can identify someone who had a significant influence on their learning and career development. But what does the term mean? When people are asked to describe their mentor they generally use phrases like 'a wise old man', 'someone who is caring and nurturing', 'a guardian angel' and such like. Rarely do their descriptions include words such as 'aggressive', 'pace-setting', 'opinionated' or 'volatile' – descriptions that do not fit the stereotypical view painted in much of the research on mentoring over the past three decades. Yet, when they are prompted to think about people who have had an influence on their learning, some will recall a teacher who was 'tough', a boss who was 'pig-headed', or a role model who was 'inspirational' but also a 'workaholic'. Often, the word 'mentor' evokes images of extraordinary characters: Merlin the magician, who mentored young Arthur to become King of Camelot; Obi-Wan Kenobi, who taught Darth Vader the ways of the Jedi Knights; or Mentor the legendary friend of Ulysses, who was entrusted to instruct his son Telemachus (and who appeared at times as Athene, the goddess of wisdom in disguise). These are historical examples that stir the imagination.

More recently and despite the increase in research since the 1970s, personal characteristics ascribed to mentors have received little attention. Researchers often collude in retaining this stereotypical view of mentors. Although history is replete with examples of mentors who influence their protégés, speculation rather than serious studies too often provides the archetypes of contemporary mentors. Hence, descriptions of mentors often paint portraits of one-dimensional, larger-than-life characters who possess a set of 'ideal' personal characteristics. Usually these one-dimensional characters are described as approachable, sensitive, empathetic, supportive and nurturing. They are almost always perceived as wiser, older men who are spiritually, intellectually and emotionally superior to their mortal charges. Such descriptions serve to enhance the archetypal image of mentors who are without flaws.

Are current-day mentors perceived as extraordinary characters like those suggested in myths and legends? Do they possess particular personality characteristics that readily identify them as mentors? More than 1000 ordinary people were asked to help answer this question, and their responses became the focus of this study.

THE STUDY

The process of data collection started by asking 1011 people (in a variety of public places) to provide three words which described a significant person at work who had a positive influence on their learning. Many words were suggested over and over by many people (kind, supportive, knowledgeable). Of the 339 total words collected, 80 of the most common words, augmented with 20 less-frequent but also highly descriptive 'negative' qualities, were arrayed in a second questionnaire and administered to a further 760 respondents, this time in work settings. The 555 respondents who reported having a mentor in their work situation were asked to circle either 'yes' or 'no' to indicate which of these 100 words described this specific person. Data was factor-analysed to examine the underlying factor structure among these key words. The final solution consisted of eight factors containing 98 words—two words failed to load strongly on any of the factors. These factors were then used to develop scale scores to produce the Dimensions of Mentoring Inventory (DOMI). These standardized scale scores were subsequently used to plot and interpret the profiles of mentors of selected protégés.

Sixteen respondents whose mentors were notably high on one or more of the mentor dimensions were selected for follow-up interviews and to investigate how these dimensions manifested themselves in relationships and in day-to-day work settings. Interviewing respondents was an opportunity to bring deeper meaning to the mentor dimensions by exploring multi-dimensional portraits and discovering similarities as well as differences. Descriptions from protégés of their mentors were illuminated through memorable incidents. While using 16 interviews limits generalizability too far beyond the immediate findings, they did provide meaningful information about how mentors who were high in one or more of the mentoring dimensions related to their protégés in mentoring relationships.

RESULTS

The eight-factor solution accounts for 40.26 per cent of the common factor variance and illuminates the key characteristics that these 555 respondents identified in their mentors (with the percentage of after-rotation variance in brackets): Authenticity (6.45 per cent), Nurturance

(5.52 per cent), Approachability (5.14 per cent), Competence (4.45 per cent), Inspiration (4.41 per cent), Conscientiousness (4.32 per cent), Hard-working (3.92 per cent), and Volatility (6.01 per cent).

The following paragraphs highlight the eight dimensions of mentoring from three different points of view: each is prefaced by a quotation from one of the 16 follow-up interviewees about their mentor; the following paragraph incorporates those of the 100 words which characterize that particular dimension, as reported by the 555 respondents who described mentors in their work settings; and finally, the bulleted items are phrases abstracted from the 16 interviewees' transcriptions of memorable incidents with their mentors.

THE AUTHENTIC DIMENSION

'She was very respected by the women and emerged as their natural leader.'

Authenticity identifies mentors who are genuine, fair, honest, supportive, understanding, loyal, helpful, principled, thoughtful, believing, respectful and empowering of others. In detailing how this authenticity manifested itself in mentoring relationships, protégés used the following phrases:

- willing to share their life stories
- direct with people and play it like it is
- genuine and real
- 'going to bat' for people
- taking a stand for what they believe is right
- having a natural sense of fair play
- taking a personal interest in others.

THE NURTURING DIMENSION

'He has my interest at heart with no ulterior motive for himself.'

Nurturance identifies mentors who are kind, sensitive, compassionate, easy-going, spiritual, patient, generous and empathetic to others. These mentors are especially not stubborn, aggressive or tough. These mentors were described by protégés as:

- having a capacity for tolerance
- individuals who are not afraid of intimacy with others
- valuing of friendship and reciprocity
- well balanced and patient with others
- active and willing listeners
- feeling a certain amount of responsibility for others
- comfortable with delegating authority and sharing power.

THE APPROACHABLE DIMENSION

'He made me laugh when I felt like crying.'

Approachability identifies mentors who are humorous, friendly, encouraging, communicative, positive, open, caring, co-operative and considerate of others. Protégés described their mentors high in this dimension as follows:

- always being available to people
- acting as though people really matter to them
- genuinely caring for others
- positive and cheerful
- great team players
- having a great sense of humour.

THE COMPETENT DIMENSION

'Roger wrote and talked like Carl Jung.'

Competence identifies mentors who are knowledgeable, bright, interested, intelligent, enthusiastic, professional, confident, experienced, insightful and informative to others. In detailing how this competence manifested itself in the mentoring relationship, protégés used the following descriptions:

- skilled, experienced and knowledgeable
- marching to their own drum
- practical and demanding of quality
- informative teachers
- giving sound advice
- tough and bright
- promoting careers.

THE INSPIRATIONAL DIMENSION

'She is a kind of hero to me.'

Inspiration identifies mentors who are risk-taking, visioning, inspiring, creative, curious, dynamic, strong, passionate, direct, brilliant, challenging and assertive. Protégés used the following words and phrases to describe their mentors:

- charismatic
- respected and admired
- often top of their field
- having personal power
- speaking simply and communicating well
- leading by example
- willing to take risks
- visionaries
- role models for many people.

THE CONSCIENTIOUS DIMENSION

'He was guided by his own conscience rather than what others thought of him.'

Conscientiousness identifies mentors who are efficient, organized, disciplined, consistent, strict and available to others. In describing their mentors considered high in this dimension, protégés used the following phrases:

- honest and fair
- accessible to people
- strong and disciplined
- having a strong work ethic
- loving to work and committed to their jobs
- telling things as they are.

THE HARD-WORKING DIMENSION

'She would work hard during the day and play hard at night'

Hard-working identifies mentors who are dedicated, motivated, committed, ambitious, energetic, driven and workaholic, who tend to be demanding of self and others. Protégés used the following phrases to describe their mentors:

- high in energy
- ambitious and successful
- either liked or disliked, admired or hated
- self-directed and admire that attribute in others
- expecting a lot from self and others
- liking to have a few like-minded people as protégés.

THE VOLATILE DIMENSION

'He was very stubborn and was up and down with his moods.'

Volatility identifies mentors who are neurotic, overbearing, egocentric, outrageous, vindictive, contradictory, self-centred, wild, eccentric, opinionated, stressed, cunning, hard and picky. In sharing their memorable incidents, protégés used the following phrases to describe their mentors:

- aggressive in business dealings
- passionate about their work
- intelligent and talented
- striving for perfection
- often changing moods and confusing people
- stubborn and opinionated
- either liked or disliked by people
- intimidating and able to intimidate.

KEY FINDINGS

MULTIDIMENSIONAL

Since all mentors are seen to exhibit greater or lesser degrees of all eight characteristics, their profiles were necessarily multidimensional. Still, there was overlap among protégés' characterizations of their mentors. Clusters of intercorrelations were found among mentors who were high in Authenticity, Nurturance and Approachability – relationship-oriented characteristics often associated with support of a more personal nature. As well, clusterings were also found among those high in Volatility, Competence and Hard-working – task-oriented characteristics often associated with career support. These cluster groupings can be seen in the correlations among the eight scale scores, as displayed in Table 3.1.

The profiles show that all mentors exhibit behaviours from all of the eight mentoring dimensions, some more than others. It is also likely that those mentors who display task-oriented rather than people-oriented behaviours evoke a more emotional response from other people, as demonstrated by the following comments: 'People either liked or disliked her, but those who didn't like her, she didn't like either, so it was mutual'; 'Some people liked him but many did not like him because he was very tough'.

For the statistically inclined, the figures in Table 3.1 are Pearson correlations among eight scale scores of mentoring characteristics, together with a ninth 'check variable' – the number of words (out of a possible 100) that respondents used to describe their mentor. The scale scores were derived from an eight-factor solution (with equamax rotation and accounting for 40.26 per cent of the common factor variance) of all 100 descriptive words which the 555 respondents used (or omitted) as descriptive of their mentor. Each of the eight factors consisted of the 9 to 16 words loading 0.30 or higher.

Table 3.1 Correlations among eight scale scores

		Authenticity	Volatility	Nurturance	Approachability	Competence	Inspiration	Conscientiousness	Hard-working	No. of words
Authenticity	1	—								
Volatility	2	−0.67	—							
Nurturance	3	0.48	−0.53	—						
Approachability	4	0.45	−0.54	0.47	—					
Competence	5	0.08	−0.23	−0.11	0.03	—				
Inspiration	6	−0.37	0.07	−0.34	−0.32	−0.12	—			
Conscientiousness	7	0.05	−0.31	−0.08	−0.14	−0.02	−0.07	—		
Hard-working	8	−0.46	0.26	−0.55	−0.37	−0.09	0.20	0.01	—	
No. of words	9	−0.11	−0.05	0.07	−11.00	−0.47	0.38	0.15	0.05	—
		1	2	3	4	5	6	7	8	9

In turn, respondents' raw data was rendered as eight scale scores by summing the number of target words for each factor which they reported as describing their mentor, dividing by the number of words in each scale and dividing again by the total number of words the respondents used ('to equate the more loquacious respondents with the taciturn ones'). Scale score means ranged from 3.18 (for Volatility) to 12.99 (for Competence). They demonstrated mean alpha reliabilities of 0.81 and mean test–retest reliabilities also of 0.81. While factor scores are by definition uncorrelated, scale scores built from those factors usually show moderate intercorrelations and may hint at second-order factors or 'cluster groupings' as discussed in the text.

MENTORING DIMENSIONS AND SOCIO-DEMOGRAPHIC VARIABLES

Non-significant variables in describing mentors

Findings in the study indicate that most people reportedly have mentors, regardless of their age, gender or status within organizations. Two thirds of respondents who had mentors reported that their mentors were older than themselves. There was no statistically significant difference between older or younger respondents who reportedly had mentors. Nor was there a statistically significant difference between women and men. However, men were more likely to act as mentors for both men and women.

Data was collected from people who had a variety of occupations and worked within a variety of organizations. Few significantly significant differences were found among industry groups and the Dimensions of Mentor Inventory (DOMI), indicating that people describe mentors in similar ways regardless of organizational or occupational groups. Hence, despite the diversity, findings were similar for most comparable variables.

PERCEPTIONS ON NURTURANCE AND COMPETENCE

Women protégés attributed higher Nurturance scores to mentors than did men, whereas men attributed higher Competence scores to mentors than did women. Higher Nurturance scores were ascribed to women than to men mentors. Same-age mentors were seen as more Nurturing than either younger or older mentors, and there were no detectable differences in Nurturance scores between those younger and older mentors. Protégés in non-management positions attributed higher Nurturance scores to mentors than those in management positions, while protégés in management positions attributed higher Competence scores to mentors than those in non-management positions.

Mentors are often portrayed as people who are high in nurturing. As this study showed, mentors more likely to be described as nurturing are women, peers and those closest to the protégé's age. On the other hand, more men than women mentors were described as competent, and protégés in management positions were more likely to describe their mentors as competent than those in non-management positions. These findings suggest that nurturing is a characteristic of those offering social support while competence is a characteristic of those offering career opportunities.

Gender studies report that men are more likely to conceive of power in terms of domination, while women are more likely to view power in terms of relationships and nurturing (Candib, 1994). Hence, women are perceived as possessing different characteristics and requirements

than their male counterparts. Clearly, regardless of any differences in characteristics between women and men mentors, protégés' perceptions differed significantly. The perception
of women as nurturing rather than competent to handle the tough leadership tasks may also be
shared by women who may feel that they do not possess the qualities necessary to advance the
learning and development of people at work or that they are not qualified to mentor (Ragins and
Cotton, 1991). Women face discrimination and identity issues throughout their careers, which
are different from those of men (Baker-Miller, 1991). When women in senior positions take
on the mentoring role there may be an attitude of discontent from male colleagues. As women
and men form mentoring (boss or non-boss) relationships, they may unconsciously collude in
familiar and stereotypical roles. Women may find themselves acting as if they need protection,
while senior men may provide more protection than they might to their male protégés.

One of the main roles of mentors has been succession planning for young leaders, since
mentoring can establish important links between leadership generations. Women remain
under-represented in that chain. There is a natural link between masculinity and authority
that places men at the head of the household and as bosses and mentors within work settings.
While this view is changing as more women enter the workforce and gain positions within
management, traditional perceptions remain strong.

LEARNING FROM FLAWS

The picture of a wise old man who dispenses pearls of wisdom is no longer an appropriate
picture of contemporary mentors. While the majority still appear to be older men, the land-
scape is changing to include women and peers who are about the same age. Clearly, there is
no one set of characteristics to describe them and many have human flaws, enabling protégés
to learn from bad as well as good behaviours and to find ways of dealing with them. It is the
Volatile dimension, more than any other, which illustrates quite clearly the active rather than
passive role of protégés within mentoring relationships. As one interviewee said: 'I think she
respected the fact that I was able to take what she threw my way and stand up for myself.' It is
this volatile side of mentors that can teach others the toughness that is sometimes required in
life, hence developing resilience.

Protégés who attributed high Volatility scores to their mentors were able to observe the
mentor's behaviour, utilize the 'best' (those actions which teach the learner how to progress
forward in an organization) and discard the worst. Yet Volatility is often left out of mentoring
descriptions. While most mentors were reported as being low on Volatility, mentoring relationships where it was high were no less potent. According to one protégé of a mentor high in Volatility: 'My mentor taught me everything. He stands out as a mentor more than anyone else in
my life.' A good mentor may be a competent person with major flaws so that one can learn what
to do and what not to do at the same time. An ability to manage mentors and bosses actively and
successfully may be a critical determinant of career-path success within organizations.

CHOOSING TO BE MENTORS

Individual characteristics appear to predispose some people to become mentors more than others. Individuals characterized as high in Nurturance, Authenticity and Approachability may be
altruistic and more relational, providing psychosocial support to others. These individuals may,

therefore, be more inclined to act as mentor for more people. On the other hand, mentors characterized as high in Inspiration, Volatility and Hard-working may be more goal-oriented and upwardly mobile and therefore more inclined to support protégés in task-related activities, particularly those associated with career development. When mentoring is task-oriented, intentional and short-term, psychosocial support is less important than the ability of the mentor to teach the protégé either new skills or how to move forward in the organization. These mentors may be drawn more by power than influence and devote little time to developing others. Hence, they are more likely to be attracted to a few protégés whom they perceive to have high potential.

COMMON THEMES

Characteristics of mentors were clearly important in the initial instigation of mentoring relationships. However, regardless of personality characteristics, there were a number of similarities that cut across most mentoring descriptions. Five themes seem common – belief and visibility; wanting to be mentored; timing; reciprocity; and affinity.

A strong feature among relations was the mentor's belief in their protégé's capacity to achieve their full potential. It is as though they were able to bring out talents in the other person because they saw something special about them that may have been invisible to others. Mentorship is in many ways spiritual as mentors help individuals learn how to 'be' as well as what to 'do', as demonstrated by the following comments from protégés:

> 'I didn't know him for long but he stands out as someone who helped me because I didn't have a lot of confidence in myself at that time and it would have been easy to give up.'

> 'She believed in me and made me incredibly visible within the company. If I get to have a position similar to hers I'd like to have the same relationship with my good staff members.'

> 'No one believed in me the way she did. I didn't have too much self-esteem and her belief in me helped me to believe in myself.'

Another theme was an eagerness on the part of protégés to want to be mentored. In fact, in many cases it was protégés who made themselves visible to their mentors and went out of their way to ensure that the relationship happened, as illustrated by the following comments from protégés:

> 'The first day she was made my supervisor I wrote her a memo telling her all of the things that I wanted out of my job and the position.'

> 'I went to this person who became my mentor and said: I think that the company needs someone to specialize in communication…and I am that person.'

Timing was important, as illustrated by the following comment: 'I guess I remember him as the main mentor in my life because it was during the time when I was really eager to learn and experience new things and he met that need for me'. In most of the mentoring stories, mentors appeared at a time when individuals were in a life transition and needed support and guidance from another person. In some cases, protégés' career paths would have been very different had they not encountered their mentors, well illustrated by one protégé who states: 'The relationship with her was absolutely fundamental to shaping my career.'

Reciprocity was another common feature of most mentoring relationships, even when mentors were obviously in more powerful situations within the organization, as demonstrated by the following statements:

'She learnt from me too. I think that I have a lot of unspoken, creative kind of attitudes that she didn't have, so in a lot of cases she looked to me for some of the spontaneity of life.'

'I know directly from him that, as I was drawing from him, picking up pointers about the job, at the same time he was drawing from me, even though I was considerably younger than him.'

Finally, within every relationship there was an affinity – a bond of warm friendship and, in most cases, a strong emotional commitment, often involving feelings of trust, loyalty and respect. 'I am able to take these risks because of the trusting relationship. I know that it's not a test with him to see me go under.' It is often an unspoken bond and an understanding of the psyches of each person. The idea that people possess an essential nature that is qualitatively different from their acquired personality is basic to psychology. Essence is often described as what is 'one's own', the potentials with which people were born, rather than what they learnt through education and schooling (Almaas, 1986). It is possible, therefore, that people unconsciously seek out others who can help them to become who they really are. This attraction does not appear to be behavioural, but of a more essential nature – sometimes spiritual, at other times intellectual or emotional. Its essence is found more within the kind of relationship that exists between the mentor and the protégés than in the roles and functions performed.

What appeared to make mentoring unique from other workplace relationships was a number of similarities found within the relationship itself. Mentors believed in their protégés and helped them to 'be' as well as to 'do'. Often mentors were encountered at a critical period when protégés were in new positions or times of transition in their lives. Mentors recognized characteristics and talents in protégés that may have been unknown to others and even to the protégés themselves. A sense of kinship developed. They offered them unique visions of themselves, motivated them to grow professionally, showed them new ways and contributed to their growth and development as people as well as supporting their careers. Protégés were often more active in their own mentoring process, especially if their mentors were high in Volatility and Hard-working. Many also seemed well equipped at managing the relationship through an understanding of their mentor's flaws as well as their strengths. Protégés effectively built zones of tolerance toward their mentors' behaviours.

The attraction of both parties appeared to be from a non-visible essence or core attraction rather than any function each mentor performed. This supports the views of Levinson *et al.* (1978) that mentoring exists as a relationship between mentor and protégé far more than any functions performed by mentors. Hence, it is the essence of the relationship itself that separates mentoring from other kinds of workplace relationships. Clearly, mentors make a difference to the working lives of ordinary people, so much so that Daloz (1986) believes that 'if mentors did not exist we would have to invent them'.

IMPLICATIONS FOR PRACTICE

PROTÉGÉS TAKE GREATER RESPONSIBILITY FOR THEIR OWN CAREER DEVELOPMENT

This study raises a number of challenges to organizations considering implementing mentoring programmes. Rather than relying on support and coaching from one mentor, people are now more likely to receive mentoring support from a number of different people, and protective functions may be of lesser importance as individuals take greater responsibility for their own career development. Rather than looking towards protective sponsorship from mentors, people may be better served by support networks of colleagues within and outside the organization. According to one respondent:

> 'It is my belief that mentors sit everywhere. They could be playmates, teachers, friends, people you meet at the store. Everyone is a potential mentor in life. You need to be open and not just looking for one saviour to pull you through life. For example, if I'd been looking for one saviour to pull me through life I might have ended up just like him (my mentor). So you need lots of examples, not just one. You also learn from bad experiences as much, if not more than, good ones.'

DON'T OVERLOOK YOUR BOSS AS A POTENTIAL MENTOR

Interestingly, more than half of the respondents to both samples reported that their mentors were their bosses (immediate supervisors or senior managers). When respondents reported their mentors as bosses, the relationships more closely resembled traditional mentoring practices – the support was reportedly more comprehensive, the relationship of longer duration and most bosses who were also mentors reportedly were more aware than non-boss mentors of the influence they had on their protégés.

The usefulness of bosses as mentors cannot be overstated. They are more accessible to their employees than non-bosses, have personal, first-hand knowledge of staff and are vested with the responsibility to be attentive to the work performance and career development of staff (Burke, 1984; Clawson, 1985; Clutterbuck, 1985; Ragins and McFarlin, 1990). Hence organizations that want to achieve high performance may need to encourage managers to become mentors to their employees. A challenge facing bosses today is to encourage, challenge and support the learning and development of all staff, equitably and evenly, rather than only those they perceive as having special abilities or those with whom they feel most comfortable. Similarly, staff need to be skilled at learning from good as well as bad role models, and to actively manage relationships. Protégés must take the initiative and make tough decisions about what feedback to get and from whom, actively pursue challenging assignments, learn to deal with bosses' aggressive behaviours and realize that workplaces are about productivity as well as relationships.

According to Bennis, 'the ideal boss for a growing leader is probably a good boss with major flaws, so that one can learn all the complex lessons of what to do and what not to do simultaneously' (Bennis, 1989, p151). It is worthwhile remembering that while all bosses have the capacity to fulfil some mentorial functions, the potential is not always realized and an 'anti-mentorial' relationship develops. It may be that knowing the art of managing bosses actively and successfully is a critical determinant of a protégé's own success within an organization.

DEVELOPING RESILIENCE

Some protégés seem to understand the foibles of their mentors and build up zones of tolerance around their behaviours and have ways of dealing with behaviours, sometimes through direct feedback and confrontation: 'I think she respected the fact that I was able to take what she threw my way and stand up for myself'. Protégés were also able to review their own beliefs and actions, often through a process of observation and reflection: 'You can spend time being goodness and light for everybody else and talking to everyone and your own work does suffer:

that's an important lesson that I learnt from her – to look after myself.' It is this volatile side of mentors that can teach others the toughness that is sometimes required in life. Yet this dimension is often left out of mentoring descriptions.

CHOOSING TO MENTOR AND BE MENTORED

Some people choose not to be mentors. As this study suggests, those high in dimensions such as Volatility, Hard-working and Inspiration are less relationship and more task-oriented. They may be high-performing managers in higher management positions who may not have the time or the inclination to mentor others. Further, studies (Ayree *et al.*, 1996a) suggest that people's motivation to mentor may be predicted by individual characteristics such as altruism and positive affectivity. The altruistic personality indicates that some people are consistently more generous, helpful and kind than others and that such people are readily perceived as more altruistic. Life-wise, positive affectivity is the tendency of people to be happy or experience positive affect across situations. Findings indicate that these individual characteristics were positively related to a person's motivation to mentor.

Kram (1985b) in her seminal work on mentoring described two main mentoring functions: psychosocial functions (role modelling; acceptance and confirmation; counselling; friendship) and career functions (sponsorship; exposure and visibility; coaching; challenging assignments). It is possible to speculate that those mentors high in Nurturance, Authenticity and Approachability are more likely to provide psychosocial support; and those high in Inspiration, Hard-working and Volatility are more likely to provide career support.

Choosing and procuring a mentor takes a degree of confidence that may evade many organizational members. By way of speculation from the findings of this study, protégés low in confidence may need to have mentors who choose to be mentors – those more likely to be nurturing and approachable. For organizations intent on developing formal mentor programmes it would also be important that protégés who are new to the organization or lack confidence are matched to mentors high in characteristics such as Nurturance, Approachability and Authenticity, while those at a higher management level or who possess a healthy dose of confidence are encouraged to find their own mentors, according to their 'just-in-time' learning and career development needs. Interestingly, protégés whose mentors were reportedly high in Volatility took an active role in the relationship and went out of their way to attract their mentor. In other words, they knew what they wanted and went for it.

SUMMARY

This study set out to explore how ordinary people perceived their mentors and whether they were seen to possess particular personality characteristics that distinguished them from their non-mentor colleagues. Earlier studies had shown that mentoring in the workplace is important. However, because most studies of mentoring have been conducted in organizations, there has been doubt about the extent to which ordinary people understood, let alone had experience of, mentoring. Ordinary citizens understand the notion of mentoring and can recall and describe their mentors in interesting and provocative ways. These people valued the uniqueness of their mentors and made explicit what we have known tacitly for a long time.

The particular contribution this study makes is to corroborate the narrative characterizations which people offer to their mentors with a method for quantitatively scaling and verifying their anecdotal descriptions.

Finally, in our search for the 'perfect mentor' we may have been too quick to judge people from a set of positive qualities and fallen into the functionalist trap of using mentoring to maintain the status quo. There is a need to construct new maps that value difference and utilize these differences so that all employees, regardless of their personality differences, can play an important role in workplace learning.

Readers may construct their own mentoring profiles at www.mentoringdimensions.com.

4 Mentor competences: a field perspective

DAVID CLUTTERBUCK

The starting point for this chapter is the experience captured on flip charts and in discussion groups of thousands of mentors, mentees and would-be mentors around the world, who have attended skills development workshops and seminars over the past decade. It is their experience that defines the behavioural dimensions, and the conceptual models of mentor competence presented. This is, therefore, a *practitioner's* account.

In addition, however, the chapter presents some of the research and connections with academic study that reinforce and/or complement these practitioner insights. It also explores the nature and role of generic competence standards in helping mentors – and those who employ them – to evaluate the individual mentor's preparedness for and ability in the role.

A PROBLEM OF DEFINITION

Before we begin to analyse, it is an issue to clarify precisely what is meant in this context by both 'mentoring' and 'coaching'.

DEFINING MENTORING

One of the recurring problems in any analysis of good practice in mentoring is the lack of precision in what activities and behaviours are being assessed. As Gill Lane's literature review illustrates (see Chapter 1), opinions vary widely about what a mentor *is* and what a mentor *does*. 'Coaching', 'counselling' and 'mentoring' have different, sometimes totally opposite, meanings according to which discipline you come from. Many managers in companies have difficulty defining which role is which. Academic studies often add to the confusion. In a random selection of 30 academic papers on mentoring, only four provided a clear definition of precisely what they were studying. In the rest, there was no indication of whether the relationship was any of the following:

- supervisory or off-line (a substantially different dynamic occurs when the helper has a decision-making influence on the junior partner's career)
- formal or informal (again, a different dynamic applies, although this aspect is more of a spectrum than two absolute differences)
- a stand-alone arrangement or part of a broader developmental support structure (perception of purpose is likely to affect both expectation and behaviour).

Another undefined variable that might have affected the results of these studies was the power distance between mentor and mentee (for example, how many hierarchical layers there were between them).

In this chapter, therefore, we will attempt to be precise in defining what we are examining. The kind of relationship we refer to is characterized thus:

- out of the reporting line
- formal in the sense that it is part of a structured programme, where there is both an *organizational purpose* and a *relationship purpose*
- one where the power and authority of the mentor are either irrelevant to the relationship or are purposefully 'parked' by the participants; where the experience gap rather than the status gap drives the processes of learning and career management

These defining criteria are core to what has become known as the 'development-focused' model of mentoring, which has emerged primarily in Europe, Australasia, Canada and southern Africa. By contrast, the 'sponsorship-focused' model still predominates in the United States – or at least in the literature emanating from North America. In this kind of mentoring relationship, it is the mentor's ability to do things on behalf of someone more junior that drives the relationship. Learning tends to flow one way, from mentor to mentee, whereas in developmental mentoring, learning is typically a mutual activity. In sponsorship-focused mentoring, the mentor plays a strong role in driving the agenda; in development-focused mentoring, the mentee is the main driver of the process (being responsible for their own development and career management), and the emphasis of the relationship is on helping them to become more self-resourceful. Not surprisingly, the language of mentoring differs between these two models, with sponsorship-focused mentoring referring to 'protégés' and development-focused mentoring to 'mentees'.

DEFINING 'COMPETENCE'

The definition of 'competence' is also not always consistent. Is a competent individual one who can do the basics of a task consistently well? Or someone who is expert at it? Is competence solely a matter of skill and application, or does it also include personality and attitude? For the purposes of this chapter, I have defined 'competence' as the consistent, observable and measurable ability to perform a defined task or an element of a task.

The development of a fully validated set of competences is a lengthy and time-consuming business. The concepts outlined here can best be described as 'proto-competences' – skills and behaviours which have high face validity, but have not so far been subjected to rigorous validation.

ADDING TO THE COMPLEXITY

Defining 'mentor competences' is also complicated by the fact that all mentoring relationships are both *situational* and *temporal* in nature. By 'situational', we mean that *the primary responsibility of the mentor is to respond to the mentee's need.* This is a bold statement to make, but it is one that is generally endorsed by all parties in a mentoring programme, both participants and the organization.

If there are different needs, it implies that there should be different responses. We can therefore infer that one of the generic competences of a mentor is to *be able to respond appropriately to the variety of needs a mentee may have.* This immediately poses problems, because the range of situations could be very wide.

Let us peel this onion one layer further. Situation may also be affected by purpose. Whose purpose? Typically the organization will have a scheme purpose, which provides the reason supporting mentoring. This purpose might be developing top talent, promoting diversity, retaining graduate recruits and so on. At the same time, the participants in the relationship will have a common purpose, which may be different from that of the organization. (The mentee may, for example, plan to leave the organization in three years' time.) The mentor may also have some learning goals from the relationship – perhaps to hone their skills in developing direct reports. So another generic competence may be *the ability to recognize and reconcile different and perhaps conflicting purposes.*

The temporal nature of mentoring refers to the way, in which relationships evolve over time. Kathy Kram, whose original and insightful studies of mentoring in the early 1980s have been the foundation for so much later research, identified four phases of evolution: initiation, cultivation, separation and redefinition (Kram, 1983). Field experience with much larger numbers than Kram's original sample suggest that, for the definition of mentoring this chapter refers to, there are potentially five phases, as shown in Figure 4.1.

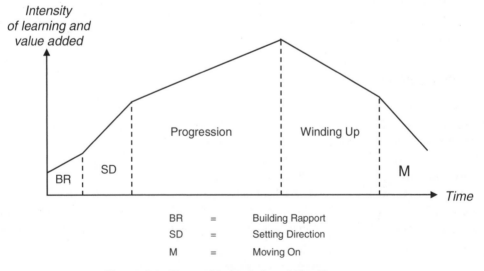

Figure 4.1 **Phases of the mentoring relationship**

Building Rapport is the initial phase, in which mentor and mentee decide whether or not they want to work with each other. If the chemistry is not right, or there is an inappropriate balance of similarity (common ground, common interests) and dissimilarity (an experience gap that provides opportunities for learning), the relationship will not progress very far under its own steam. As important as the skills of achieving rapport is the ability of the mentor to recognize and manage positively a lack of rapport – confronting the issue openly and reviewing with the mentee what kind of person might better meet their needs. At this stage, also, mentor and mentee negotiate how the relationship will be conducted – what each expects of the other, particularly in terms of behaviours.

Setting direction is the phase in which mentor and mentee achieve clarity about what each aims to achieve from the relationship, and how. Goals may change with circumstances or as they are achieved and replaced with new ones. However, having a sense of purpose for the relationship is fundamental to achieving commitment to it.

Progression is the hard core of the mentoring relationship – where most of the time and energy is expended. Having helped the mentee to define and commit to personal change, the mentor has to goad and support them as needed. Most of this effort will take place within the mentoring meetings, but much may also occur through telephone conversations and via e-mail. The portfolio of potential skills required here is as wide as the variety of potential applications of mentoring. Where practical and within the role, the mentor will wish to provide the particular type of help that is needed, when it is asked for. Most, if not all, of these behaviours are covered later in this chapter, see page 46.

Winding up occurs as the relationship has delivered or helped to deliver the desired outcomes, or when the mentee begins to outgrow the mentor. It is not always obvious when the time has come for the mentee to leave the comfort of the mentoring nest. The mentor needs to be sensitive to this issue and to some extent pre-emptive, reviewing the added value of the relationship with the mentee from time to time. Having a vision of where the relationship might go (although not one that restricts or restrains its potential by being too fixed or too narrow) also helps the mentor plan an effective, positive ending.

Moving on from a mentoring relationship into a less committed, more casual relationship, or professional friendship, demands potentially complex skills of redefinition. These have been likened to changes in relationship between parent and child. Some such relationships never progress beyond parent–child behaviours, even when the child has grown up and become a parent in turn. Old habits die hard. Other parent-child relationships dissolve into conflict: instead of dependence, the child's need to self-express leads to counter-dependence – a rejection of the parent. In a healthy relationship, however, the child achieves independence and their interaction with the parent becomes collegial. The greater the element of sponsorship and power-broking within a relationship, the more difficult it appears to be for both parties to achieve the positive independence of each other that underlies a continuing professional friendship.

Each phase requires a modification of the mentor's behaviours and, by inference therefore, of the competences required. The skills of rapport-building differ substantially from those required in helping someone clarify and commit to specific career or personal development goals. The skills required in managing a relationship which has settled into an effective routine are different from those required in bringing the formal phase of the relationship to a positive close. And, should the relationship evolve into more of a long-term supportive friendship, it may call for different behaviours again. Another generic competence, therefore, may be *recognizing and adapting appropriately to the phases of the mentoring relationship.*

SOME SUGGESTED COMPETENCES FOR EACH PHASE OF THE MENTORING RELATIONSHIP

Building rapport is a behaviour set, which has been relatively well researched. It includes the skills of active listening, empathizing and giving positive regard; of offering openness and trust to elicit reciprocal behaviour; and of identifying and valuing both common ground and differences.

Setting direction requires a portfolio of skills, including goal identification, clarification and management; personal project planning; and testing the mentee's level of commitment to specific goals. Reality testing – helping the mentee focus on a few, achievable goals rather than on many pipedreams – is as important as helping the mentee raise their horizons to set more ambitious personal targets than they might otherwise have done.

Progression requires a further shift of behaviours. Among competence issues raised by mentors and mentees in reviewing their experience at this stage are:

- sustaining commitment
- ensuring sufficient challenge in the mentoring dialogue
- helping the mentee take increasing responsibility for managing the relationship
- being available and understanding in helping the mentee cope with setbacks.

Winding up was the theme of a recent study (Clutterbuck and Megginson, 2001) of 44 mentors' experiences, across a wide spectrum of situations, with mentors being both internal and external to the organization (see Chapter 15). Virtually all those relationships, which had been allowed simply to drift away, were viewed by participants as unsatisfactory; while those that had managed the dissolution process were almost all regarded positively.

Moving on to a *professional friendship* has not been studied in detail since Kram's original review of mentoring relationships. However, it appears likely that a core competence of this phase of the mentoring relationship may well be *the ability to redefine the relationship when it has run its formal course.*

GENERIC COMPETENCES FOR MENTORS: A ROLE AND BEHAVIOUR MODEL

While some informal mentoring relationships operate in an isolated context, most workplace mentoring occurs as one element in a complex network of developmental relationships. People learn from a wide variety of colleagues – from their immediate superior, their peers, their direct reports, from technical specialists and training professionals, to name but a few. People may also play a variety of roles in helping others to learn.

All developmental relationships at work appear to be defined by two dimensions. One relates to the degree of directiveness applied. In some circumstances, the more experienced person may take the lead, suggesting things the less experienced person could experiment with, giving direct advice, suggesting topics to discuss and perhaps giving feedback. The more of these behaviours the more experienced partner exhibits, the more directive the relationship. If, on the other hand, the relationship is one of similar but different experience, or the less experienced person sets the agenda, generates their own feedback (or brings to the discussion feedback they have gathered from elsewhere) and/or takes the lead in managing the relationship, it can be said to be relatively non-directive.

The second dimension has its origins in the personality of the figure behind the mortal Mentor in the Greek story – the goddess Athena, who represented both warlike, challenging behaviours and the nurturing, supportive behaviours appropriate to the goddess of handicrafts and agriculture. Stretching people through challenging assignments, then supporting them as they gain confidence and new skills, has been shown to be a core capability for line managers in a creative environment (Microsoft, 1997).

As with any other developer, a core competence for the mentor must be to *respond to the learner's needs with the appropriate level of directiveness and the appropriate balance of stretch and nurture.*

Each of the four quadrants created by the two developmental dimensions suggests a common role, as follows (Figure 4.2):

- Directive stretching suggests the role of *coach*. Coaches encourage people to try new things, demonstrate what to do, give feedback and act as a critical friend. In general, the process is mainly in the hands of the coach (although some of our observations of coachee behaviours suggest that the coachee can strongly influence the coach's response to requests for help.) In traditional coaching, where the emphasis is on observation and feedback by the coach, the goals are also owned or at least proposed by the coach; in the more recent evolutions of coaching, which aim to generate intrinsic feedback by the learner, ownership of the goals rests more with the learner.
- Non-directive nurturing suggests the role of *counsellor.* Counsellors help people to cope, and to make career and personal plans. They provide a sounding board, a shoulder to cry on, and sometimes, someone to just listen. In workplace counselling, it is the person being helped who sets their goals – indeed it could be argued that counselling of this kind is a precursor to effective coaching.
- Directive nurturing suggests a role we can call *guardian* – someone who takes a protective interest, gives grandfatherly advice and is a role model in some areas, which the less experienced person may wish to emulate. At the extreme, the guardian may be a kind of godfather figure, 'fixing' things on the less experienced person's behalf, putting them forward for high-profile projects that will benefit their career, and so on. In effect, the guardian is more hands-on than the counsellor.
- Non-directive stretching aims to help the less experienced person become more self-resourceful. In particular, it helps them build more extensive networks of people and places, to which they can turn for learning and support. We typically call this role *facilitator* or *networker-facilitator.*

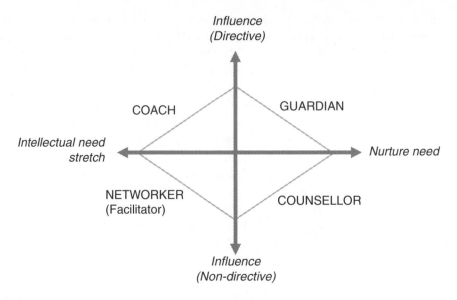

Figure 4.2 Dimensions of mentoring

One of the most practical ways of looking at mentoring is as a broadly holistic process that draws heavily on all four of these roles, according to the learner's needs. From the earliest studies of mentoring by Kram (1983) and Alleman *et al.* (1984), the elements of these roles have been recognized. However, there is not complete overlap. Mentors do not normally set goals for the learner, nor give feedback based on observation of the learner's work. Rather, they work with the learner's own perspectives and try to help them develop better skills of intrinsic observation. While mentors may need some of the skills of counselling, they are not therapists (and even were they clinically qualified, it is usually unwise to mix roles in such circumstances). And, in the definition of mentoring with which we are working, sponsorship would be outside the role, although fully permissible for a guardian.

A further competence set, then, can be posited as *the ability to recognize different developmental roles, the flexibility to move between roles appropriately and comfortably, and the ability to recognize the boundaries between mentoring and those elements of other roles which are not normally part of the mentoring experience.*

A FIELD PERSPECTIVE

The behavioural model suggests that mentoring requires a situational set of competences. At the same time, fieldwork suggests that there are also generic competences. Several years ago, we began to gather perceptions of managers, professional executive mentors and human resource professionals about those behaviours and abilities which had proven most useful in executive mentoring. In parallel, we gathered feedback from initial training sessions, review workshops and questionnaires to both programme participants and programme co-ordinators

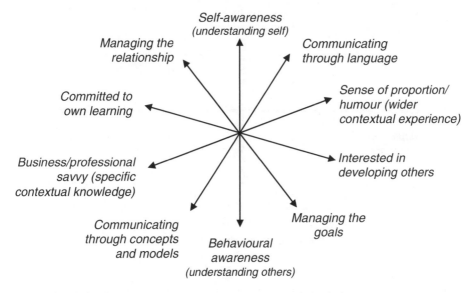

Figure 4.3 Five competency pairs of mentor competences

for a variety of other work-based programmes – for equal opportunities, graduate induction, succession planning and so on – across a wide swathe of industries and nationalities.

The research method was highly informal. In the initial training workshop, mentors and mentees were asked to complete a list of the characteristics that they would *least* expect in an effective mentor – 'the mentor from hell' – and then of the characteristics that they would *most* expect in an effective mentor.

We found five pairs of matched capabilities, which were commonly associated with the most efficacious mentors (Figure 4.3). These were:

- self-awareness *and* behavioural awareness
- business/professional savvy *and* sense of proportion
- communication *and* conceptual modelling
- commitment to own learning *and* interest in helping others to learn
- relationship management *and* goal clarity.

These five dimensions, considered in turn below, give rise to another ten potential competences.

SELF-AWARENESS AND BEHAVIOURAL AWARENESS

This might more easily be expressed as 'mentors need a relatively high level of emotional intelligence', although only two elements of emotional intelligence are represented here (Goleman, 1996). Mentors need high self-awareness in order to recognize and manage their own behaviours within the helping relationship and to use empathy appropriately. Self-awareness helps them recognize when there is a dissonance between what they are advising the mentee to do and what they do themselves. It is also essential to the processes of analysing one's own behaviour and motivations. One of the common problems we find in mentoring relationships

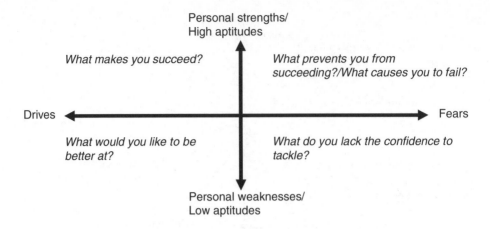

Figure 4.4 Building self-awareness

is that the mentor sees the mentee's issues in the light of the mentor's own problems and preoccupations, rather than from the mentee's perspective. Such transference may lead to dangerously inapt guidance.

Given that the mentor's role is often at least in part to help the mentee grow their own self-awareness, being an effective role model for self-perceptiveness could be regarded as an essential skill. By the same token, having an understanding of and insight into other people's behaviour and motivations is equally important. To help others manage their relationships, the mentor must have reasonably good insight into patterns of behaviour between individuals and groups of people. Predicting the consequences of specific behaviours or courses of action is one of the many practical applications of this insight. It is not normally essential for the mentor to have a deep understanding of behavioural psychology, but it does help for them to be able to relate issues to some of the basic concepts of motivation, social exchange and learning processes. Helping someone else work through such issues frequently results in the mentor reflecting more deeply on similar issues of their own.

Some of the questions which mentors may usefully ask themselves and their mentees to build self-awareness are illustrated in Figure 4.4.

BUSINESS/PROFESSIONAL SAVVY AND SENSE OF PROPORTION

Savvy is the intuitive wisdom a person gathers from extensive and varied experience and reflection on that experience. It could also be referred to as specific contextual knowledge. The mentee's need for access to that wisdom may be very broad (an overview of good business practice) or quite narrow (making better use of a computer). Savvy may be technical, strategic, political or systemic. It helps the mentee avoid problems, which they might not have foreseen; find better strategies for getting round obstacles; and it is the source of those 'killer' questions that force people to reshape their thinking. In short, savvy is the link between experience and being able to use experience to guide another person effectively.

Sense of proportion (wider contextual experience) is a broader perspective that places the organization's goals and culture in the wider social and business context. It is, in effect, the other side of wisdom – the ability to step back from the detail, to identify what is really important and to link together apparently discrete issues. It also encompasses the ability to project good humour, helping the mentee recognize the elements of incongruity in situations and laugh at themself, where appropriate. Mentees frequently find this to be one of the most valuable competences of a mentor – very often the mentee is so close to their issues that they cannot easily put them into perspective without skilled help.

COMMUNICATION AND CONCEPT MODELLING

Communication isn't a single skill; it is a combination of a number of skills. Those most important for mentors include:

- listening – opening the mind to what the other person is saying, demonstrating interest/ attention, encouraging them to speak, holding back on filling the silences
- observing as receiver – being open to the visual and other non-verbal signals, recognizing what is *not* said
- parallel processing – analysing what the other person is saying, reflecting on it, preparing responses (effective communicators do all of these in parallel, slowing down the dialogue as needed to ensure that they do not overemphasize preparing responses at the expense of analysis and reflection; equally, they avoid becoming so mired in their internal thoughts that they respond inadequately or too slowly)
- projecting – crafting words and their emotional 'wrapping' in a manner appropriate for the situation and the recipient
- observing as projector – being open to the visual and other non-verbal signals, as clues to what the recipient is hearing/understanding, and adapting tone, volume, pace and language appropriately
- exiting – concluding a dialogue or segment of dialogue with clarity and alignment of understanding (ensuring message received in both directions).

The most effective mentors place far more emphasis on listening and encouraging the mentee to speak than on talking themselves. They are also adept at the use of silence, at times suggesting the mentee pause to reflect on an issue; at other times simply allowing silence to take over, giving the mentee space to think matters through.

Effective mentors have a portfolio of models they can draw upon to help the mentee understand the issues they face. These models can be self-generated (that is, the result of personal experience), drawn from elsewhere (for example, models of company structure, interpersonal behaviours, strategic planning, career planning) or – at the highest level of competence – generated on the spot as an immediate response.

According to the situation and the learning styles of the mentee, it may be appropriate to present these models in verbal or visual form. Or the mentor may not present them at all, but simply use them as the framework for asking penetrating questions.

COMMITMENT TO OWN LEARNING AND INTEREST IN HELPING OTHERS TO LEARN

Effective developmental mentors become role models for self-managed learning. They seize opportunities to experiment and take part in new experiences. They read widely and are reasonably efficient at setting and following personal development plans. They actively seek and use behavioural feedback from others. Within the context of the mentoring relationship, they perceive this as a significant opportunity for mutual learning. They may articulate their learning needs to the mentee and from time to time share what they have learned from the relationship.

At the same time, effective mentors have an innate interest in achieving through others and in helping others recognize and achieve their potential. This instinctive response is important in establishing and maintaining rapport and in enthusing the mentee, building their confidence in what they could become. There is a danger here, however. The more the relationship is driven by the mentor's need to feel useful, the easier it is to overshadow the mentee's need to achieve independence. Mentors (particularly in a sponsorship-based model) may end up trying to relive their own careers through someone else. Altruism can be a highly self-serving attitude of mind, if it is not moderated by a sense of social exchange. The overt recognition of mutual learning objectives largely overcomes this problem.

RELATIONSHIP MANAGEMETN AND GOAL CLARITY

Both of these areas have been largely covered in the analysis of the various phases of a mentoring relationship. Among the key abilities in relationship management are to establish and maintain rapport, to set and adhere to a schedule of meetings, and to step back and review the relationship from time to time. Mentees rate their mentors highly on relationship management when the latter clearly place an importance on the relationship and demonstrate that they have continued to think about the mentee's issues between meetings.

Goal clarity is important, because the mentor must be able to help the learner sort out what they want to achieve and why. Goal clarity appears to derive from a mixture of skills including systematic analysis and decisiveness. Mentors who lack the skills to set and pursue clear goals of their own are likely to struggle to help someone else. Yet most mentors seem to find that helping someone else achieve goal clarity has a positive effect on how they perceive and work towards their own goals.

THE BROADER ISSUE OF STANDARDS

The issue of standards in mentoring has arisen for two reasons. First, the rapid spread of mentoring programmes aimed at young and vulnerable people requires close attention to risk management, and government-supported programmes require standards as an element of impact measurement. Second, the rapid growth of executive coaching and mentoring inevitably gives rise to calls for regulation, given that anyone can claim to have the necessary skills and experience. The increasing volume of qualifications offered in coaching and mentoring does not necessarily help, as they tend not to be specific about the level of competence required (length of experience does not equate to quality of performance!), or about the audience specific factors that may demand additional competences (for example, knowledge of cognitive development and skills in behaviour management for mentors of children and persons with special needs).

There does, however, seem to be room for a generic or core set of mentoring standards, which will apply with minimal adaptation to most or all situations and to which situation-specific competences can be added as appropriate. One valiant attempt to do this is the *Draft Occupational Standards on Mentoring*, produced by the University of North London, in association with a variety of other academic and practitioner bodies. This was evaluated in over 300 mentoring schemes in all sectors of education, government and business.

More recently, a set of standards for mentoring programmes has been generated and subjected to public consultation on behalf of the European Mentoring and Coaching Council.

Standards codify competences into a framework that can be used to assess how well an individual performs against them. The virtue of this framework is that it provides a structure upon which evidence of competence can be gathered, in terms of both knowledge and effective practice. Unlike most qualification-based programmes, they provide an objective, independent measure. How useful that measure is depends on how credible the standards are perceived to be by programme participants and organizations using mentoring. It is probably fair to say that the jury is still out on this issue.

THE PERSONALITY ISSUE

Personality is not by itself a competence of a mentor, although some traits – such as empathy – may predispose towards positive mentoring behaviours. Alleman *et al.* (1984) found that traditional approaches to personality measurement did not have significant impact on relationship outcomes. Engstrom and Mykletun (1999) used a different measure of personality factors (see chapter 6).

When we ask mentors and mentees to describe the kind of personal attributes which make for a good (or for a disastrous) mentor, they usually respond with a mixture of personality factors, attitudes and behaviours. Some of the most common are listed in Table 4.1.

Table 4.1 Qualities attributed by mentors and mentees to good and poor mentors

Positive attributes	Negative attributes
Friendly	Distant
Committed	Obligated
Empathetic	Self-preoccupied
Sees benefits to self	Sees only a one-way exchange
Encouraging/positive	Discouraging/negative
Self-confident	Arrogant
Open/trustful	Distrustful
Challenging	Either combative or passive
Reliable	Inconsistent
Astute	Cynical/political

This is by no means an exhaustive list. However, together these items form the basis for a set of behavioural competences, which might be described as *establishing a positive, dynamic atmosphere within the relationship.*

COMPETENCES AND OUTCOMES

A competence is of little value unless it assists in achieving some form of intended or desirable outcome. In mentoring terms, desirable outcomes can be cast into four basic categories, each of which applies (to a greater or lesser extent) to both mentor and mentee. These categories are detailed in Table 4.2.

Table 4.2 Desirable outcomes of mentoring

General	Career management	Enabling	Emotional
Knowledge acquisition	Achievement of specific career goals	Increased self-awareness	Increased confidence
Improvement in technical competence	Being in greater control of career	Increased visibility	Opportunities to reflect
Improvement in behavioural competence	Increased confidence in being able to achieve career goals	Better understanding of organizational politics	Intellectual challenge
		Clarity of personal goals	Improved feeling of being valued by the organization

An obvious implication of these categories is that some, at least, will demand specific competences. Many of the potential competences we have already identified are relevant here.

MACRO COMPETENCES VERSUS MICRO-COMPETENCES

As the box opposite illustrates, these multiple approaches to identifying the competences of a mentor give rise to a long list, with considerable duplication. From a practitioner perspective and/or from the perspective of someone who helps mentors and mentees equip themselves with the skills for the role, this is not necessarily a problem. We know that this is a complex, intuitive, multiskilled role that requires a very wide spectrum of life skills and purpose-specific skills. The reduction of the list into macro and micro is to some extent arbitrary, but all the items listed under macro-competences are generic – they are essential for effective role management in all mentoring relationships. The micro-elements, by contrast, all have some aspects of situationality – they are specific to a phase of the relationship, or they are a constituent behaviour or skill which will enhance the relationship, but not necessarily one that all relationships will require in significant measure. Very few mentors out of a potential population are likely to be excellent in all of these micro-competences – indeed, they may use the mentoring relationship as one means to develop in those areas where they are least strong.

POTENTIAL COMPETENCES IN FULL

Macro-competences

- Being able to respond appropriately to the variety of needs a mentee may have
- Having the ability to recognize and reconcile different and perhaps conflicting purposes
- Recognizing and adapting appropriately to the phases of the mentoring relationship
- Responding to the learner's needs with the appropriate level of directiveness and the appropriate balance of stretch and nurture
- Recognizing different developmental roles, and having the flexibility to move between roles appropriately and comfortably
- Recognizing the boundaries between mentoring and those elements of other roles which are not normally part of the mentoring experience
- Establishing a positive, dynamic atmosphere within the relationship (motivational skills).

Micro-competences

- Building rapport – active listening, empathizing and giving positive regard; offering openness and trust to elicit reciprocal behaviour; identifying and valuing both common ground and differences
- Setting direction – goal identification, clarification and management; personal project planning; testing the mentee's level of commitment to specific goals; reality testing
- Progression – sustaining commitment; ensuring sufficient challenge in the mentoring dialogue; helping the mentee take increasing responsibility for managing the relationship; being available and understanding in helping the mentee cope with setbacks
- Winding down – the ability to review the relationship formally and celebrate what has been achieved
- Moving on – the ability to redefine the relationship when it has run its formal course..
- Self-awareness
- Behavioural awareness
- Business/professional savvy
- Sense of proportion
- Communication
- Conceptual modelling
- Commitment to own learning (being a role model for good practice in self-development)
- Interest in helping others to learn
- Relationship management
- Goal clarity.

Recognizing the ideal, however, provides a platform for development, which both individuals and mentoring scheme co-ordinators can use.

From an academic perspective, I hope this analysis provides a starting point for continued research to refine the notion of mentoring competences. Certainly, some greater clarity around which competences are generic in *all* forms of mentoring would be helpful, along with a credible diagnostic process to map the micro-competences of mentoring against the requirements of specific situations and forms of mentoring.

CONCLUSION

This chapter has not set out to achieve a comprehensive, neat framework of mentor competences. Rather, I have tried to illustrate the complexity of such a task and some of the elements such a framework would likely need to include. Herein lies a dilemma, however. The more we formalize and measure mentoring, the more we distance it from its informal, intuitive origins. Like the rainbow in Keats's poem (see introduction), our drive to analyse and standardize may destroy what we admire and aim to preserve. On the other hand, the greater our understanding of the competences of an effective mentor, the better we can help prospective and practising mentors raise the quality of what they do. There is a balance to be struck here, and I hope we can learn to reach and sustain it.

A quantitative view of mentor competence

5

GILL LANE

Given the range of literature around roles and activities of mentors, this chapter outlines how those roles and activities were formed into an initial model of mentor competence and presented to focus groups, from which a refined model and quantitative survey emerged. The study involved a wide range of organizations and sectors, including responses from mentors, mentees and academics interested in mentoring, and looked at both behavioural and personal competence approaches to determine the core skills and abilities that make for effective mentors. The methodology involved literature review, an initial model of mentor competence, focus groups, two case studies and a quantitative study.

The chapter is divided into the following sections:

- the rationale for undertaking the research
- focus of research and hypothesis
- the research methodology – a literature review, testing of an initial model of mentor competence, focus groups, two case studies and a detailed questionnaire
- findings and the developed model of mentor competence
- implications and summary.

The chapter looks at the research done and the emergent results, and considers the implications for mentoring, whether as a mentor, mentee or for those engaged in setting up mentoring programmes.

The doctoral-level research was undertaken through Henley Management College in conjunction with Brunel University.

THE RATIONALE FOR UNDERTAKING THE RESEARCH

At the start of the study there was almost nothing in terms of investigation into the competence required of a mentor. Because much was being made of competence development for managers at that time and the interest in mentoring was continuing to grow, it seemed appropriate to see if a specific mix of competences was relevant and then to consider whether that mix of competences was appropriate to specific mentoring situations.

From the initial literature review into the roles and activities of mentors, it was confirmed that little written work was available on specific competences or competence structures around which major research could be structured. Others who have written in this area were undoubtedly having similar thoughts at around the same time and thus a number of competence approaches emerged within a few years of one another (see Chapter 1 for further details).

If one could determine a suite of competences that made for an effective mentor, then that suite of competences could be applied to a number of situations. Training programmes, standards for mentors and companies internally recruiting mentors and matching with mentees could all benefit. In addition, mentors would be able to assess themselves against the 'effectiveness' competence set to see whether they might need to place their energies into slightly different mentoring approaches in order to really help their mentees develop.

It is assumed that mentor competence can be applicable to non-work mentoring as well as mentoring relationships within the work environment.

FOCUS OF RESEARCH AND HYPOTHESIS

The research came from interest in and knowledge of both mentoring and competence generation. The latter had been the subject of intensive focus group research with senior managers, and initially the research into mentor competence focused on the senior manager as mentor, the initial hypothesis being that those in senior management use specific competences as mentors.

As the study progressed it became apparent that the seniority of manager level in those acting as mentors was irrelevant with regard to the range of mentor competence. It may still apply, however, in respect of emphasis, an example being where a mentor is helping a mentee who is in a senior position: networking may have a higher prominence for that mentee because of the seniority of their position and the need for more networking in career terms, the higher one rises in seniority. Networking may be applicable to all levels in mentoring relationships but its emphasis as a developmental tool at the higher levels of management may influence the higher level of input in mentoring relationships of more senior positions.

The study began by looking at some of the vast array of literature on the roles and activities of the mentor and at the underpinning skills, abilities and knowledge required for effectiveness in mentoring. It split the list of potential mentor competence into two, taking its lead from a number of competence approaches: functional competence (often referred to as behavioural competence) and personal competence (or personal characteristics). This gives us the combination of the practical 'doing' type approaches and the 'being' type approaches, the mixture of which is essential to performance.

It should be noted that this twofold competence structure based on the two aspects of functional and personal competence followed the research of Richard Boyatzis (1982) and Woodruffe (1990). Boyatzis defined competence as broadly 'an underlying characteristic of a person', which Woodruffe believes could be a 'motive, trait, skill, aspect of one's self-image or social role or a body of knowledge which he or she uses'. A further examination of Boyatzis's work talks of competence as being:

- occupational competence: the aspects of a job that have to be performed competently
- personal competence: what people need to bring to the job in order to perform the aspects to the required level of competence.

These two distinctions have become known as functional or personal competence. This research follows these distinctions in differentiating between the two lists of competences for further analysis.

Taking these functional and personal competence models from the research work on the competence of senior management (Lane, 1996), the research drew from the roles and activities outlined in mentoring literature. It looked at whether both mentors and mentees considered them to be of significant importance in the respective three areas of mentoring activity:

- career focus
- current role focus
- personal development.

The study considered whether the range of competences required was generic to mentoring, irrespective of the focus of discussion/situation and equally whether a range of competences fell within each of the three distinct mentoring approaches. As the literature was explored, it became apparent that the roles and activities needed in each distinct area were not necessarily repeated in the other two areask, and thus the underlying functional competence might vary from one part of the mentoring emphasis to another. The same could be said of the underlying personal competence. If these assumptions were found to be accurate then it was feasible that a distinct suite of functional and personal competences existed for each of the three situational contexts.

With this potential outcome, training arrangements for mentors could be specifically tailored to the type of mentor functions that the mentor is likely to perform in any given situation. Those setting up mentoring schemes in companies or recruiting mentors to existing schemes can establish the type of functions to be performed and appoint based on the specific competence set required. Existing senior managers seeking peer mentors might seek peers displaying the range of competences that links to the specific mentoring they seek at a specific time.

The further development of the model shows the addition of the more generic competences and these together with the discrete competences for the three key areas can help the overall training, recruitment and self-assessment by mentors referred to earlier.

The hypothesis therefore became that there was a distinct suite of competences for mentors when operating within each of the three distinct areas of career focus, current role focus and personal development in addition to a generic set of competences. The emphasis on what the core generic competence set should consist of for effectiveness only emerged towards the final stages of the research.

THE RESEARCH METHODOLOGY

This section looks at how the quantitative research was conducted through a literature review, testing of an initial model of mentor competence, focus groups, two case studies and a detailed questionnaire.

A qualitative approach was initially undertaken to inform the methodology. This consisted of the literature review followed by preparation of an initial model of mentor competence. This, together with the research concept, was tested with a number of focus groups. A questionnaire followed, tested with a pilot group prior to circulation. Two case studies were developed using the questionnaire as the baseline for specific target audiences.

A LITERATURE REVIEW

Details of a selection of the literature can be found in Chapter 1. The literature review began with mainly hard text copy, leading to the development of the initial model of mentor competence, and was then extended to take in further literature including articles relevant to the topic. Many writers were considered and, at first trawl, the literature seemed divided into consideration of relationships in mentoring, gender issues, the process of mentoring, and finally the roles and activities of the mentor. This latter area of roles and activities formed the research focus.

The research started in 1995 and predominantly looked at writers of that period and earlier. A number of writers referred to roles and activities of mentors across one, two or all three of the three distinct areas referred to earlier, namely: career focus, current role focus and personal development. Writers giving strength to this approach include Baird (1993), Bennett (1992), Caldwell and Carter (1993), Caruso (1992), Clutterbuck (1985), Kram (1988), Lane and Robinson (1992), Levinson *et al.* (1978), Leeds Metropolitan University (1995), Mumford (1989), Noe (1988), Parsloe (1992), Schein (1978), Simosko (1991) and Wiggans (1995). (More details can be found in Chapter 1.)

From these writers an initial model of mentor competence emerged, and further reading into various articles and other books (again see Chapter 1) supported and strengthened the model.

The concept of separating the mentor competence into discrete parts of the model was supported by Green and Bauer (1995), who researched Supervisory Mentoring with doctoral students in a longitudinal study of 233 PhD students and found that not all required all the mentoring functions provided to the mentees. Their study examined the relationship between the student potential for mentoring and their research productivity and commitment. They were able to distinguish between what they termed 'psychosocial mentoring', akin to the personal development focus of this research model; 'career mentoring', as in career focus; and 'research collaboration', which relates to the current role focus, given that the PhD was the current role focus for the students. They considered that mentoring for some mentees might not need all three functions of mentoring, and in some contexts mentoring might take on compensatory characteristics where emphasis on one function might compensate for the lack of other functions. This was noted in Chapter 1 and reenforced the altered hypothesis of different competences being important to different situations, as per this research.

Table 5.1   Lane's initial combined mentor competence model showing potential differences (Lane, 1997)

Current role focus	Career focus	Personal development
Trainer	Opener of doors	Counsellor
Confidence builder	Networker	Encourager
Director	Political mover	Supporter
	Role model	Evaluator
	Career developer	

TESTING OF AN INITIAL MODEL OF MENTOR COMPETENCE

Following the early literature review, an initial model of mentor competence was developed as a 'taster' of what might emerge from more detailed research. At later stages this was to be developed into a more complex model as a result of empirical data collection and analysis. The initial model took the three facets of mentoring as shown from the key literature references, and demonstrated potential competence attributed to each of the three areas given the findings from the initial literature trawl. These were first put into separate models for the functional competence set and then for the personal competence set. Then the differences alone were pulled together into the combined initial model (Table 5.1). The model showed some of the key roles and functions attributed to only one of each of the three areas as found in the literature review. No attempt was taken to provide a comprehensive list, as it was merely a vehicle at this stage to test the potential for further research into specific competences within such a mentor approach. Equally, no attempt was made to break down the roles and activities further into the underpinning competence for each role/activity, as the main purpose was to identify the potential for such a model with division between the three differing mentoring aspects. The generic list of roles and activities attributive to all three areas was excluded from the initial model as a means of testing whether such a variation in role/activity differences was a sound approach on which to develop the research further.

This initial model demonstrating differences in roles and activities dependent on the mentoring approach was tested with a number of focus groups before forming the basis of a questionnaire inviting a more detailed response.

FOCUS GROUPS

During the early research phase, I was undertaking other development work with a UK utility company, a UK national security firm and Henley Management College, a UK-based international business school. This enabled the setting up of a number of focus groups to test out the concept of the model and the potential detailed research focus.

Each of the companies involved in the focus group discussions had mentors and mentees in a mixture of formal and informal relationships.

Groups with the utility company had between five and ten members within each of the four groups involved. All participants were at senior- or middle-level management within their organization. The security company offered a number of groups totalling 30 participants across divisional and branch manager level. The third group, from Henley Management College, were managers working as mentors with an in-house NVQ programme from within the college staff, no academic mentors being chosen at this stage so as not to bias the results into an academic dimension.

The positive qualitative feedback from each of the focus groups encouraged the formation of a quantitative-based questionnaire to build further on the idea of the initial model. The format for the final model diagram was formulated after the focus groups, though at this stage the impact of the findings from the questionnaire remained unknown.

TWO CASE STUDIES

Two case studies were undertaken, within a major international engineering and vehicle manufacturing company, and within Henley Management College. The latter case study was later dropped from the doctoral research as two cases studies were not statistically required given the amount of other statistically based evidence amassed throughout the research study.

The case study with the international firm involved initial discussion followed by questionnaires sent to two groups: their International Management Development Programme and their Graduate Programme. Further discussion then took place with the company to present the findings in relation to them, and discuss the potential implications for their mentoring relationships over the two programmes and in other mentoring pairs across the company.

The respondents were made up of mentors and mentees and, as was the case for all questionnaire respondents to this and the main survey, they had to be active within a mentoring relationship at the time of responding or within the previous six-month period to ensure currency.

The questionnaire invited respondents to provide data on the type and extent of their mentoring relationships with which they were or had been involved. In addition, it invited respondents to indicate a level of importance for an extensive list of both functional and personal competences. Mentors and mentees were further invited to provide an example of a specific mentoring incident outlining the mentor competences demonstrated plus the most influential competence. A final question asked for a list of mentor competences that the company mentors and mentees considered to be essential for mentors to possess.

Within this case study alone 42 respondents returned replies with 71.4 per cent being mentors and 26.2 per cent being mentees. The remaining 2.4 per cent had been both mentors and mentees within the period specified. Thirty-eight were male, four female. The age range was spread between under 30, up to 50 and over. As was to be expected given the programmes identified to take part, a mix of levels responded, although 63.4 per cent were from director and above, with 24.4 per cent being middle and junior management and 12.2 per cent trainees.

Mentors stated that their mentoring relationships totalled 31, with five of the respondents saying they had had more than six mentor–mentee relationships within their career. As mentees the respondents had all had less than five mentoring relationships.

The length of the mentoring relationship was queried with 12.2 per cent showing less than one year, 46.3 per cent one to two years, 34.1 per cent three to five years and 7.4 per cent having maintained one or more of their mentoring relationships for six years or more.

Frequency of meetings showed a range from monthly to less than once a year with the majority (61.9 per cent) meeting quarterly. Three quarters felt their mentoring relationships

Table 5.2   Rating scale for functional and personal competences

Very important	5
Important	4
Of some importance	3
Of little importance	2
Of no importance	1

were part of a formal scheme only, with the remainder having a mix of formal and informal. All confirmed they operated across the spectrum of the three distinct areas of career focus, current role focus and personal development.

The respondents were asked to rate a list of roles, activities, skills and knowledge (functional/behavioural competences) and a list of characteristics (personal competences) of mentors against the criteria shown in Table 5.2.

In response, 32 functional competences were offered for consideration, plus 30 personal competences. For every competence respondents were asked to give a rating of importance in each of the columns against career focus, current role focus and personal development.

The findings and the impact on the overall model of mentor competence can be found in the later section in this chapter on findings and then the section on implications. It is significant to say here that the findings of the case study survey correspond with the findings of the main survey – they are fully consistent.

A final report and presentation was given to the company with the focus on implications for each of the participating mentoring programmes. The findings and implications informed both the existing mentor programmes and future mentoring relationships.

The second case study was undertaken but dropped from the doctoral research results for the reasons mentioned above. The findings were, however, consistent with the first case study and with the main research questionnaire.

A DETAILED QUESTIONNAIRE

Alongside the case study questionnaire, the main survey was undertaken using the same questionnaire tool. After a pilot study of the questionnaire with a small group of mentors, mentees and academics from Henley Management College, the document was used for both the case studies mentioned above and for the main bulk of the respondents outside of the case study companies. The main questionnaire structure was as for the case study outlined above. Any potential bias in the questions was eliminated and the competence words were mixed at random to avoid respondents clustering their responses. The questionnaire allowed for qualitative comments.

One section was devoted to two separate lists of functional and personal competences for rating purposes. The lists drew from over 90 functional competences and over 70 personal competences, which had been identified during the literature review. Each competence set was clustered down to just over thirty for each, with an attempt at short definitions throughout to help the respondents to take a considered view before rating their level of importance to each competence within each of the three mentoring approaches (career focus, current role focus, personal development).

The detailed questionnaire was sent to 577 mentors and mentees across a number of organizations, sectors and countries from those currently or recently (within previous six months to ensure currency) operating as mentors, mentees or as both at the same time. It included mentors and mentees within formal company mentoring programmes, those within informal arrangements, those operating as external mentors and a small number of academics with an interest in mentoring from their own experience. It also included the 42 from the case study mentioned earlier. All respondents had to be active within a mentoring relationship at the time of responding or to have been active within the previous six-month period.

The total audience whilst worldwide was predominantly European, with some African, Far Eastern and US respondents. A 22.2 per cent response rate was achieved (see later section on findings for details). Of the respondents, 62 per cent were mentors, 25 per cent were mentees and 13 per cent were both mentors and mentees.

The respondents were asked to self-assess their level within the organization irrespective of whether they replied as mentor or mentee or both. The response was:

- director/senior manager level: 57%
- manager: 26%
- trainee: 11%
- other: 6%

It is obvious that the more senior levels had the higher proportion of mentors to mentees but middle management levels were equally spilt between mentor or mentee or both.

The age range for respondents showed two thirds male to one third female responding; over age 40 the responses were also split two thirds male to one third female, the under-40 age range being split the same way. Under 30 and over 50 showed a higher proportion of male to female.

A host of clustered roles, activities, knowledge, interpersonal skills and personal characteristics were presented as part of the questionnaire forming the base for both functional and personal competence. Respondents were invited to rate the level of importance to effective mentoring for each individual competence within each of the three areas of mentoring. The range was a standard set from five (very important) to one (of no importance). The findings appear in the later section of this chapter.

For the interest of mentors, mentees, HR developers and academics reading this text, the two clustered-down lists of competences are set out below (Tables 5.3 and 5.4). They may still seem long and may still be repetitious, but they served as the final lists upon which the respondents rated the importance of the respective competences to the effectiveness of the mentor.

You as the reader might like to rate each competence in respect of importance to the mentoring relationships with which you are currently or have recently been involved, bearing in mind that you are looking at their importance to the effectiveness of the mentor. Using the rating scale in Table 5.2 to do this. For your convenience, the boxes in which to rate the competences have been reproduced in Table 5.3 and 5.4.

Table 5.3 Functional competences

1	Opener of doors – gives access to others
2	Networker – belongs to chain of interconnected persons
3	Political role – has status or influence
4	Positive role model – is worthy of imitation
5	Career developer – helps growth of career
6	Sponsor – is responsible for mentee/lends support
7	Draws on own experience
8	Gives direction – guides mentee
9	Collaborates– works jointly with mentee
10	Balances own job with mentoring
11	Supporter – encourages mentee
12	Assessor – estimates value or quality of work
13	Protector – defends mentee
14	Takes planned approach
15	Adviser – offers advice, gives opinions
16	Guides mentee – shows the way
17	Coaches – trains, gives hints, primes with facts
18	Is knowledgeable on own subject
19	Brings different perspective
20	Facilitates learning, growth and development
21	Helps mentee realize potential
22	Acts as sounding board – listens to ideas
23	Monitors progress – listens and reports back to mentee
24	Provides feedback – responds about results
25	Counsels – advises mentee
26	Develops relationship
27	Manages relationship
28	Invests time
29	Agrees action
30	Builds mentee interest
31	Helps build confidence
32	Encourages reflection

There are no right or wrong answers with these tables, as each respondent to the research questionnaire gave their own views, dependent on their own mentoring experiences. In the actual questionnaire, respondents were invited to rate each line of the lists within three columns corresponding to the three key mentoring areas of career focus, current role focus and personal development. You may want to revisit your overall ratings above and see if you would want to change them for any of the three focus areas.

Table 5.4 Personal competences

1	Critical friend – remarks on faults	
2	Succinct – briefly expresses comments	
3	Caring listener – listens with concern and interest	
4	Shows concern and interest in mentee	
5	Persuasive – induces mentee into action	
6	Has strategic vision	
7	Assertive – positive, insists on own rights/opinions	
8	Influential – powerful	
9	Empathetic – understands mentee	
10	Energetic	
11	Achievement-orientated – works towards accomplishment	
12	Team builder	
13	Takes/shows initiative – takes action without prompting	
14	Tolerant – allows mentee to exist without interference	
15	Adaptable – adjusts to mentee's needs	
16	Independent – doesn't depend on others	
17	Demonstrates integrity – shows uprightness and honesty	
18	Resilient – springs back, recovers	
19	Tenacious – resolute, holds on to principles	
20	Methodological – brings order to activity	
21	Precise – accurate, definite	
22	Individually focused – concentrates on mentee	
23	Sense of humour	
24	Patient	
25	Self-confident	
26	Self-aware – conscious of self	
27	Challenges – invites to discuss	
28	Stimulates – excites to action	
29	Encourages – urges, stimulates	
30	Shows genuine interest	
31	Non-judgemental	
32	Values others	
33	Trustworthy – reliable	

FINDINGS AND THE DEVELOPED MODEL OF MENTOR COMPETENCE

The analysis of the returned questionnaires involved the usual battery of statistical tests. The most interesting finding was that the generic list of competences for both functional and personal competences far outweighed the separate lists for the three key mentor approaches of career focus, current role focus or personal development. So the initial model and hypothesis were not proved.

Whilst the findings do not directly relate to the initial model of mentor competence as proposed, the results are nonetheless significant. A developed model emerged together with a list of what really makes the difference in mentor effectiveness over and above the wealth of mentor competence identified by respondents.

There were, however, some differences. Looking at the responses where competences scored 70 per cent or above at the 'important' and 'very important' end of the rating scale, the following differences emerged, almost exclusively under the personal development heading. There are generic competences too, but these will be shown later.

For the current role focus only, the generic list of competences applies, nothing being shown as discrete to this mentoring focus alone.

For the career focus, it is not surprising that the 'career developer' emerged as the key discrete competence with an overall rating of 71.9 per cent. It is however the only one to emerge as a discrete competence. The competence 'challenges – invites to discuss' scored 75.2 per cent under career focus and 71.3 per cent under personal development, but it failed to score more than 70 per cent under current role focus, achieving the slightly lower rating of 69.6 per cent.

For personal development, the discrete competences to emerge at 70 per cent or above are far greater in number, these being:

- brings different perspective
- facilitates learning, growth and development
- invests time
- helps mentee realize potential
- individually focused – concentrates on mentee
- encourages reflection
- non-judgemental
- values others.

Role modelling is often referred to as a key aspect of mentoring. This research only showed role modelling in relation to personal development and not at a sufficiently high level to warrant inclusion. It did not appear in the other two areas of career focus and current role focus at a high enough level of importance compared to the other competences listed in the generic conclusions.

The generic list of those competences that 'mattered', namely those competences that were rated 'important' or 'very important' by more than 70 per cent of respondents, whether mentor or mentee, is reproduced below. What may be surprising are the many aspects of mentoring from the earlier full lists of clustered functional and personal competences that are not included here.

The generic competences that matter are:

- helps build confidence
- caring listener – listens with concern and interest
- shows concern and interest in mentee
- encourages – urges, stimulates
- empathetic – understands the mentee
- demonstrates integrity –shows uprightness and honesty
- shows genuine interest
- supporter – encourages mentee
- acts as sounding board – listens to ideas
- trustworthy – reliable.

From the above list, the breakdown between the functional and personal competences was then made. Although the functional competence of 'career developer' only occurred in the career focus area, it still had a high score on the scale of importance to the mentor and mentee when operating in that area, so in terms of saying what makes a mentor effective it should be included. The same could be said of the personal competence 'challenges – invites to discuss', for whilst this appeared as a high score in only two out of the three areas, it should nevertheless be included in the list of effective mentor characteristics. Again, the specific list that emerged for personal development as outlined earlier showed certain competences of high importance rating, so as long as the mentor was aware of the particular area for those competences they should be added to the 'effectiveness' list. Thus the combination of the generic competences and the area-specific competences gives us the following nineteen, in three lists, that together combine for overall mentor effectiveness.

In all three areas:

- helps build confidence
- caring listener – listens with concern and interest
- shows concern and interest in mentee
- encourages – urges, stimulates
- empathetic – understands the mentee
- demonstrates integrity –shows uprightness and honesty
- shows genuine interest
- supporter – encourages mentee
- acts as sounding board – listens to ideas
- trustworthy – reliable.

In the two areas of career focus and personal development, but not current role focus:

- challenges – invites to discuss.

In the area of personal development not specifically focused on career or current role:

- brings different perspective
- facilitates learning, growth and development
- invests time
- helps mentee realize potential
- individually focused – concentrates on mentee
- encourages reflection
- non-judgemental
- values others.

Out of these, eight come from the list of functional competences and eleven from the list of personal competences, suggesting that how a mentor *is* (the 'being' type competence) rather than what a mentor *does* (the 'doing' type competence) matters more to effectiveness as a mentor and to the outcome as perceived by the mentee.

This result does not mean that the other competences are not valid or relevant from the lists included within the questionnaire, merely that they are not of such significance when mentors and mentees consider effectiveness in helping the mentee.

The developed model of mentor competence was then prepared for the purpose of illustration and discussion.

LANE'S DEVELOPED MODEL OF MENTOR COMPETENCE

The initial model was revisited to form a developed model taking into its framework the findings from the research. To develop the final model, two models were outlined as being relevant to the separate functional and personal competences. They still exist but the combination of the two such models has become the final demonstration of the research findings.

The model in Figure 5.1 below shows the three areas of mentoring as the key circles of focus. They are joined by the arms of the model which link any two of the three areas. The core of the model, the central triangle, is reserved for the overall combination of the three key areas.

Looking at the model, the specific competence related exclusively to any one of the three areas will appear next to that circle of focus. The competence relevant to two of the key focus areas will appear in the appropriate linking arm of the model. The central triangle is reserved for the generic competences relevant to all three of the focus areas.

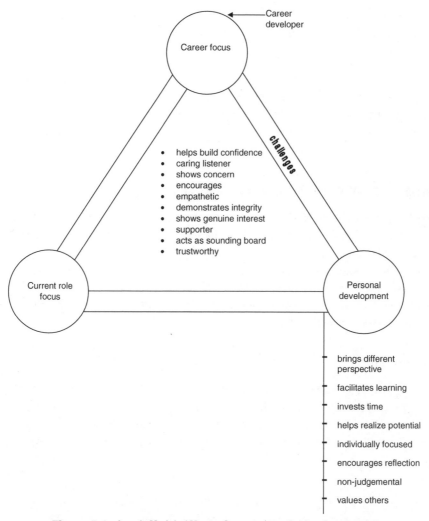

Figure 5.1 Lane's Model of Mentor Competence – the developed model

IMPLICATIONS

SO WHERE DOES THAT LEAD IN TERMS OF THE IMPLICATIONS FOR MENTORING?

Empirical research of this nature plays an important part in determining what the various stakeholders consider to be important. Those involved in mentoring should think about the impact of the findings in relation to their own areas of interest, such as:

- choice of mentors by individual mentees
- recruitment of mentors to company schemes
- mentor training
- mentor focus
- mentee expectations
- mentee needs in respect of career focus, current role focus and personal development.

We now take each of these in turn.

CHOICE OF MENTORS BY INDIVIDUAL MENTEES

A mentor may currently be chosen by what perception the mentee has of that person as a manager within their organization rather than as a mentor. The findings of the research may help the mentee focus on what they want from a mentor, and what they expect of the mentor in order to help them be effective as a mentee. The list of personal competences may help the mentee to consider such attributes of the mentor, rather than looking to what position the mentor may hold within the hierarchy.

RECRUITMENT OF MENTORS TO COMPANY SCHEMES

HR directors, in considering whom to invite to become mentors within internal company mentoring relationships, may have looked at the hierarchical position of a mentor. They will have considered that the prospective mentor may have acted as a mentor previously, that they may know 'what it takes' to act as a mentor to help others develop their potential. Again, the research outcome puts the focus on the personal competences that the mentor brings to the mentoring relationship rather than what they may physically 'do', and may help HR directors focus attention on those competences.

MENTOR TRAINING

Training programmes could focus on the main competences that make a difference. This would not mean ignoring the other competences, but the emphasis should be for the mentor to understand the importance of the key competences within both the functional and personal competence areas and to know that the research places greater emphasis on the competences.

MENTOR FOCUS

The mentor can focus on the three areas of mentoring – career focus, current role focus and personal development – but take into account the approaches, techniques and skills that relate to each of the distinct areas.

MENTEE EXPECTATION

Mentees can draw similar conclusions from the research to the above. In addition, mentees may choose to use the findings to help them in their process of mentor selection and in the process of looking to the mentor to use specific skills and competences that will in turn help mentees to achieve their full potential within the mentoring relationship.

MENTEE NEEDS IN RESPECT OF CAREER FOCUS, CURRENT ROLE FOCUS AND PERSONAL DEVELOPMENT

Mentees may use the research findings to inform themselves and the mentor of the competences that relate to a particular mentoring approach.

SUMMARY

In summary, this chapter introduced the research undertaken into mentor competence, the rationale for undertaking the research and the focus of research and hypothesis, together with details of the research methodology through a literature review, testing of an initial model of mentor competence, focus groups, two case studies and a detailed questionnaire. It then outlined the findings and the developed model of mentor competence before suggesting potential implications.

There is scope for further research into both generic and specific competences for given mentoring situations.

6 What about mentee competences?

DAVID CLUTTERBUCK

It takes two to tango. Mentoring relationships succeed because both parties contribute to making them work. A television documentary on mentoring, produced and screened several years ago, took the title *Consenting Adults* to emphasize the fact that this kind of helping relationship was a mutual endeavour. (And possibly to boost viewer ratings!) Yet where the academic literature on mentor competences is relatively thin, that on mentee competences is almost transparent. Very few books or articles give more than passing comments on how the mentee gets the most out of the relationship; or to be more precise, how they help the mentor help them.

In this chapter, I attempt to draw together the thinking around the nature and concept of mentee competences and suggest a framework for developing practical competences, which mentees can be helped to develop before or during their mentoring relationships.

One reason that mentee competences have not attracted a great deal of interest to date is a perception that it is unreasonable to expect mentees to be fully functional – or why would they need help? But, as we shall see from what literature there is, a certain level of competence (or a set of expressed attributes) is important in establishing and maintaining the relationship. The mentee's preparedness for being mentored can be argued to be a significant factor in the success of the relationship. For example, here is a fairly typical quote from a memo generated within an international oil company: 'Results would have been better, if protégés had been trained to make better use of the opportunity mentoring offered'.

In Chapter 4, I followed the phases of a mentoring relationship (Kram, 1983) to examine the kind of competences that could be valuable at each phase. In this chapter, I have chosen to simplify the phase model, because it is not practical to assign competences (or to be more accurate proto-competences) into so many categories without a high level of duplication. The three phases that work from a practical perspective, and which align with what few academic references there are, I have chosen to call:

- initiation of mentoring
- relationship management and
- learning maturity/disengagement.

The literature reviewed below does not in most cases purport to define competences. However, it does provide clues to the specific behaviours which may contribute towards competences.

INITIATION OF MENTORING

One of the many aspects of mentoring we do not have adequate data on is what proportion of informal mentoring relationships do not take root – in other words, how many frogs a prospective mentee needs to kiss before one turns into a prince! Even within formal mentoring schemes, the evidence for the proportion of relationships that do or do not gel is patchy at best. What academic studies there are, are North American in origin (such as Ragins, 1989, 1999) and tend to focus on 'sponsoring' mentoring, a largely one-way form of learning in which the influence of the mentor on the protégé's career is significant. 'Developmental' mentoring, in which there is more mutual learning and the mentee is not looking for hands-on career help, is more common in Europe and the British Commonwealth. The focus of this chapter is on developmental mentoring. Another weakness of the academic literature is the lack of longitudinal research. Although it is logical that the competences required of a mentee would evolve with the progress of the relationship, there has been no systematic examination of the process.

For the mentee, the ability to capture the mentor's interest and commitment is the precursor to rapport between mentor and mentee, which is in turn crucial to the subsequent maintenance of the relationship. Kram (1983) describes the protégé as a young manager, who 'quickly comes to represent someone with potential, someone who is "coachable" and someone who is enjoyable to work with'. The successful protégé is likely to exhibit more masculine traits, regardless of gender, than feminine traits, according to a study of 387 university professors and their mentoring relationships. The proposed explanation for this result is that 'masculine and/or androgynous behavior is associated with effective leadership and management' – in other words, mentors are drawn to people who most closely match the mentor's perception of potential future leaders.

Kalbfleisch and Davies (1993) summarize the research on receipt of mentoring. A variety of studies suggests that 'demographic factors such as gender (Daniels and Logan, 1983; Ragins, 1989; Sands *et al.* 1991) and race (Kalbfleisch and Davies, 1991) may predict the likelihood of having a mentor.' However, O'Neill (2001) in summarizing the evidence on these issues concludes that the majority of studies do not indicate significant differences on race or gender grounds for receipt of mentoring.

Kalbfleisch and Davies's analysis (1993) is more useful, however, where it examines factors such as communication competence and self-esteem in the mentee, both of which they found to be related to participation in mentoring relationships. They quote Wiemann (1977) who 'defines communication competence as "the ability of an interactant to choose among available communicative behaviors in order that he may successfully accomplish his own goals during an encounter, while maintaining the face and line of his fellow interactants within the constraints of the situation".' Among definitions of self-esteem is that it is 'composed of perceptions of self-worth and perceptions of power and ability'. Self-worth originates from a sense of social approval, and perceptions of power and ability arise from feelings of effectiveness (Franks and Marolla, 1976).

A proposed intervening variable between communication competence and self-esteem is perceived risk in intimacy. Mentors and mentees may need to expose their own feelings and hidden experiences, in order to encourage the other party to reciprocate. Kram (1985a) and Bullis and Bach (1989) both report this psychological intimacy as an element of mentoring relationships. The primary conclusions of Kalbfleisch and Davies's study (1993) are that 'individuals with higher degrees of communication competence and self esteem, who perceive less risk in intimacy, are more likely to participate in mentoring relationships.... Conversely...individuals, who may very much need mentoring relationships may not be as likely to be involved in those relationship as individuals who are more communicatively competent, have higher self esteem and perceive less risk in being intimate.' Studies of self-efficacy (Bandura, 1982) also support the position that confident, competent people find relationship-building easier than less confident, less competent peers.

Fagenson (1992) studied the needs of protégés and non-protégés for power, achievement, autonomy and affiliation. She found that people who became protégés tended to have higher needs for power and achievement, but not for autonomy and affiliation. It should be noted, however, that personality characteristics do not necessarily equate with competences. It is quite possible for someone to have a personality that makes them attractive as a mentee, but not the skills to make effective use of the relationship – and vice versa.

RELATIONSHIP MANAGEMENT

Effectiveness within the mentoring relationship, once it is established, has been related to a variety of factors.

Aryee *et al.* (1996b) examine ingratiation behaviours in the context of mentoring. (Ingratiation in this meaning is not necessarily a negative behaviour; rather it consists of a wide spectrum of reputation management behaviours.) They note the link in other studies between ingratiatory behaviours and career success.

Communication skills, already identified above as a factor in the initiation stage, were recorded by Kram (1985a) as a factor in relationship success for both mentors and mentees. Small field experiments I and colleagues have carried out with coaches suggest that the way the learner presents an issue for discussion strongly influences the nature and quality of the response. Saying 'I have a problem', for example, is likely to switch on advice mode; indicating the need for a sounding board to review thinking already partly done is likely to precipitate a more discursive, reflective dialogue.

Engstrom (Engstrom and Mykletun, 1999) compared personality factors of mentors and mentees in the success of mentoring relationships. High scores of agreeableness, extroversion and openness to experience on the part of the mentee correlated with positive relationship outcomes, although the personality interaction between mentor and mentee was also a significant factor with respect to each of the personality dimensions.

LEARNING MATURITY/DISENGAGEMENT

We have not been able to find any studies which investigate the skills required in managing the mature mentoring relationship, or in managing the relationship ending from the mentee perspective. Kram & Bragar (1992) talks of experiencing 'new independence and autonomy' and of the need to 'test his or her ability to function effectively without close guidance and support'. However, she does not explore how the mentee contributes towards achieving these attributes.

Managing the closure of the relationship and moving on is an important element in the satisfaction of both parties. A recent study (Clutterbuck and Megginson, 2001) of relationship endings found that a planned, positive winding down was more effective than a gradual drifting away (see Chapter 15). It would seem logical, given that the mentee is expected to take more and more responsibility for driving the relationship, that they should also play a role in bringing it to a close. Kram discusses the pain of separation, comparing it to bereavement. Some clues to the management of the separation process may therefore be gained from the counselling literature that deals with processes for letting go.

A FRAMEWORK OF COMPETENCES

As with mentors, it seems that competences for mentees may arise from a number of paired characteristics, which can be considered to be generic pairs of behaviours. In some cases – perhaps all – these pairs are in essence probably dimensions; however, it would be presumptuous to elevate them to that status without considerable further investigation. Those suggested by my analysis of the literature and by field experience in mentor and mentee training, as well as review meetings, appear to fall into the three categories above, relating to the mentee's stage of development and the stage of relationship development. There seem to be three pairs of competences at the initiation level (Figure 6.1) and four each at the relationship management (Figure 6.2) and learning maturity/disengagement levels (Figure 6.3).

THE COMPETENCE IDENTIFICATION PROCESS

Given the paucity of data from desk research, a high emphasis needs to be placed on field research. The process of data gathering in the field has been in three main forms: two highly informal and subjective; one more formal and more objective. First, mentors and mentees have been asked to discuss and record those characteristics they would expect to value and those they do not value, in both roles. Typical responses include an aversion among mentees to a mentor who talks at them rather than with them; and among mentors an aversion to people who expect too much of the relationship, people who do not respond (variously described as 'black holes' or 'puddings') and people who are unwilling to give commitment. A second phase involves review meetings, where mentors and mentees discuss their actual experiences, with a view to improving both the scheme process and their own skills in the roles. Over the past two years, I have also been gathering data on mentor and mentee expectations, behaviours and outcomes, in a continuing longitudinal study. At the time of writing, the data from this study is not ready for detailed statistical analysis, but it appears to support the broad thrust of the previous two phases.

THE MENTORING CONTEXT

As with the mentor competences suggested in Chapter 4, the proto-competences for mentees explored here belong to the specific context of developmental mentoring and to structured mentoring programmes. By developmental mentoring, I mean off-line relationships, where there is no expectation of sponsorship and a concentration on helping the less experienced person achieve independence. By structured programmes, I mean those where there is a process for assisting people (and in particular those who are at a racial, gender or other disadvantage) to find a suitable mentor, some training for participants to help them use the relationship well and some form of ongoing background support for participants.

It may well be that other forms of mentoring – for example, relationships that emphasize sponsorship, or which take place electronically (e-mentoring) – may be sufficiently different in their dynamics that these competences do not apply, or that there are other competences which would need to be included in those contexts. That, however, is beyond the scope of this exploration.

RELATIONSHIP INITIATION COMPETENCES

Focus – proactivity

Focus relates to having some ideas about what you want to achieve (how do you want you or your circumstances to be different? what do you want to become?) and/or a willingness to work with the mentor to put some clarity behind the relationship purpose.

Proactivity relates to a willingness to take the initiative, to contact the mentor rather than wait to be contacted and to seek the opinion of others in determining what issues to bring to the mentor. The proactive mentee will already at least have thought about how to achieve their goals and ideally taken some steps towards achieving them. Mentors are also impressed by the perception of relationship commitment – behaviours that demonstrate that the mentee really wants the relationship to work and is prepared to invest in it.

Respect – self-respect

Respect and self-respect go hand in hand. Rogers' concept of mutual common regard indicates the necessity of reciprocated respect as a core constituent of rapport (1961). A mentee can demonstrate respect by showing that they value the mentor's advice and/or insights, by being attentive and by using the mentor's time and effort wisely (for example, by not making inappropriate demands).

Self-respect may be an emergent characteristic of the mentee, rather than a starting competence, but, as the research above indicates, the relationship may establish itself more easily if the mentee is relatively self-confident. There are, of course, extremes – self-confidence to the point of arrogance is unlikely to be attractive to a mentor. Equally, in community mentoring schemes, mentors often report that the greatest satisfaction comes from watching mentees grow in self-esteem and self-confidence.

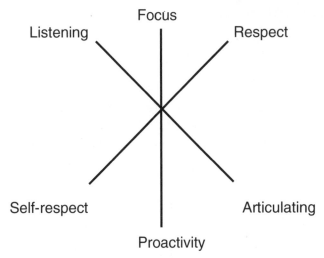

Figure 6.1 Three competence pairs for relationship initiation

Listening – articulating

Although some mentees may not have great communication skills, the willingness to listen and to try to communicate their goals, feelings and values goes a long way towards establishing a relationship.

RELATIONSHIP MANAGEMENT (BASIC COMPETENCES FOR MENTEES)

Learn – teach

The mentee must have a commitment to learning and a purpose for doing so which shapes their requests of the mentor and gives the mentor a sense of direction for the relationship. They must value the learning they may acquire from the mentor and demonstrate that they do so. At the same time, they need to be aware of the mentor's needs and prepared to share their experiences, learning and insights, where these will be of interest and value to the mentor.

Challenge – be challenged

The mentee must be willing and able to engage in constructive dialogue. This requires occasional challenge – not simply accepting advice from the oracle, but delving deeper and exploring the reasoning behind advice and guidance given. At the same time, they must be open to examining issues about which they feel fearful or otherwise uncomfortable, in the cause of gaining greater understanding.

Open – questioning

Mentees must be prepared to be honest with themselves and their mentors, both providing an accurate description of issues they face and being willing to consider different perspectives and approaches. At the same time, they need the appropriate skills to pose questions to mentors in ways that make it clear what kind of help they need at this time – a sounding board, direct advice, counselling or some combination of these.

Prepare – reflect

This could perhaps be described as reflect and reflect, for it is important that the mentee spend quiet thinking time both before the mentoring session (to prepare what they want to discuss and why) and after (to review what they have learned and extract further lessons from it). Reflection also encompasses willingness to examine one's own motives, drives, attitudes and behaviour.

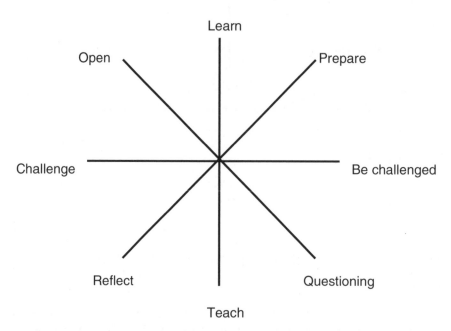

Figure 6.2 Four competence pairs for relationship management

LEARNING MATURITY/DISENGAGEMENT (ADVANCED COMPETENCES FOR MENTEES)

The four dimensions of advanced competences suggested by both field experience and mentoring case studies are outlined below.

Acknowledge the debt – pay forward the debt

There is a substantial difference between demonstrating gratitude and ingratiation. The level of mutual respect required in the relationship should make ingratiation untenable as a behaviour, but the mentee should be able to express their appreciation for the mentor's time and thoughtfulness. They may also be able to reciprocate in more practical ways – for example, one of my mentees keeps an eye open for public platforms I might find it commercially useful to speak at, although there is no obligation for her to do so.

Paying forward the debt is a reflection of a phenomenon noted in much of our field research. People who have been effective mentees frequently wish to become mentors in turn. Indeed, this is one of the core measurements of the success of a mentoring relationship or scheme. It is also a key goal for community mentoring in the UK (Miller, 2002).

Process awareness – process management

An awareness of the process is essentially a contextual competence. Field interviews suggest strongly that mentees learn more and reflect more, if they understand what the mentor is trying to do and why. Mentoring therefore becomes a collusive activity, in which the mentee takes an active role in helping the mentor help them. For example, if the mentee may recognize that a period of silence is an opportunity for them to reflect; or the mentee may craft the way an issue is presented to the mentor, in order to stimulate the kind of response that will be most useful to them (saying 'I've got a problem' is likely to trigger direct advice; saying 'I'd value your help in testing my thinking about…' is more likely to trigger exploratory dialogue).

The process of empowerment in the mentoring relationship requires that the mentee take responsibility for the management of the process. The mature learner, or the mentee with high self-esteem and high goal clarity, may begin the relationship by setting the agenda, steering the mentor towards appropriate responses and actively drawing upon the mentor's knowledge, experience and networks.

Extrinsic and intrinsic feedback

Receiving feedback from others can be one of the most difficult skills to learn. It demands a certain level of trust, which is not always easy to give, and a willingness to accept and address one's weaknesses. People who appear self-defensive and oversensitive to criticism make it more difficult for the mentor to relax and behave naturally towards them. A relationship where one or both sides is constantly having to assess whether or not what they say will offend, will struggle. Indeed, it may not even get off the ground in extreme cases. As the relationship progresses, the need typically increases to accept the mentor as a critical friend and to encourage 'cruel but kind' feedback. In addition, the mentee should become more comfortable with giving honest personal feedback about the mentor's performance in their role, especially when the mentor specifically seeks it.

The mentee should also be able to move beyond feedback from others to develop their intrinsic feedback skills. Learning how to listen to yourself or observe yourself in action takes time. With each new area of skill, you may need to begin the process again, learning what to listen for, how to recognize positive and negative patterns, and how to assess the impact of experimental changes. For example, a teenager with problems of anger control learned to watch out for the tightening of muscles that indicated he would repeat a cycle of verbal abuse followed by violence. By experimenting with different reactions to these early physical cues, he was able to learn a different set of instinctive behaviours that not only helped him control himself, but also gave him more control over the situation that threatened to cause the anger. The same principles of intrinsic feedback can be applied to almost any personal performance issue at work, from time management to giving presentations or motivating colleagues.

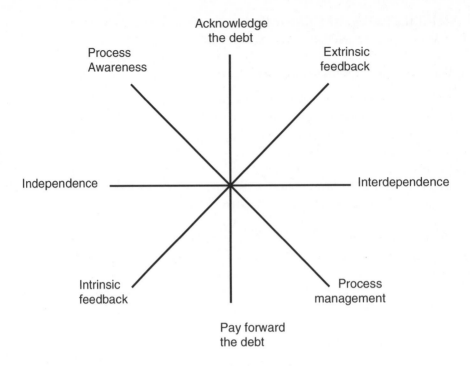

Figure 6.3   Four competence pairs for learning maturity/disengagement

Independence – interdependence

Being self-motivated, self-reliant, self-resourceful and self-confident are all elements of maturity, in life as well as in learning. The more capable the mentee is in each of these areas, the less dependent they will be on the mentor. A comment I often hear from 'mature' mentees is: 'When I was faced by a dilemma, I thought, "How would my mentor have approached this?" and I soon had the answer.' This phenomenon of role model in absentia appears to characterize those relationships where the mentee has expanded both the scope and the portfolio of their responses to learning opportunities. Independence is likely to be accompanied by a shift from using the mentor as adviser to using them as sounding board. It is also likely to involve an increasing confidence in their own ability to manage their career planning and progress towards career objectives.

Developing a wide range of support resources is also a sign of learning maturity. With the mentor's help initially, and gradually through their own ingenuity, the mentee builds a network of advisers – sources of information, influence and encouragement – upon which they call for different needs and in different circumstances. The mentee also develops the skill to sustain and enhance relationships within this network and may reciprocate to the mentor by passing on information and contacts from outside the mentor's sphere.

CONCLUSIONS AND IMPLICATIONS

A number of writers on mentoring have linked mentor competences with the phases of re-lationship development, suggesting that specific skills should be addressed as they become necessary in the management of the relationship (for example, Pascarelli, 1998). However, none, so far as I have been able to ascertain, has applied the same principle to the development of mentee competences.

Of course, we can't expect the mentee to have all of these competences. But we can help them acquire and reinforce each of the competences. Issues that need further explanation here include the timing and extent of help, and whether it should be given by the mentor or by a source outside the relationship. With regard to timing, much will depend upon the mentee's starting point. We might expect a mentee who is mature in the sense of learning capability and who has prior experience of being mentored to begin with a much fuller competence set than one who is a neophyte in both respects. According to Yan Lu (2002), previous experience of a mentor-type relationship with a school teacher as a young student correlates strongly with subsequent development of positive mentoring relationships. Figure 6.4 attempts to put this into context. The mentee who is low in both previous experience of mentoring and learning maturity (A) will presumably require more support upfront and more tolerance from the men-tor than someone who is high on both counts. In general, the mentee who has low learning maturity and experience of being mentored will need a wider range of support and encourage-ment simply to embark on the relationship.

Someone with high learning maturity and little experience in mentoring (C) should swiftly adapt to the relationship, but many require a high degree of initial clarity about what to expect.

A mentee who has low learning maturity and a lot of experience in mentoring (D) is a less likely combination. However, we have encountered people who have had an ineffective men-toring relationship. Here the mentor may need to spend time early in the relationship building their credibility with the mentee.

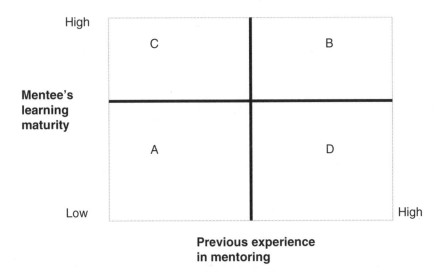

Figure 6.4 Where is the mentee starting from?

Finally, someone with high learning maturity and previous experience of mentoring may be regarded as a 'natural' – able to engage rapidly and effectively with the process from the beginning.

Although all of the proposed competences described have face validity, there is still a great deal of research to be done to establish the validity using more rigorous measures. In the meantime, however, having at least a tentative framework of mentee competences should help scheme co-ordinators design training that helps mentees present themselves more effectively to their mentors and engage more fully in the initiation of the relationship. It should also help to deliver mentee training more closely in phase with evolving needs. Finally, it should also be useful in making mentors more aware of what to expect from mentees – and how they can work with them to help them gain more from the relationship.

7 Competences of building the developmental relationship

TERRI A SCANDURA and EKIN K PELLEGRINI

A mentor is traditionally defined as an influential individual with advanced knowledge who is committed to providing upward support and mobility to their protégé's career (Levinson *et al.*, 1978). Mentoring has been found to be an important relationship in the development of a person's career identity (Kram, 1983). Research on mentoring has indicated relationships between having a mentor (and the functions a mentor provides) and outcomes of job performance, promotions, salary, job satisfaction, reduced stress and lower turnover (Baugh *et al.*, 1996; Dreher and Ash, 1990; Lankau and Scandura, 2002; Scandura, 1992). Mentoring functions have been conceptualized as vocational (career coaching), social support and role modelling (Kram, 1983; Burke, 1984; Scandura, 1992). Recently, Lankau and Scandura (2002) identified another mentoring correlate, which is the enhancement of the personal learning of the protégé. There has been much theory and research on mentoring in the last two decades (see Scandura and Hamilton, 2002, for a review). Some research has identified personality correlates of mentoring (Fagenson, 1992; Turban and Dougherty, 1994) which may suggest some antecedents of effective mentoring relationships. However, there has been little research regarding how mentoring relationships develop in early phases.

Recently, the traditional one-on-one definition of mentoring has been reconceptualized into a 'multiple relationships' phenomena (Baugh and Scandura, 1999; Higgins and Kram, 2001) where a protégé has a network of mentors, each providing different functions. Furthermore, Eby (1997) proposed alternative models of mentoring based on the form of relationship (lateral and hierarchical) and the type of skill developed (job-related and career-related). The mentoring literature has thus taken new directions, suggesting more complex networks of relationships. However, the question of why some protégés (and mentors) may be more predisposed to mentoring relationships still remains relatively unexplored.

The emergence of mentoring, as with any other close personal relationship, is in part a function of the individual's basic orientation towards the development of relationships. Hence, this paper proposes a new model of mentoring that integrates concepts drawn from attachment theory. Incorporating attachment theory broadens the theoretical base of mentoring to consider long-term developmental processes that may influence attitudes and behaviour at work. Also, this framework expands the emerging literature on attachment theory to incorporate work relationships. Levinson *et al.* (1978) described the mentor–protégé relationship in terms of parent–child interaction. Over the years, the mentoring literature has moved away from this conceptualization and more towards a model of mentoring as a tool for training and development (Hunt and Michael, 1983) or as a vehicle for protégés' upward mobility (Dreher and Ash, 1990; Scandura, 1992). Introducing attachment theory may help to refocus the literature on the developmental nature of mentoring.

ATTACHMENT THEORY

Attachment theory is an emerging field for the study of interpersonal relationships throughout the course of life (Ainsworth, 1991). Based upon a sound theoretical base and over 20 years of empirical research, attachment theory focuses on the development of an individual's basic orientation towards relationship formation. Empirical evidence from the field of social psychology clearly supports the proposition that attachment styles remain stable over the adult lifespan. Recently, attachment theory has been applied to job satisfaction (Hazan and Shaver, 1990), career development (Blustein *et al.*, 1995), transformational leadership (Popper *et al.*, 2000) and work versus family concerns (Sumer and Knight, 2001). Attachment theory has implications for the development of mentoring relationships at work. This paper presents a theoretical framework that extends mentoring theory by integrating the patterns of attachment style (Hazan and Shaver, 1987) with the functions and phases of mentoring in the workplace.

Adult attachment mainly stems from the individual's relatively stable tendency to seek safety and security. Internal working models of attachment regulate the tendency to search for and maintain proximity with specific individuals, who are perceived to have the potential for providing security (Berman and Sperling, 1994). Internal working models are models of self and attachment figures that are built during infancy and carried over to adulthood. These 'working models' characterize the world, and establish expectations of how others will respond in specific circumstances (Bowlby, 1979). The individual develops responses using information gathered from these internally constructed working models that develop from childhood attachment relationships.

Bowlby's work (1979) suggests that the representational models of self and others persist over the lifespan. Infants build internal models of self and attachment figures, which are then projected onto new relationships in adult life, such as spouse and employer. In fact, results of a 25-year longitudinal study demonstrate that the three attachment groups (Hazan and Shaver, 1987) maintained distinct internal models from age 27 to 52 (Klohnen and John, 1998). Given the relatively stable pattern of attachment styles throughout the lifespan, it is clearly important to observe the extent to which the working models of adults are products of childhood experiences with attachment figures (Bowlby, 1979). The focus of the present chapter will be limited to adult attachment relationships, which is relevant to mentoring at work.

ATTACHMENT STYLES

Attachment behaviour results in achieving closeness to another individual, who is perceived to be capable of providing safety and security when needs arise. Although Bowlby mainly studied childhood attachment behaviour, he nevertheless considered attachment to 'characterize human beings from the cradle to the grave' (Bowlby, 1988, p129). Thus attachment theory attempts to explain not only attachment behaviour, but also the stability of attachment relationships. An important aspect of attachment relationships is the concept of a 'secure base' (Ainsworth *et al.*, 1978) from which the individual safely goes out to explore, knowing that they can return to the base any time they need protection and care. According to Bowlby, the concept of the 'secure base' is fundamental in understanding how an individual develops emotional stability. Exploratory activity may thus sound antithetical to attachment behaviour. However, this is where Bowlby's definition of emotional stability becomes relevant, as it is the healthy child who can normally alternate the two kinds of behaviour (Bowlby, 1979).

Ainsworth *et al.* (1978) identified three major patterns of attachment. The *securely* attached individual was confident in the attachment figure's availability and responsiveness should the individual need protection. *Avoidant* attachment was identified in individuals who had no confidence that the attachment figure would be responsive when the individual was in need of care. These individuals are likely to grow up to be emotionally self-sufficient and to try to live without the support of others (Bowlby, 1988). The third pattern of attachment is the *anxious/ ambivalent* style in which the individual cannot predict whether the attachment figure will be available and responsive when needed.

According to Hazan and Shaver (1994) different attachment styles, mediated by working models of self, underlie many interpersonal differences. Hazan and Shaver (1987) utilized attachment theory, specifically the three attachment patterns identified by Ainsworth *et al.* (1978) to study the development of close relationships and how they change over time. They also related Bowlby's exploration activity to work activity (Hazan and Shaver, 1990) and studied the relationship between adult attachment type and job satisfaction, including satisfaction with salary and co-workers, job security, and opportunities for challenge.

The three attachment styles (secure, avoidant, anxious/ambivalent) identified by Ainsworth in her infant–mother attachment studies (Ainsworth *et al.*, 1978) were carried into the adulthood realm by Hazan and Shaver (1987) in their forced-choice self-report measure. Hazan and Shaver wrote descriptions of these three styles focusing on adult attachment in romantic relationships, and suggested that the three attachment styles are roughly the same in adulthood as in infancy and the three kinds of adults differ predictably in the way they experience romantic love.

Bartholomew and Horowitz (1991) modified this measure. They argued for an expanded four-style model of adult attachment and added a second type of avoidance (dismissing-avoidance) to the Hazan and Shaver (1987, 1990) measure of attachment styles. The four attachment patterns (secure, preoccupied, dismissing, and fearful) were defined using combinations of a person's self-image (positive or negative; the self as worthy of love and support or not) and image of others (positive or negative; other people are seen as trustworthy and available versus unreliable and rejecting).

Feeney *et al.* (1994) proposed another measure of adult attachment style that argued for a five-dimensional model of attachment styles: confidence (in self and others), discomfort with closeness, need for approval, preoccupation with relationships, and relationships as secondary (to achievement). The authors suggest that confidence represents secure attachment, and each of the other four scales represents a particular aspect of insecure attachment.

The measure proposed by Fraley *et al.* (2000) appears the most suitable for the study of attachment theory and mentoring relationships. This measure needs to be slightly modified to reflect the mentoring relationship and the context of work. Also, the length of the measure (36 items) requires reduction. It is clear that the first step in researching mentoring and attachment

Table 7.1   Proposed revision of Hazan and Shaver (1990), Bartholomew and Horowitz (1991) and Fraley *et al.* (2000) attachment style scales

Proposed item revision Fraley *et al.* (2000) ANXIETY	Proposed item revision Fraley *et al.* (2000) AVOIDANCE
I'm afraid that I will lose my mentor's attention.	I prefer not to show my mentor how I feel deep down.
I often worry that my mentor doesn't really like me.	I find it difficult to allow myself to depend on my mentor.
My mentor only seems to notice me when I'm angry.	I don't feel comfortable opening up to my mentor.
My mentor makes me doubt myself.	I prefer not to be too close to people.
It makes me mad that I don't get the attention and support I need from my mentor.	I get uncomfortable when someone wants to be very close.
I worry that I won't measure up to other people.	I am nervous when people get too close to me.
Proposed item revision **Hazan and Shaver (1990)** **SECURITY**	**Proposed item revision** **Bartholomew and Horowitz (1991)** **SECURITY**
I find it relatively easy to get close to others.	It is easy for me to become emotionally close to others.
I am comfortable depending on others and having them depend on me.	I am comfortable being close to others.
I don't worry about someone getting too close to me.	I don't worry about being alone.

styles is the development of a reliable and content-valid measure. We therefore revised the two 18-item scales into two 6-item scales as shown in Table 7.1. Clearly, these measures need to be empirically examined for reliability and construct validity. Fraley *et al.* (2000) note that these items assess insecurity better than security. Thus we suggest a separate measure of security, based upon Hazan and Shaver (1990) and Bartholomew and Horowitz (1991) (see Table 7.1).

ATTACHMENT PROTOTYPES IN THE WORKPLACE

In utilizing different prototypes of adult attachments for explaining behaviour in adult relationships, it is important to consider whether the relationship can actually be conceptualized as an attachment relationship. Ainsworth (1991) distinguishes affectional bonding from other relationships. She suggests that although affectional bonds develop from dyadic relationships, they are internalized by the individual and not the dyad per se (as in other relationships). Also, affectional bonds tend to persist over the lifespan, whereas specific relationships may be of either long or short duration. Weiss (1991) asserts that some of these other relationships are also likely to be attachment relationships depending on the properties of the relationship. Berman and Sperling (1994) suggest that a relationship may be considered as an attachment depending upon the dimensions of the relationship. They distinguish five dimensions of adult attachment: intensity, security/reliability, sensitivity, activation, and frustration tolerance (the role of anger).

There is a growing literature investigating attachment styles in the work environment. Hazan and Shaver (1990) examined the relationship of attachment styles (secure, avoidant, anxious/ambivalent) and job satisfaction. Individuals with a secure attachment style approach work with confidence and are more likely to report that they enjoy their work. Also, they reported the highest income of the three groups. Avoidant respondents were found to use work to avoid social interaction. These individuals demonstrated a 'workaholic' orientation towards work. They reported incomes comparable to the secure group. However, they also reported dissatisfaction with too much work, lack of challenge and co-workers. Anxious/ambivalent respondents reported dissatisfaction with job security, advancement and recognition opportunities, and had the lowest average income of all three groups. These results suggest that individual reactions to the workplace may be a function of the ability to develop close personal relationships with others, which in turn may affect job satisfaction, income and other work outcomes. Perhaps the most interesting aspect of their work, for which they have found substantial evidence, is that many dysfunctional relationships, in all spheres of adult life, might be the outcome of insecure attachment styles.

Popper *et al.* (2000) examined attachment theory in the context of transformational leadership. They found similarities in the characteristics associated with the secure attachment style and the transformational leadership behaviour pattern. Three studies, conducted in military settings (that is, involving officer training) found that secure attachment was associated with charisma, individualized consideration and intellectual stimulation. These findings were replicated with ratings of these transformational leadership behaviours from both supervisors and subordinates. These results further support the idea that attachment styles are relevant in the workplace.

Recently, Sumer and Knight (2001) investigated the relationship of attachment styles to perceptions of balance between work and family. They found that individuals with a preoccupied attachment style (anxious/ambivalent) reported more negative spillover from the family to the work domain. These respondents were less likely to use coping strategies, which partition from family life. Secure respondents experienced more positive spillover in both work and family than the other two groups. The authors concluded that 'job attitudes and behaviors may reflect underlying personality attributes or orientations more than individuals' objective job situations' (Sumer and Knight, 2001, p661). This study further supports the contention that attachment styles may help explain individual reactions to the work environment and the relationships they encounter there.

Blustein *et al.* (1995) have also related attachment theory to career development. These authors reviewed the literature on career counselling and development, noting that attachment theory has been applied to issues of work identity formation, career choice and occupational stress. They also reviewed studies suggesting the potential influence of gender and cultural factors on the relationship of attachment style and career development. However, there are few studies in this area, rendering conclusions about the role of diversity variables in models of attachment theory and careers tenuous at the present time. Blustein *et al.* (1995) clearly indicate that attachment theory has implications for the development of interpersonal relationships at work. They specifically refer to mentoring relationships in this context:

"Whereas not all mentors or supportive work relationships contain the full array of properties of attachment relationships (Ainsworth, 1989), some of the interpersonal bonds developed at work may resemble selected aspects of attachment relationships or may actually become attachment relationships" (p426).

Based upon this suggestion, we propose a model of attachment theory and mentoring where mentoring will be expected to mediate the relationship between attachment styles and work outcomes. We propose a typology of mentoring relationships consisting of four distinct types, by combining the mentor's and protégé's attachment styles. We then suggest that these four combinations will lead to different work outcomes through the mediation of mentoring functions. We expect that the direct influence of attachment style may be lower in the presence of the mentoring functions provided.

Recently, there have also been attempts to study the attachment literature from a dependency perspective (Kahn and Kram, 1994). This synthesis of the two literatures is therefore reflected in the proposed model. The next section will review the dependency literature and how it relates to the attachment styles. Then a framework that integrates the attachment, dependency and mentoring literatures will be introduced.

DEPENDENCY RELATIONSHIPS

The goal of this chapter is to address the issue of why some protégés (and mentors) may be more predisposed to the development of mentoring relationships than others. To explain this variability, we have mainly utilized the internal models of attachment relationships that develop in childhood and affect the adult throughout life. Others have also utilized the same 'internal model' concept, in an attempt to explain how childhood factors shape the adult's authority (dependency) relations in the context of work relationships (Kahn and Kram, 1994). According to Hirschhorn (1990), authority (dependency) models are 'internalized models' that are enacted across various roles and positions. As has been suggested by Bowlby (1979), people internalize the models from their unresolved dynamics of past relationships, and act as if those dynamics are the result of present relationships. Therefore, adults have internal models of dependency relations that shape how they behave in social systems, including the adult's dependency relationships in the context of work. These models are also relevant for mentoring relationships at work.

Kahn and Kram (1994) proposed three enduring internal models of authority: dependence, counterdependence and interdependence. Dependent people 'seek dependency on those in formal authority, deauthorizing themselves to take responsibility for managing themselves' (p28). Counterdependent people 'dismiss or undermine hierarchically determined role interactions' and also 'seek to step outside the boundaries of role-determined relations' (p29). On the other hand, interdependent people 'tend to establish relationships in which there are aspects of both dependence on hierarchical authority and independence from that authority' (p30). These models act as a template for expectations in dependency relationships (that is, mentoring relationships). Others have also suggested different models of dependency: anticonformity, independence, passivity, interdependence (Scandura, 2002); co-dependency (Davidhizar and Eshleman, 1992); and interdependent, counterdependent, overdependent (Joplin *et al.*, 1999).

Internal models of dependency correspond to the patterns of attachment behaviour (Quick *et al.*, 1987; Joplin *et al.*, 1999; Kahn and Kram, 1994). Dependent people (anxious/ambivalent attachment) are likely to seek a mentor's advice, and thus will benefit from the initial stages of the mentoring relationship, but the relationship may turn dysfunctional, as dependent protégés may resist entering the separation phase of the relationship which is essential to the protégé's independence and growth. Counterdependent people (avoidant attachment) will be more likely to resolve challenges alone, and not seek help from a mentor. Kahn and Kram (1994) also suggest that even if counterdependent (avoidant) people can overcome this resistance to seeking help, they may be more unwilling to exhibit the self-disclosure that is essential for fostering mentoring relations. It may be difficult to manage a counterdependent person, especially when the mentor tends to be directive or authoritarian (Gabarro & Kotter, 1992). Therefore, mentoring relations involving counterdependent (avoidant) or dependent (anxious/ambivalent) people either as protégés or mentors will be less likely to develop. A mentoring relationship will not emerge or will become 'marginal' (Ragins *et al.*, 2000) or dysfunctional (Scandura, 1998) during the initial phase. On the other hand, an interdependent (secure) person is secure about the availability and responsiveness of others, and confident in authority relations. Thus it is expected that interdependence (secure attachment) is most likely to result in functional mentoring relationships that will benefit both the mentor and the protégé as the relationship develops (Kahn and Kram, 1994).

Based upon the correspondence between the dependency and attachment styles, we integrate dependency models into the proposed model of attachment theory and mentoring relationships (Figure 7.1).

As shown in Figure 7.1, the secure (interdependent) style, either as a protégé or as a mentor, relates to the emergence of a mentoring relationship. Secure individuals are comfortable developing relationships with others. Also, they are not threatened when asking for help from others. In the workplace, it can be expected that such individuals will both seek the advice of more experienced senior managers, or offer help to the less experienced protégés.

In sharp contrast to the secure attachment prototype, it is expected that avoidant (counterdependent) people will be less likely to report having a mentor. These individuals are uncomfortable developing close interpersonal relationships and may not develop relationships with senior members of the organization. Asking for help is an admission of vulnerability and

POTENTIAL MENTOR

		SECURE (INTERDEPENDENT)	ANXIOUS/AMBIVALENT (DEPENDENT)	AVOIDANT (COUNTERDEPENDENT)
POTENTIAL PROTÉGÉ	SECURE (INTERDEPENDENT)	O	O	⊗
	ANXIOUS/AMBIVALENT (DEPENDENT)	O	O	⊗
	AVOIDANT (COUNTERDEPENDENT)	⊗	⊗	⊗

Figure 7.1 The effect of attachment styles on the formation of a mentoring relationship
(Note: O = mentoring relation will occur; ⊗ = mentoring relation will not occur.)

avoidant people might see this as a threat to their self-esteem. Or they simply may not consider that help from others is available, and expect to go it alone. It is also expected that avoidant people will not offer help and they will not likely serve as mentors.

Anxious/ambivalent (dependent) individuals worry more about how others view them, and are more likely to seek out the feedback of a senior person via the mentoring relationship. Uncertainty is an aversive state for such individuals, and feedback may reduce ambiguity by giving them information about appropriate behaviours (Ashford and Black, 1996). Anxious/ ambivalent people lack confidence and often see themselves as misunderstood (Simpson, 1990). Thus they may seek feedback to obtain key information in developing their self-concept (Sully de Luque and Sommer, 2000). The mentor may help to alleviate some of their anxiety about work performance or how others see them in the workplace. The anxious person may spend more time considering the choice of a mentor and worry about the consequences of not having a mentor that can best advance their career. As mentors, these individuals may be willing to offer coaching and support, but they may have problems in developing the relationship into a functional one.

Attachment style should also be related to the mentoring functions provided. We suggest a typology of mentoring relationships by combining the mentor's and protégé's attachment/ dependency styles. This typology presents four distinct types of mentoring relationships (Figure 7.2). The model also proposes that mentoring functions mediate the relationship between the mentor's and protégé's attachment/dependency styles and work outcomes (Figure 7.3).

As has been mentioned above, anxious/ambivalent people will be willing to offer their help and establish mentoring relationships, but they will have problems in developing the relationship into a functional one. The relationship may either evolve into a dysfunctional one (Scandura, 1998) and dissolve relatively quickly, or it may evolve into a 'marginal mentoring relationship' (Ragins *et al.*, 2000) that is limited in the degree or scope of mentoring functions provided. In such a relationship the outcomes shown in Figure 7.3 are not likely to be attained.

When an anxious/ambivalent (dependent) mentor is in a relationship with a secure (interdependent) protégé, the mentoring relationship may develop into a marginal one. The secure protégé's desire to function interdependently may be resisted by the anxious/ambivalent (dependent) mentor. This type of mentor may resist the separation phase, which is vital to the protégé's development. Thus this relationship will be marginal, as the dependent mentor will not provide the protégé with the career support functions that will prepare the protégé for future independence. In such relationships the desired work outcomes will likely not be achieved. In fact, Ragins *et al.* (2000) found that the attitudes of protégés in marginal relationships were

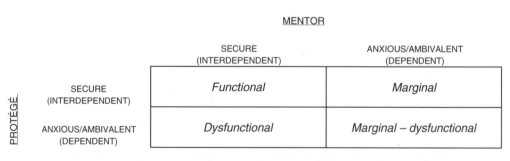

Figure 7.2 A typology of mentoring relationships

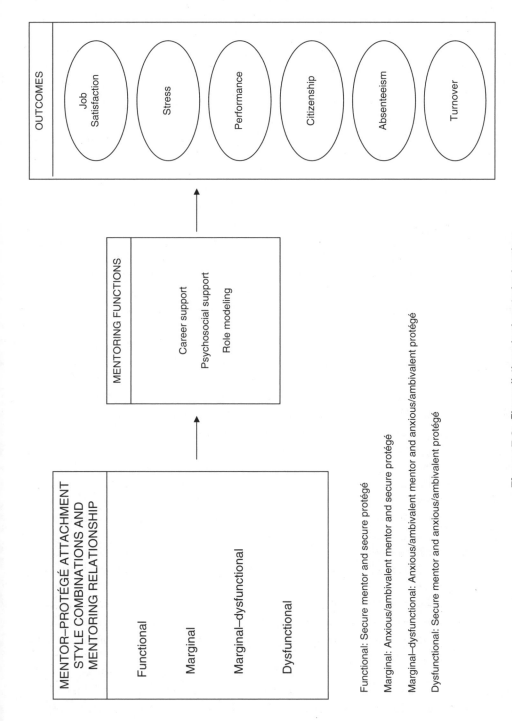

Figure 7.3 The mediating role of mentoring functions

equivalent to those of non-mentored individuals.

Another category in the proposed typology concerns the relationship between an anxious/ambivalent (dependent) mentor and an anxious/ambivalent (dependent) protégé. In this type of relationship, neither the mentor nor the protégé will be willing to experience the separation phase where the protégé starts to function independently. Thus the relationship may evolve into a dysfunctional one. It may terminate during the initial phases, as not only will the mentor not coach, but also the protégé will not be willing to acquire the vital skills in becoming more independent. However, this relationship may also evolve into a marginal one, as both members of the dyad have the same style and are likely to be satisfied with the relationship. Also, since both the mentor and the protégé have the same attachment styles, the protégé may perceive the mentor as a role model. If this is the case, then the relation will evolve into a marginal one that will not meet most of the protégé's developmental needs, including coaching towards functioning more independently.

Mentoring relationships may become dysfunctional, in which the needs of one or both parties are not being met (Scandura, 1998). Clearly, this result is a property of the relationship. However, attachment theory may help explain the precursors to dysfunctional mentoring relationships. The typology presented here suggests that a secure (interdependent) mentor and an anxious/ambivalent (dependent) protégé are likely to result in a dysfunctional relationship. In such a relationship, the secure mentor is likely to expect the protégé to show some responsibility in self-management and to function more interdependently rather than being solely reliant on the mentor. However, as anxious/ambivalent individuals worry about not being able to measure up to other people, these individuals are likely to resist a any attempt that will reduce their dependency on their mentor. With different expectations from the relationship, the mentor may cease investing in the relationship.

The final category in the proposed typology is the one that results in a functional mentoring relationship. Secure mentors and protégés can be expected to report higher levels of vocational support, social support and role modelling in comparison with other groups. Secure persons would be comfortable asking for career advice, or help in difficult situations. For these individuals, the mentoring relationship may easily make the transition into a peer friendship (Kram, 1985a). They may be more comfortable exchanging information about themselves and their family, for example. These communication patterns increase rapport and trust within the mentoring relationship. Also, only secure mentors can effectively provide mentoring functions, as only the interdependent (secure attachment) orientation is negatively related to social dysfunction (Joplin et al., 1999). Secure mentors may effectively delegate tasks, and be able to trust others, which are essential for the development of a functional mentoring relationship (Quick et al., 1987).

As shown in Figure 7.3, mentoring should mediate the relationship between attachment/dependency styles and outcomes. The development of a mentoring relationship has been related to the outcomes shown in Figure 7.3 (Baugh et al., 1996; Lankau and Scandura, 2002) with the exception of absenteeism. The influence of attachment styles may be lessened in the presence of a mentor and the functions provided. Once mentoring functions are activated, the impact of attachment styles is eliminated. The effect of attachment styles should thus be more salient during the initiation phase. Mentoring functions, such as career support, and psychosocial support may represent relationships during the cultivation phase.

CONCLUSION

Mentoring theory needs to further address the issue of why some protégés (and mentors) may be more predisposed to the development of mentoring relationships than others. Attachment theory may provide some new directions by introducing concepts from developmental psychology into mentoring theory.

The model proposed here should also be useful for HR practitioners, especially when conducting training needs analysis and/or matching newcomers with potential mentors. As can be seen from Figure 7.2, only the secure (interdependent) mentor and secure (interdependent) protégé dyad attains the desired outcomes. As mentioned above, a person's attachment/dependency style is a 'working model' and can be changed if the person becomes aware of it and is eager to change it. The importance of providing potential mentors with thorough training and making them aware of how internal models of people have the potential to affect the relationship seems clear. As a result of effective mentor training, mentors will become aware of their own predispositions, and will work to correct them. They can also make their protégés become aware and alter their own automatic actions that are based on these unconscious internal models. Therefore, this chapter suggests that with the help of formalized, effective training it is indeed possible to turn potential dysfunctional and marginal relationships into functional ones and attain the desired work outcomes.

8 Development and supervision for mentors

DAVID MEGGINSON and PAUL STOKES

In this chapter we explore the practice of developing mentor competences. We offer conceptual frameworks for the development of mentors and also elaborate practical guidelines, drawing on our own practice and the literature. We then go on to consider the issues in organizing the supervision of mentors, a new and rapidly growing field of practice.

MENTOR DEVELOPMENT

In a project that the Mentoring and Coaching Research Group at Sheffield Hallam University has recently carried out for the European Foundation for Management Development (efmd), in conjunction with practitioners and researchers in Germany and Switzerland, we have developed a new framework for developing mentor competences. What we found in this international collaboration was that there is a diverse range of approaches to developing mentors. In our work we highlighted three in particular:

- a skills approach
- developing the business case
- a conscious seeking-out of each mentor's own way.

Each of these approaches will be outlined below. First we will discuss how practitioners can orient themselves to the approaches. One option is to choose just one approach. Each has strengths and advantages, so developers might select one of them and go with that. The features, principles and advantages of the three approaches are outlined in Table 8.1.

An alternative approach to using the three approaches is to blend them, seeking to gain the advantages of each and compensate for their weaknesses. This was the approach adopted in the efmd project.

Table 8.1   Features, principles and advantages of three approaches to mentor development

Approach	Features	Principles	Advantages
Skills	Common skills for all. Build capability by putting together building blocks. Skills can be practised. Skills acquisition can prepare mentors for most eventualities.	Atomism. Universality.	Intellectually simple. Trainers can offer standard package. Can produce good enough mentors from varied quality mentors.
Business case	Assumes widely held capability for mentoring. Requirement is in specific context and business purpose. Integrates with other initiatives.	Skilfulness of mentors. Situated learning.	Persuasive for business leaders. Unequivocal link to business benefit. Balances interest of mentee and business.
Conscious seeking	Mentors identify their own current capability. They develop a process of their own. They find ways of adapting their process to the needs of mentees.	Start from where the learner is. Every mentor has a process (container). Individuality and consciousness.	Flexibility. Congruent with mentoring practice. Helps deal with unknowable future.

SKILLS APPROACH

This way of organizing mentor development is the principle underlining most of this book. Readers can find much practical advice and frameworks in other chapters, particularly Chapter 9 (Insights from the psychology of executive and life coaching), Chapter 7 (Competences of building the developmental relationship) and Chapter 4 (Mentor competences: a field perspective).

If, say, the ten competences identified by Clutterbuck in Chapter 4 are adopted, then training will be organized around that framework. Skills exercises can be used to develop the competences. Here there are two approaches:

- specific exercises for each skill
- a general skills development process with feedback focused upon the specified competences.

The specific skills method is one with a long history and one of our early books (on coaching) pioneered this (Megginson and Boydell, 1979), with activities to develop the following skills:

- attending
- giving and receiving feedback
- drawing out
- silence
- suspending judgement
- recognizing and expressing feelings
- paraphrasing.

In Megginson and Clutterbuck (1995) we elaborated the skills of mentoring for each of four phases of the process, as outlined below.

Establishing rapport:

- suspend judgement
- be open to hints and concerns
- be clear about what must be open and what can be left out
- establish formal contract
- agree way of working
- set up details of future meetings
- achieve rapport.

Direction-setting:

- use and interpret diagnostic tools
- encourage thinking-through of implications of diagnosis
- set up gaining information from third parties
- help selection of initial area for work
- give feedback/set objectives/plan
- be clear about next step.

Progress-making:

- monitor progress
- review and renegotiate relationship
- recognize achievements/objectives attained
- time and manage the evolution of the relationship.

Moving on:

- address feelings of loss
- develop next phase and/or
- orchestrate a good ending
- think through and generalize learning
- establish friendship.

One obvious difference between these two lists is that the four-phase list is greatly elaborated compared with the first. A design consideration in using the skills approach is to decide how fine-grained the description of the skills will be. If you adopt too general a level, then key aspects of managing the relationship may be omitted. If you are too specific, then the essential wholeness and integrity of the mentoring process may be lost. Too much detail leads to an atomistic approach, which stands against the holistic nature of mentoring (see the third approach, 'conscious seeking', below).

Another difference between the two approaches above is that the second list is much more contextualized than the first. It is explicit in describing what kind of relationship the mentor and mentee are expected to develop. 'Establish formal contract'; 'use and interpret diagnostic tools'; 'review and renegotiate relationship' and 'think through and generalize learning' all imply a particular way of doing the helping that does not come though in the other list to the same extent. If you are a practitioner designing mentor development, it is important to note this feature of many competence frameworks – they carry with them a set of values and principles which can be imported into a scheme unnoticed. So, particularly if you are using someone else's framework, ask if it embodies the kind of mentoring that you want.

The general skills method does not practise each skill in turn, but uses 'real play', rather than 'role play' and gets participants doing a whole piece of mentoring in pairs or (with an observer) in triads. The competence framework in this case is used to provide a template for those giving feedback – whether it is the mentee, the observer or the course tutor. Specific practice activities may be carried out to focus on different stages of the relationship. However, in practice, it is often found that real play requires those practising to move outside any narrow brief that we may set for them. Garvey and Galloway (2002) offer an example of a corporate case adopting the real-play approach.

BUSINESS CASE

The focus in the business case approach is on helping learner mentors to relate the mentoring that they are to do to the context in which their organization is embedded. In our experience, this context is often articulated in terms of schemes, initiatives and change programmes which the organization is undertaking. In a public sector context, an added layer of complexity is the government policy (for example, the modernization agenda) within which departmental or authority programmes are meant to fit.

A critical feature of the usefulness of this approach is the vigour with which the mentoring scheme organizers test the framework and ensure that it has enough buy-in to be valued and respected by those participating as mentors and as mentees. If a scheme is a whim of a senior manager, or a bugbear of the HR function, then linking up to it is like falling on a broken reed, which will end up doing more harm than good. Eaton and Brown (2002) give an example of a thorough linkage with other initiatives in their work in Vodaphone.

Another issue to be born in mind when adopting the business approach is that some business contexts conflict with the values built in to a mentoring approach. Mentoring implies giving a great deal of space to the learner's dream (Caruso, 1996). Caruso says: 'Quite often the protégé's dream is replaced by either a mentor objective or an organizational goal' (p72). Caruso follows Levinson *et al.* (1978), in seeing the pursuit of the dream by the protégé as activating the mentoring relationship, which therefore needs to be bottom-up rather than top-down.

However, given these provisos, it is frequently found that the organization's agenda can provide a container or framework within which the mentoring pair can pursue their legitimated personal agendas. Some researchers suggest that there is no tension here, for example Kleinman *et al.* (2001), but other authorities suggest that it is by no means straightforward to negotiate the rocks and whirlpools in these waters. For example, a compelling account of the complexities of the interrelationships between personal and organizational agendas can be found in Covaleski *et al.* (1998).

CONSCIOUS SEEKING

Megginson and Clutterbuck (2002) undertook a study of written accounts by mentors of individual mentoring sessions to identify the benefits that they experienced from mentoring. An unintended by-product of this analysis was the recognition that different mentors frame their accounts in differing levels of consciousness. Six levels were identified, namely:

- JDI (just doing it) – no reflection on learning
- aware of what the learner is taught
- aware of what the learner is making sense of and how
- aware of interaction between mentor and mentee, and its effects
- questioning and considering behaviour and alternatives for both mentor and mentee
- seeing these alternatives in context, and that the context itself can also be addressed.

Within this framework the development task is seen as supporting mentors (and, indeed, mentees) in moving to greater levels of consciousness, represented by a progression from 'JDI' to 'addressing the context as well as the relationships'.

We start this approach to mentor development with the mentor group sharing their past experiences, both as people who have helped and been helped. The purpose of this sharing is to highlight that they already know a lot about helping and being helped – very often, they have articulated what works and what does not work. Often they are also conscious of the situations in which particular approaches or styles are more or less appropriate.

We make a distinction between mentoring as a learner-centred approach to helping and coaching as a more focused, skills-based approach where goal-setting is shared between coach and coachee (Megginson, 1988). For coach training, it is often appropriate to give coaches a standard process. The Goals Reality Actions Wrap-up (GROW) model (Downey, 1999) is perhaps the best-known framework for coaching. However, for mentors as opposed to coaches, we argue (Clutterbuck and Megginson, 1999) that one thing that good mentors have in common is that they have a good process, which acts as a container for the anxieties and ambiguities that can afflict both parties in the relationship. However, we found (pp149–150) that it is 'also clear that their processes were markedly different for each mentor'. So there is a need for each mentor to build their own process. Again, then, consciousness is seen as the critical issue. First the learner mentor needs to be aware of whether or not they have a process. If they haven't got one, they need to build one. When they have built and become confident in using it they need to recognize when it needs adaptation and change. Developers working with mentors can help this process by offering a range of processes (Megginson and Stokes, 2000). One framework for this can be the seven roles identified by Clutterbuck and Megginson (1999, pp14–15) of sounding board, critical friend, listener, counsellor, career adviser, networker and coach. At a more fundamental level, however, mentors can usefully develop their own process or way of going on, bringing together whatever set of resources they have developed in the course of their career. Some of the components that might be included are:

- models for appraising business proposals
- quality management frameworks
- organization change or development models
- general helping, counselling or development models
- neurolinguistic programming (NLP) or other transformation frameworks.

We particularly like Nigel Harrison's model, which is outlined fully in Harrison, 2000. It includes the following key stages:

- Who is involved?
- What do you do now?
- What do you want to be able to do?
- What is the cost of the gap?
- What are the causes and reasons?
- Knowledge, skills, motivation, environment.
- Action plan.

When we are offering a range of examples, we also talk about our own frameworks – not as a right answer, but as a possible example to contrast with others. The material from the Mentoring for Export programme that we currently use is given in an abbreviated form in the box below.

EXAMPLES OF MENTOR PROCESSES FROM THE MENTORING FOR EXPORT PROGRAMME

Every good mentor has a process…
…but no two mentors work in the same way.
Here are outlines of three mentors' views of their process. These are examples only.
Yours might be quite different. Research shows that the best mentors all have a model,
though these vary considerably. Some are like Example A, and are quite specific; others are more like Example B (David's approach) and are exploratory and relatively open.
What is your model?

Example A

Is this role too close to that of the international trade adviser? Which parts are legitimate for a mentor?

- Clarify nature of business, and its strengths and weaknesses.
- Establish intentions around export.
- Test robustness of export intentions.
- Explore costs and benefits of proposal, and financial feasibility.
- Explore governance and legal implications.
- Explore marketing and product development implications.
- Explore staffing implications and likely personal impact.
- Help mentee to develop plan to deal with these issues.
- Help mentee work on this plan.

To take a metaphor from the way that an artist works, mentoring is like what Shirley
Hughes, a children's writer and illustrator, does when she depicts a broad scene spread
across two pages of one of her books. She seeks 'to create a simple whole, very easily accessible and satisfying, but, like an onion, many layered within' (Hughes, 2002).

Example B

Is this framework too loose or too close to counselling for you?

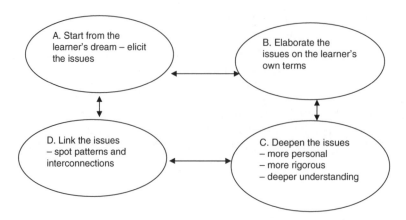

Example C

Is this prescription from an experienced mentor something that you could live up to?

'The initial role is to set the tone and create a climate where both can agree a purpose for the relationship. It is not a cosy role and, while simple in concept, it is complex in practice evolving uniquely in each case. The relationship is like weaving a Fair Isle sweater – looking equally harmonious on both sides, and all the colours fitting with each other. It is a holistic process… Every relationship is different, but the mentor is in charge of facilitating the process. Within each meeting, we usually start with a catch-up, where they talk about what they have done since the last time. They get a bit from me about what has been happening to me, so there is some reciprocity, without me using the time to deal with my own stuff. Then we identify a theme – "What would you like today to be about?" We explore what they want from me related to this theme, and then we work upon it. The mentor's job is to attend to this agreement, the purposes, boundaries, processes and benchmarks and to restate them if things go too far off track or become erratic.'

Dame Rennie Fritchie, from *Mentoring Executives and Directors*
by Clutterbuck and Megginson (1999).

Activity

- Outline your own process for how you would go about mentoring for export.
- Discuss it with colleagues.
- Amend it in the light of feedback that you find useful.
- Review it in the light of experience in exercises or in practice.

CONCLUSION

Garvey and Alred (2000) summarize the content in order of frequency from what they found among 25 mentor development programmes in a survey that they undertook, as:

- personal qualities of mentors
- mentoring process, skills of mentoring
- personal experiences of mentee
- personal experiences of mentor
- models of mentoring
- advantages of mentoring
- roles and responsibilities of mentors
- abuses of mentoring.

This illustrates that the mentoring literature seems to focus on the skills and consciousness approaches; the coaching literature (for example, Eaton and Brown, 2002), on the other hand, makes greater play with the business case approach. All three have their place in an integrated scheme.

IMPLICATIONS FOR MENTOR SUPERVISION

Whatever approach is adopted, each has issues for the supervision of mentors. First of all, it is important to make some distinctions between the various terms used in both the literature and in practice. When we talk about a mentoring supervisor, we are clearly differentiating that person from a scheme organizer. The latter is a vital role in any successful mentoring scheme and involves scheme promotion and recruitment, registration and other important administration tasks.

A mentoring supervisor is what is often referred to as a 'grandfather' relationship in the mentoring literature; this is where the mentor – already engaged in a mentoring relationship with their mentee(s) – receives supervision in a mentoring way from the mentoring supervisor. The term 'supervision' is one that has been borrowed from other helping professions, for example counselling, psychotherapy, education, medicine and social work. In each of these professions, however, there are different understandings of what is meant by supervision. For example, Marrow *et al.* (1997) and Hyrkas *et al.* (2002) both focus on clinical supervision in the health profession, which appears to place a significant emphasis on the quality control of their supervisees. However, Blase and Blase (2002), in their thorough discussion of supervision in education, incorporate 'direct assistance to teachers, group development, staff development, curriculum development and action research' (p12), whilst Maidment and Cooper (2002) draw our attention to the importance of challenging oppression and acknowledging diversity in social work. There are other definitions and contributions from psychotherapy and counselling (see Schur (2002) or Kutter (2002) for useful reviews of this area). However, our agenda is not to engage in a fully blown discussion of supervision and its different connotations but to offer some useful frameworks and strategies to those wanting to incorporate the supervision of mentors in their scheme.

A FRAMEWORK FOR SUPERVISION

We have come across several models of mentoring supervision in both our review of the literature and in our own practice, but one of the most useful discussions is offered by Hawkins and Shohet (2000) in their book on supervision in the helping professions.

Using frameworks adopted from Kadushin (1976) and Proctor (1988), they develop the following three categories of help that a supervisor can provide to a helper:

1 Educative/formative – focused on developing the skills, understanding and abilities of the supervisees. The superviser helps the supervisee by encouraging reflection on the skills practice they have done with the person they are helping.
2 Supportive/restorative – focused on how the supervisee deals with their own responses to the person they are helping. The supervisor helps by drawing attention to ways in which the supervisee has been affected by the emotional issues of the person being helped, both in terms of being a container for any emotional pain as well as any restimulation of the supervisee's own issues that may have resulted.
3 Managerial/normative – focused on ensuring that supervisees adhere to the appropriate professional and/or organizational standards when they operate as helpers, that is. implementing quality control. The supervisor helps by drawing the supervisee's attention to their behaviour and actions in terms of standards and/or the ethical frameworks of the project, organization or profession.

This has implications for, and linkages with, the model developed in Table 8.1, which are incorporated into Table 8.2.

Table 8.2   Features, principles and advantages of three approaches to supervision

Approach	Supervision category	Focus of attention	Advantages
Skills	Educative/formative	Helping the mentor to audit themself and their skills against a set of competences. Gives agenda for improvement.	Clear development path for both supervisor and supervisee.
Business case	Managerial/normative	Ensuring that the mentor is working with their mentee in a way that is congruent with the goals of the project/ organization/profession.	Ensures that mentor is 'good enough'. Enables deselection or retraining of mentors who do not fit with the agenda.
Conscious seeking	Supportive/restorative	Helping the mentor to recognize their own responses to the mentee and the issues these raise for their relationship.	Enables the mentor to use their own responses as data for their and the mentee's development.

This table summarizes the linkages that we see between the different modes of supervision and the approaches framework developed earlier. The skills approaches seems to fit closely with the educative/formative mode of supervision, which enables the supervisor to draw on the skills practice from real/role play to identify areas for development, for example, 'I notice you talked first every time there was a silence. Have you tried using silence as a way of drawing more responses from the mentee instead of filling the gaps yourself?'

The business case model seems particularly pertinent to the managerial/normative style of supervision where the supervisor acts as a guardian of the organization's interests and/or of the goals of the project. Here, the supervisor might suggest that certain behaviours or responses are inappropriate on the part of the mentor and may suggest alternatives in a sounding board role (Clutterbuck and Megginson, 1999). However, there is potential for difficulty for the supervisory relationship if the agenda is understood and enacted differently by the mentor and the supervisor.

Finally, the conscious seeking approach seems best suited to the supportive/restorative process. This is where the mentor is trying to find a style or approach (or even a repertoire of approaches) that best suits them and may need to recognize and reflect on their own development needs and issues in order to be comfortable with the approach that they are using.

In our work on a peer mentoring scheme with managing directors of firms involved in export (see Megginson and Stokes (2000) for a full account), we found that the conscious seeking approach was the most appropriate, as we were dealing with people who were very confident in what they did (both mentors and mentees) but who had little direct experience of formal mentoring schemes. Hence, they would not have tolerated a skills approach, as they felt they used many of the appropriate skills already. However, they did welcome the opportunity to reflect on those skills and processes in a more focused way. Although being successful in exporting was perceived to have some generic components, a business case approach was not appropriate as they all operated in very different businesses and as managing directors did not need teaching about this by us. Following the logic of our linkages between mentor development and supervision, our chosen approach to supervision was by way of peer-group supervision (Hawkins and Shohet, 2000) using a supportive/restorative agenda, as we felt that this was congruent with our agenda of adding to the mentors' repertoire of skills and behaviours. The next section includes part of a transcript from this event.

DATA FROM A GATHERING

The following extract is taken from Megginson and Stokes (2000) and contains a transcript of a team mentoring session held as part of a peer-group supervision session, which we called a gathering.

> *Mentors*
>
> *A = Mentor 1, whose issue was the focus of this discussion*
>
> *B = Mentor 2*
>
> *C = Mentor 3*
>
> *D = Mentor 4*
>
> *E = Adviser from export agency and supporter of the scheme*
>
> *F = Researcher*
>
> *A: I have a challenge rather than a problem – which is finding the right level of advice to be useful. For example, in practical terms, it's no use saying to my mentee, 'Here's a classic marketing plan – read it and learn!' He'll say 'Push off!' In the workshops you (F) talked about helping mentees to work things out for themselves, but you have to be helpful enough to enable him to do something. Also, you've got to deal with the complexity of what he's got to do – in my mentee's case finding a market that he can sell to competitively and where his products are culturally acceptable.*
>
> *B: Does he have expectations of what mentoring and exporting will do for the firm?*
>
> *A: I think he wants to grow incrementally through exporting. He's got a bit of time to play with as MD of an established company, though he's on a steep learning curve as far as exporting's concerned.*
>
> *D: Mine's the same, though it's in a smaller company. At our next meeting I'll get him to think about a business plan.*
>
> *C: Is A's mentee's product exportable?*
>
> *B: He doesn't know what he's selling – whether it is a locale, a service or one-stop shopping.*
>
> *E: It's a service.*
>
> *C: It'll be the authorities in the countries he's exporting to that he needs to work on.*
>
> *E: Yes, I talked to him about that before he went on the trade mission. I could get someone to do an export audit for him – free of charge.*
>
> *A: What would that involve?*
>
> *E: A half-day survey of the firm and its products.*
>
> *A: Send me the details and put it through me. I was thinking of creating models for him to work around – to help him think through the critical factors that he has to consider.*
>
> *C: I'm interested in his motivation. I'm not sure he's committed! Why isn't he here tonight?*
>
> *B: I think A has said things to indicate that he is committed. My experience is that in the early stage of a relationship – you've got to be totally honest – like when you first go out with a girl; or you get yourself into a lot of trouble.*
>
> *A: As a result of the information you gave us, F, I said to my mentee, 'I'm not here to tell you what to do – let's see how it goes!'*
>
> *C: Has he looked into exporting a lot? Is he frightened of it?*
>
> *A: His current idea seems to be to sell to what you might call 'the expatriate market' in Hong Kong, South Africa, Australia. I'm saying to him, 'Think more widely – that may not be the right route.'*
>
> *C: I've dealt with educational suppliers: the Irish buy from Britain by the boatload.*
>
> *D: Your mentee could link with integrated exporters. I knew of an example where one exporter was given a contract to totally equip six schools in Ethiopia.*
>
> *C: But success will come through gaining access to the authorities in the country of his choice.*

DISCUSSION OF EXTRACT

In this extract, our analysis suggests that A is dealing with conscious choice about how to mentor, and is opening himself up to the tension between offering solutions versus asking open questions. He is being helped in this process by B, who is modelling both sharing his experience and asking open-ended questions. Both C and D are, in this context, keen to offer concrete, pragmatic advice, grounded in their experience.

A couple of other points arise from this rich extract. First, there was a strong temptation for two of the mentors to make inferences about the motivation of A's mentee. C saw the mentee's commitment as suspect; B thought that A had provided evidence that the mentee was committed. One of the findings of the literature is that mentees value having a relationship without judgement where they can just *be*, and that this creates an opportunity for entering and using personal reflective space (Clutterbuck and Megginson, 1999, pp8–10).

Second, the extract confirms the usefulness of having meetings of mentors with open, problem-solving agendas, in the manner of action learning. We were able to use the meeting to feed back to the parties concerned what we had observed of their interaction and the inferences that might be drawn from them. In this sense, *all* of the participants took from the meeting questions and ideas for their own mentoring practice.

IMPLICATIONS AND CONCLUSIONS

In the preceding analysis, we categorized mentor development into three different approaches: skills, business case and conscious seeking. We then mapped three modes of supervision onto these approaches: educative/formative, managerial/normative and supportive/restorative. However, as the extract shows, all three approaches have their place within an integrated scheme. Our supervision session had elements of an educative/formative approach with our feedback to the mentors, but also had a managerial/normative element where we as scheme developers tried to model good mentoring and uphold the standards of the scheme. Finally, the fact that the conversation happened at all was born out of the mentor's frustration and impatience with his mentee, and his need to be supported in dealing with that and to have some practical suggestions to work with.

In conclusion, whichever approach to supervision dominates, or whether it is all three approaches, Barrett's work on mentor supervision (Barrett, 2002) is helpful in offering some validation of this framework. His evaluation work on mentor supervision suggested the following benefits of developing and supervising mentors from the point of view of the mentor themselves (p283). Mentor supervision and development were seen as:

- preventing personal burnout
- a celebration of what I do
- demonstrating skill/knowledge
- helping me focus on my blind spot(s)
- discovering my own pattern of behaviours
- developing skills as a mentor
- a quality control issue

- a quality control process
- providing a different angle on an issue.

Finally, we would like to echo Barrett's sentiments and call for others to engage in this extremely important debate.

9

Insights from the psychology of executive and life coaching

ANTHONY M GRANT PhD

Although definitions of mentoring vary somewhat, mentoring can be understood as a developmental relationship in which a more advanced or senior individual (the mentor) provides help and support for career, professional and personal development to a less experienced individual (the protégé or mentee). Thus mentoring relationships typically involve the passing on of domain-specific personalized knowledge from a more experienced mentor to the less experienced protégé.

Coaching is closely related to mentoring. In its broadest sense, workplace coaching can be understood as a solution-focused, results-oriented process in which the coach facilitates the enhancement of work performance, self-directed learning and personal and professional growth of the protégé.

A key distinguishing factor between mentoring and coaching is that the mentor has personal domain-specific expertise. For example if you want to become a great lawyer, you would seek to be mentored by a great lawyer. Coaching differs in that the coach need not have the same domain-specific knowledge – the coach need only be expert in facilitating the protégé's skill or knowledge acquisition. (Precisely the opposite distinction would be used in many contexts.)

A recent development within the behavioural sciences has been the emergence of a new sub-discipline of psychology – coaching psychology. Coaching psychology encompasses the application of the theory, research and practice of behavioural science to the enhancement of work performance, life experience, self-directed learning and personal growth of normal (i.e., non-clinical) populations.

Clearly there are important overlaps between coaching and the mentoring process. The aim of this chapter is to contribute to the discussion on what makes a mentor, by drawing on the research and practice of coaching psychology, and highlighting how aspects of coaching psychology can inform and help enhance the mentoring process.

HOW CAN COACHING PSYCHOLOGY CONTRIBUTE TO SUCCESSFUL MENTORING PRACTICE?

There has been considerable research indicating that mentoring, done well, can have positive effects on the personal and professional development of protégés. There has been less research that investigates the negative aspects of mentoring.

Eby *et al.* (2000) found that some of the key factors in negative mentoring relationships were mismatches in values and personality, and mentors' lack of skills in facilitating the protégé's learning. Ineffective mentors tended to be authoritarian, and to been seen as autocratically dispensing options. Further, ineffective mentors were inclined to be either too aggressive, pushy or distant. Feldman (1999) also noted the need for mentors to be more flexible in the way that they relate to and work with their protégés.

Those factors mentioned by Eby *et al.* (2000) may have less negative impact within informal mentoring relationships where the mentor–protégé relationship is voluntary and protégés seek out mentors with whom they have a natural affinity. However, lack of mentoring skills may be a significant barrier to success within formal mentoring programmes.

Typically, protégés experience greater anxiety and confusion in formal programmes (Scandura, 1998), and so the development of good mentoring skills and the ability to work effectively with a wide range of individuals may be a crucial factor in the making of a successful formal mentoring relationship.

To be effective, mentors need a measure of psychology-mindedness – that is, mentors need to have the ability to understand why people think, feel and behave in the way that they do. Effective mentors also need an understanding of how to help protégés systematically set, and then work towards, their goals. Advice-giving alone is not sufficient. Mentors need to actively manage the relationship and supervise their protégés' progress towards their goals.

In short, mentors need to be active and informed agents of change. To be an effective agent of change, one needs to have an understanding of the psychological and behavioural mechanisms by which human transitions and change can be purposefully constructed and maintained. Thus the frameworks, theories and techniques used in coaching psychology may well prove to be useful both as means of enhancing the mentoring process, and as important information in the making of mentors themselves.

A PSYCHOLOGICAL FRAMEWORK FOR FACILITATING THE MENTORING PROCESS

What are the essential criteria of a framework that would facilitate the mentoring process? As in coaching psychology, the key elements are:

- a model of self-regulation which allows delineation of the processes inherent in self-regulation, goal-setting and goal attainment;
- a model of how behaviour, thoughts and feelings can be altered to facilitate goal attainment;
- an empirically validated model of change.

SELF-REGULATION, GOAL ATTAINMENT AND MENTORING

Mentoring is essentially about helping protégés regulate and direct their interpersonal and intrapersonal resources to better attain their learning and developmental goals. Such self-regulation has a long and well-researched history in psychology (e.g. Collier, 1957).

The core constructs of goal-directed self-regulation are a series of processes in which the individual sets a goal, develops a plan of action, begins action, monitors their performance, evaluates their performance by comparison to a standard and, based on this evaluation, changes their actions to further enhance their performance and better reach their goals.

In relation to mentoring, the mentor's role is to facilitate the protégé's movement through the self-regulatory cycle. Thus a clear understanding of the behavioural science of self-regulation is invaluable in the making of an effective mentor. Figure 9.1 depicts a generic model of self-regulation.

In practice, the steps in the self-regulatory cycle are not discrete and separate stages; rather there is significant overlap between each stage and the next. Thus each step should facilitate the enactment of the next step. For example, goal-setting should be done in such a way as to facilitate the implementation of an action plan; the action plan should be designed to motivate the individual into action, and should incorporate means of monitoring and evaluating performance in addition to incorporating regular follow-up mentoring sessions (Figure 9.1).

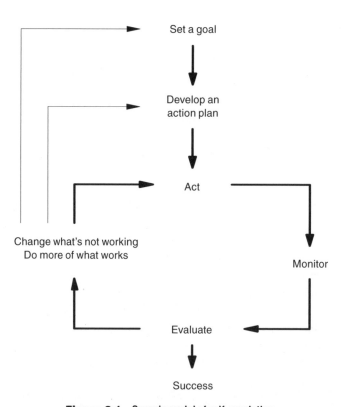

Figure 9.1   Generic model of self-regulation

GOAL-SETTING

If mentors are to be effective in helping their protégés reach their learning and developmental goals, careful attention must also be paid to the process of goal-setting.

Goal-setting is the foundation of successful self-regulation. Although there is a voluminous literature on goal-setting (Rawsthorne and Elliott, 1999), little of this has been explicitly discussed in the mentoring literature. Locke's seminal review of goal-setting research (Locke, 1996) summarizes a range of findings which usefully inform the mentoring process.

According to Locke, for individuals who are committed and have the necessary ability and knowledge, goals that are difficult and are specifically and explicitly defined allow performance to be precisely regulated and lead to high performance.

Commitment to goals is critical (Hollenbeck and Brief, 1987), and high commitment is attained when the goal is perceived as being attainable and important, or when the individual participates in determining outcomes. Goal-setting is most effective when there is feedback showing progress in relation to the goal, for goals stimulate planning in general, and often the planning quality is higher than that which occurs without goals. Furthermore, the effects of goal-setting can be long-lasting. For example, Howard and Bray (1988) found that managers' goals for the number of levels of future promotion was a significant predictor of the number of promotions received over a 25-year time span.

The implications of Locke's findings for mentoring practice is that mentors should strive to help their protégés set stretching, specific, attractive, realistic and time-framed goals which are easily operationalized and developed into action plans, and to give regular feedback to their protégés. Mentors may do well to explicitly incorporate Locke's findings into the mentoring process.

ACTION PLANNING AND ACTION

Goal-setting is a necessary, but not sufficient, part of the mentoring process – action plans must be developed and enacted. Action planning is the process of developing a systemic means of attaining goals.

VandeWalle *et al.* (1999) found that systematic action planning was associated with sales performance, and good action planning is particularly important for individuals who have low self-regulatory skills (Kirschenbaum *et al.*, 1981). The mentor's role in the action-planning stage is to help the development of the protégé's skills in developing a realistic and workable plan of action.

One key outcome of successful action planning is the facilitation of the protégé's transition from a deliberative mindset to an implementational mindset (Gollwitzer, 1996).

The *deliberative* mindset is characterized by a careful weighing of the pros and cons of action and a careful examination of competing goals or courses of action (Carver and Scheier, 1998). The *implementational* mindset is engaged once the decision to act has been made. This mindset has a determined, focused quality, and is biased in favour of thinking about success rather than failure. The shift from the deliberative to the implementational mindset is important, not least because individuals in implementation tend to perceive themselves as being in control of their outcomes (Gollwitzer and Kinney, 1989), and experience a positive and optimistic view of their chances of success (Taylor and Gollwitzer, 1996). Such cognitions themselves are associated with higher levels of self-efficacy, self-regulation and goal attainment (Bandura, 1982).

MONITORING, EVALUATION AND CHANGE: THE ROLE OF SELF-AWARENESS

Goal-setting and action planning need to be complemented by monitoring and evaluation. Because self-monitoring and self-evaluation are key components of the self-regulatory cycle, it is important to have an understanding of the sociocognitive mechanisms involved, and how they impact on mentoring practice and outcomes.

Self-monitoring and self-evaluation are metacognitive processes, metacognition being the process of thinking about one's thoughts, feelings and behaviours. As Carver and Scheier (1998) note, key abilities mediating effective self-monitoring and self-evaluation include self-awareness and self-consciousness.

Self-awareness refers to focusing attention on some aspect of the self or one's experiences (Wicklund, 1975), and *attention* refers to the selective processing of sensory input and information. Self-awareness is thus the selective processing of information about the self (Fenigstein *et al.*, 1975). *Self-consciousness* refers to an individual's propensity or ability to be self-aware. Fenigstein *et al.* differentiate between private self-consciousness, which is concerned with attending to one's own inner thoughts and feelings, and public self-consciousness, which is a general awareness of oneself as a social object that has an effect on others.

In relation to the self-regulatory cycle, focusing attention on the self allows the individual to better access the internalized mental representations of the standards and reference values by which they evaluate their performance.

Thus, individuals who are high in private self-consciousness should perform better than those low in private self-consciousness, and the difference between those with high and low levels of private self-consciousness should be particularly noticeable when the standards are salient or of personal importance (Carver, 1996).

Indeed, higher levels of private self-consciousness were found to be related to sales performance for salespersons for whom sales performance was important (Hollenbeck and Williams, 1987), and Church (1997) found that high-performing managers were significantly more self-aware than low-performing managers. Further, individuals with high levels of private self-consciousness appear to hold more functional (i.e. stable and internal) attributions for success than individuals low in private self-consciousness (Briere and Vallerand, 1990) and they tend to be less negatively affected by negative feedback (Doherty and Schlenker, 1991).

The development of an individual's private self-consciousness through mentoring may be particularly important when the mentoring relationship is directed at enhancing interpersonal skills, for example for leadership development (Church, 1997; Sosik and Dworakivsky, 1998). This is because the development of intra- and interpersonal skills may well be limited by low self-awareness or a lack of interest in the psychological or emotional aspects of human experience and interaction (Bar-On and Handley, 1999).

However, it should be noted that although high levels of private self-consciousness are associated with accurate and extensive self-knowledge, higher levels of self-consciousness are often associated with anxiety, stress, psychopathological rumination and depression (Trapnell and Campbell, 1999).

Indeed, in a study of the impact of life coaching on goal attainment and private self-consciousness, Grant (2001a) found that as individuals were coached through the self-regulation cycle their levels of private self-consciousness decreased, and this decrease was associated with better goal attainment. The implication of this for mentoring practice is to emphasize that an excessive focus on self-reflection may be counterproductive in terms of facilitating goal attainment.

WHAT IS REGULATED IN MENTORING, AND HOW?

Human experience encompasses four dimensions – thoughts, feelings, behaviour and the situation (or environment). There is a quadratic reciprocity between these four dimensions. For example, how we think impacts on how we feel, how we feel affects the way we behave (Ellis and Harper, 1961), and situations and environments can elicit specific behaviours (Skinner, 1963). Figure 9.2 illustrates the reciprocity between the four dimensions and their relation to goal attainment.

Drawing on this conceptual foundation, clinical, counselling and coaching psychologists have developed an extensive repertoire of techniques designed to enhance self-regulation in each of these domains, and these may well be useful for mentoring practice.

Burns (1989) details about 50 techniques which enhance the self-regulation of thoughts, feelings and behaviour. These include self-monitoring (in which behaviours, thoughts or feelings are observed and recorded), cognitive restructuring (the altering of unhelpful thoughts) and behavioural skills training protocols.

Self-monitoring alone – that is, self-monitoring in the absence of other self-regulatory techniques – has been found to be an effective tool for change for a wide range of behaviours, including inappropriate social behaviour (Pope and Jones, 1996), learning in young students (Lalli and Shapiro, 1990) and poor time management for small business owners (Gaetani *et al.*, 1983). However, self-monitoring is often more effective when combined with other strategies such as behavioural skills training and cognitive restructuring (Febbraro and Clum, 1998).

All human experience is contextualized and takes place within a specific environment. The situation or environment can have a powerful influence over behaviour (Bargh and Gollwitzer, 1996). For example, ex-addicts are more likely to relapse if prematurely exposed to the environment in which they developed their addiction (Klingemann, 1994). However, environ-

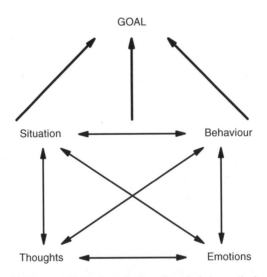

Figure 9.2 The 'House of Change': quadratic reciprocity between the four dimensions of human experience and goals

ments can be regulated and structured to facilitate the adoption of specific behaviour (Chesney *et al.*, 2001), and environmental structuring is particularly effective when combined with self-monitoring and behavioural skills training (Dean *et al.*, 1983). In addition, behavioural skills training is an effective way of inducing change in a wide range of dysfunctional and clinical populations (Murphy, 1984).

Further, in an investigation of the impact of the purposeful regulation of all four domains in coaching, Grant (2001b) found that when coaching trainee accountants to improve their performance, the purposeful regulation of all four domains was associated with significantly higher levels of goal attainments.

The implications of these findings for mentoring practice is that mentors should seek to work with their protégés in order to help them regulate all four domains. Thus, in the mentoring process, mentors may find it useful to ask themselves the following questions:

- Does the protégé have the necessary behavioural skills? If not, what do they need to do to develop them?
- Do the protégé's thoughts and feelings facilitate or impede their progress towards their goals? If not, what are more useful ways to think and feel about the goal?
- Does the situation or environment facilitate goal attainment? If not, how can the situation or environment be restructured?

SOLUTION-FOCUSED APPROACHES

One important issue stemming from the use of such psychological techniques is that they can lead to a pseudo-therapeutic discourse, one where the mentor may fall into playing the amateur psychologist. This is clearly not a desirable outcome.

One way to circumvent this issue is to use a solution-focused approach (de Shazer, 1988). O'Connell (1998) cites the following as being central characteristics of a solution-focused approach and these might well be useful in mentoring practice:

- *Use of a non-pathological model:* problems are not indications of pathology or dysfunctionality, rather they stem from a limited repertoire of behaviour.
- *A focus on constructing solutions:* the focus in on the construction of solutions rather than trying to understand the aetiology of any presenting problem.
- *Utilization:* the mobilization and utilization of any part of the protégé's life experience which could help facilitate goal attainment.
- *Action orientation:* there is a fundamental expectation that positive change will occur, and that the protégé will act to create this change outside the mentoring session.
- *Clear, specific goal setting:* setting of attainable goals within a specific time frame.
- *Assumption that change can happen in a short period of time:* this stands in contrast to schools of thought that assume that any problems must be worked on over a long period of time.
- *Future orientation:* the emphasis is more on the future (what the protégé wants to have happen) than the present or the past.
- *Enchantment:* the mentoring is conducted in a way that is attractive and engaging for the protégé.

A MODEL OF CHANGE FOR MENTORING PRACTICE

Mentoring is about facilitating purposeful change. Yet there has been little discussion in the mentoring literature about models of change which can be used in the mentoring process. In the psychological literature there are two key models of change that have been applied to individual career development, life changes and organizational change: the transition model (Bridges, 1986) and the transtheoretical model (Prochaska and DiClemente, 1984).

BRIDGES' TRANSITION MODEL

Bridges' model focuses on the role of emotional reactions to change, and makes a key distinction between *change* and *transition*. This distinction may be useful for mentors who are mentoring protégés through transitions periods.

For Bridges, change is both situational and external. Change happens when something starts or stops. For example, the physical act of moving from home is a change. On the other hand, transition is the internal experience of the psychological reorientation process as one adapts to change. In Bridges' model there are three stages to transitions: endings, a neutral zone and new beginnings.

Fundamental to the model is the recognition that transitions start with an ending – one thing must end for something else to begin. The endings stage is about letting go of the past. There may be a sense of loss, mourning, and even anger and resentment. Bridges recommends that individuals at the endings stage give themselves time to complete the process.

The next stage is the neutral zone, the core of the transition process. This stage is characterized by a sense of confusion and uncertainty about the future. Bridges again cautions against prematurely moving out of the neutral zone, and suggests that the neutral zone is a place of promise and opportunity, which represents a great chance for creativity and renewal. The final stage in the model is new beginnings. Here the new vision for the future is developed and enacted. Fear and disorientation turn into excitement about new opportunities. Bridges suggests that individuals at this stage need to maintain the focus on achieving results, become more aware of their thoughts and emotions, and be open to the need to alter plans in response to unexpected events.

Bridges' model is useful for mentors as it provides a framework for understanding and working with protégés' differential emotional reactions as they work through transitions.

THE TRANSTHEORETICAL MODEL OF CHANGE

The transtheoretical model (TTM) was originally developed by Prochaska and DiClemente (1984) as a means of understanding addictive behaviours such as smoking, and drug and alcohol misuse, and is somewhat more sophisticated than Bridges' model. Over time the model has been successfully applied to a wide range of other behaviours. In the TTM, change is not seen as an all-or-nothing dichotomous process. Rather, change is a progressive transition through a series of five identifiable, although somewhat overlapping, stages.

Progression through these stages can eventuate in permanent change. However, for most individuals change is a cyclic rather than a linear process, and many individuals relapse into old behavioural patterns before the new behaviour is permanently maintained. The stages of change are:

1 *Pre-contemplation*: at this stage there is no intention to change in the foreseeable future. Individuals are often completely unaware of the need to change.

2 *Contemplation:* individuals at this stage are considering making changes, but have not yet done so. The primary characteristic of this stage is ambivalence – the weighing up of the pros and cons of change.

3 *Preparation*: individuals at this stage have increased their commitment to change, intend to make changes in the near future and often have started to make small changes.

4 *Action:* individuals at this stage are engaging in the new behaviours, but have made such changes for only a short period of time (less than six months for addictive behaviours).

5 *Maintenance:* individuals at this stage have been consistently engaging in the new behaviours over a period of time (six months for addictive behaviours).

As individuals move through these five stages, they experience a number of shifts in the way they think and feel. One such shift is in the perceived costs and benefits of change – decisional balance. The decisional balance construct describes how individuals weigh up the pros (perceived benefits) and cons (perceived costs) of making change.

It has been found that for individuals at the pre-contemplation stage, the cons of change are more salient than the pros, and that this decisional balance is gradually reversed as individuals move through the stages (Prochaska and DiClemente, 1986). For individuals at the action and maintenance stages, the pros of change will be more important than the cons.

Figure 9.3 illustrates the typical pattern of pros and cons over the stages of change. Similar patterns have been observed for a wide range of behaviours.

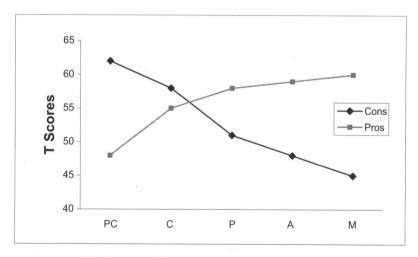

Figure 9.3 A typical pattern of pros and cons across the stages of change
(Note: PC = pre-contemplation; C = contemplation; P = preparation; A = action; M = maintenance). T scores (or standardized scores) are a conversion (transformation) of raw individual scores into a standard form. They are the result of standardized tests that attempt to measure an individual's performance compared to a population of similar individuals, in order to establish norms of performance which are representative scores for members of that population. T scores are best used for averages and (in this case) averages over time, allowing for the study of change. In the above diagram, those in the survey on average rated the cons higher than the pros in the pre-contemplation stage. Over time, this trend reverses, with pros rated increasingly higher than cons as they move from the contemplation stage into the preparation, action and maintenance stages.)

Another core construct in the TTM is self-efficacy. Self-efficacy is the belief in one's ability to perform a specific task, and is an important factor in determining whether individuals decide to make changes, the amount of effort they expend and the degree to which they persevere in the face of adversity (Velicer *et al.*, 1990). Not surprisingly, it has been found that self-efficacy substantially increases as individuals move through the stages of change.

Implications of the transtheoretical model for mentoring practice

The TTM has important implications for guiding mentoring practice as it suggests that mentors should work differentially with protégés, depending on their specific stage of change. Prochaska *et al.* (1998) outline a number of guidelines for facilitating change based on the TTM:

1 *Avoid treating all individuals as though they were at the action stage:* a fundamental mistake made by many agents of change is to assume that all presenting candidates for change are ready and willing to actively engage in the work of change. As many mentors know all too well, this is simply not the case. Many mentors will have had the experience of making useful suggestions for action, only to find that the protégé's resistance to change increases.

2 One reason for this increased resistance is that individuals at the pre-contemplation and contemplation stages have high levels of emotional investment in maintaining the decisional balance status quo. Mentors need to explicitly assess their protégé's readiness for change and, having developed an understanding of the protégé's stage of change, tailor their approach to match the dynamics of that specific stage of change. Such assessment can be conducted by written questionnaire, behavioural observation or (possibly of most use to mentors) by verbal self-report.

3 Self-reports can involve asking the protégé a simple series of questions such as: 'Do you think behaviour X is a problem for you right now?' If the answer is 'yes', then the protégé is at the contemplation, preparation or action stage; if 'no', then the protégé is at the maintenance or precontemplation stage.

4 The other question to be asked is: 'When do you intend to change behaviour X?' If the answer is 'at some point' or 'not soon', the protégé is at the contemplation stage; if they answer 'in the next month or so', then they are probably at the preparation stage, and if the answer is 'now', then they are probably at the action stage.

5 Individuals at the action stage are likely to achieve better and quicker outcomes than those at the contemplation and preparation stages. Individuals at the action stage are more motivated, with greater self-efficacy and than thus can cope with (and often welcome) more challenging behavioural change assignments and more difficult goals than people at the contemplation stage.

6 *Facilitate the insight–action crossover:* individuals who are reluctant to make changes are typically at the contemplation or preparation stages (Grimley and Lee, 1997) and spend more time thinking about their problems than actually changing their behaviour. For such protégés it is important that mentors focus on facilitating a shift from thinking about problems to behavioural change.

7 *Anticipate relapse:* for most people, relapse – slipping back into old behaviour – is a normal part of the change process. The mentor needs to include relapse-prevention strategies, prepare the protégé for possible setbacks and minimize guilt and shame if relapse does occur, helping them move back into action as quickly as possible.

Some stage-specific tactics for fostering change

At the *pre-contemplation stage*, the general principle is 'Raise awareness.' Here the mentor needs to ask the 'better' question, 'In what way would this change make things better for you?', or if necessary, 'You'd better change or else…'

At the *contemplation stage*, the general principle is again 'Raise awareness.' The mentor should not confront resistance – rather, roll with the resistance. One tactic that works well is *amplified reflection* – 'so what you're saying is that you'll *never* change…' *Double-sided reflection* is also effective. The mentor simply reflects back to the protégé both sides of the protégé's ambivalence – 'So on the one hand you feel that the change would benefit you because of xxxxx, but on the other hand you feel xxxxx…'

Interestingly, for many people at the contemplation stage, such double-sided reflection may be the first time they will have heard their ambivalence clearly articulated. By providing a personal reflective space, skilful double-sided reflection is often sufficient to help many people move through into preparation and action. In addition, mentors may find it useful to reframe the protégé's perceptions to facilitate moves towards change, for example, reframe fear of change as being a normal part of the change process.

At the *preparation*, *action* and *maintenance stages*, the general principle is to increase self-directed change. Protégés at the preparation stage will need less stretching goals, more structured support and more ongoing monitoring than those at the action and maintenance stages.

At the *relapse stage*, the general principle is to normalize and move the protégé back into action as soon as possible. Here the protégé can reframe relapse as a normal part of the change process, and minimize shame and embarrassment. It is often useful to look for past successes and build on those, whilst abandoning past failed 'solutions' – try something new.

SUMMARY

Mentors need to be active and well-informed agents of change, with a good understanding of the psychological and behavioural mechanisms by which human transitions and change can be purposefully constructed and maintained. The mentor's role is to help the protégé set appropriate goals which will lead to the protégé's personal and/or professional development, and for this they need an understanding of the core issues in goal attainment, self-regulation and self-reflection.

Whilst the opportunity to engage in self-reflection is an important part of profession development and of the mentoring relationship, excessive self-reflection may be counterproductive in terms of facilitating goal attainment.

Mentors also need the ability to work holistically with their protégés – helping them to regulate all four dimensions of human experience (thoughts, feelings, behaviour and the situation) in order to best facilitate goal attainment. In addition, transition and stages models of change provide mentors with useful insights about how best to work with protégés who are at different points in the change process.

The frameworks, theories and techniques used in coaching psychology can be seen to be useful both as means of enhancing and researching the mentoring process, and as important developmental tools in the making of mentors themselves.

10 Developmental relationships: a mentoring approach to organizational learning and knowledge creation

LIZ BORREDON and MARC INGHAM

Our objective in this chapter is to consider the characteristics of a relationship between a scientific leader in the field of technological innovation and his research and development team. Focusing our discussion on the leader, we identify the nature of the developmental context that they create, their understanding of a learning team and how they use conversation as a means for learning and development.

We have examined this dynamic through the lens of a mentoring approach to organizational learning and knowledge creation. Our study is unusual in as much as research on knowledge creation and research on mentoring have developed separately and in parallel. While some research investigates the role of personal learning in mentoring relationships, it is rare to combine these two 'disciplines' and yet, as we have discovered, there is much to learn from how the mentor contributes to the collective learning process.

POSITIONING MENTORING AND LEARNING

Managers at all levels deal with complexity, uncertainty and value conflicts. Rapid technology change, downsizing, and globalization mean that all individuals in organizations are faced with the challenge of learning new skills, combining mastery of highly technical expertise with critically reflecting on, and then changing, their own organizational practices. As Argyris says, 'the nuts and bolts of management increasingly consists of guiding, and integrating the autonomous and interconnected work of highly skilled people' (Argyris, 1991, p100).

Mentoring, with its career and psychosocial functions, sits within a new age of management that emerged in the 1980s after research indicated it promoted career success, personal growth, leadership development and increased organizational productivity. A North American survey in 1996 indicated that the percentage of business and planned mentoring programmes doubled between 1995 and 1996 (Darwin, 2000). More recent literature suggests that the mentoring process also includes functions that are more explicitly oriented to learning and knowledge creation or to making significant transitions in knowledge, work or thinking, transitions required to deal with changing environments. These call for developing research and practice in these areas (Lankau and Scandura, 2002; Higgins and Kram, 2001; Darwin, 2000, Clutterbuck and Megginson, 1999; Garvey, 1999; Bartunek and Kram, 1997; Ragins, 1997).

It is interesting to note that the term 'mentor' is initially used by Homer in his epic poem *The Odyssey*, where the goddess Athene, with her power in higher circles, takes on a human form to become the nurturer of wisdom and courage, suggesting that the role assumed by any 'mentor' varies in accordance with the circumstances and the protégé's needs.

We could also say that mentoring is a complex relationship or unique alliance enabling the engagement of the 'self' in the process of learning. 'Complex' because the relationship will change focus and the mentor will respond according to what the learner or situation needs rather than be bound by habitual behavioural or functional relationship or thinking routines.

Routines can be one of the main obstacles to learning unless they transform themselves gradually in step with the organization acquiring expertise within its environment. They ensure that, in time, organizational behaviour remains stable and homogeneous. In this sense, the organization's objective, even if subconscious, is to evolve functions and routines that are already in place through incessantly striving to incrementally improve operations in a consistent and regular manner. In an environment which is constantly challenged by disorder, unexpected fluctuations, and sometimes radical and abrupt change, consistency and regularity might not be appropriate, as they bind an organization to what is called 'single-loop learning' (Argyris and Schön, 1978). Such learning ensures the normal functioning of business development, which implies improvement without modification of an organization's functional framework for action or their fundamental beliefs. And yet, in a phase when an organization or process is in transition, these models no longer provide a sense-making function for individuals or the work they undertake. So we come to the limit of single-loop learning when the hypotheses which underpin our approach to a given situation cease to be valid or efficient.

Mentors can contribute to promoting 'social order' or the types of learning described above. However, when conditions which permit the individual to reflect on their work bring to the surface potentially threatening or embarrassing information that brings about a need for real change, the mentor has a very specific role. This includes providing the source of challenge which results in the painful acceptance of abandoning assumptions, attitudes and thought patterns in order to adopt others which are better adapted to the existing organizational reality. The transition from single-loop learning (Argyris, 1993) gives rise to anxiety and fear which threatens the stability of the organization and its members. They will impulsively activate defensive mechanisms or seek refuge in deep-rooted organizational routines and procedures that play a stabilizing role in moderating behaviours.

'Double-loop learning' (Argyris and Schön, 1978; Senge, 1992) consists in the organization transforming its fundamental frames of reference as well as its system for interpretation and thus its mental models. This is not incremental learning; it is much more a result of unexpected constraint, or disorder which forces a change of thinking. Mentors do not collude with defensive mechanisms, neither do they maintain the comfort zone. Tension and contained anxiety are elements which liberate potential, and courage is needed to overcome inevitable doubts. The role of the mentor alternates between sustaining courage and confronting assumptions with the aim of understanding the nature of the 'whole' and unfragmented situation.

There is another level of learning referred to as 'triple-loop learning' (Bateson, 1971). Through a process of intentional inquiry, engagement in the learning process is strengthened by seeing the need to transcend mindsets, values or paradigm limitations. We usually consider intelligence a measure of how fast or easily we assimilate theories, information or concepts. Here, intelligence is understood as a source of ideas or creativity, accessible through the process of unlearning or, put differently, the process of making space through suspension of habitual 'knowing'. Bateson (1971) and Pauchant (1996) claim that accessing new levels of intelligence and creativity depends on freeing up energies normally restrained by rigid thought patterns and binary thinking. Removing the barriers that inhibit organizational learning does not only reside in perceiving the need for triple-loop learning, but also creating contexts that make such learning possible. Considered as a contained meeting of minds in pursuit of understanding the meaning of what is said, dialogue is one such context.

'Dialogue' consists of suspending assumptions, having them discussed and called into question. This is not the same as 'debate', which is to beat down, or 'consensus', which is to create a measure of agreement. In dialogue we learn to preserve all diversity and difference between those present. Many authors (Bohm, 1990; de Maré *et al.*, 1991) claim that dialogue holds the potential for allowing entirely new collective intelligence to emerge because it underpins questioning of the presuppositions attending any given problem, providing a shared space that serves as a foundation for knowledge creation. Nonaka and Konno (1998) claim that knowledge is embedded in such a space or 'Ba'. We would like to take this approach further by suggesting that if we consider the mentor as a catalyst in the learning process, then they are involved and not separate from this process.

Darwin asserts that there is more to mentoring research than 'surveys that attempt to link programme initiatives with work-related outcomes' (Darwin, 2000, p209). She calls for a major shift in understanding mentoring. Knowledge, she says, needs to be viewed as an active process, where learning becomes dynamic, reciprocal and participatory, with change more likely to occur as a result of individual learning. She sees in mentoring the opportunity for dialogue where expert and learner demarcations disappear and a learning partnership emerges, with recognition of different ways to structure meaning. Thus mentoring would become one of a number of strategies in moving from tacit to explicit knowledge creation, which would suggest learning referred to as transformational, or triple-loop.

We now move on to new product development that involves learning and knowledge creation. Usually, developing a new product concept is a complex process based on the interplay, conversion and interaction between tacit and explicit components of individual and 'collective' knowledge (Nonaka and Takeuchi, 1995). In recent R&D and innovation literature, authors emphasize tacit aspects of knowledge and their conversion into explicit knowledge through externalization (consisting of articulation and codification): 'The externalization mode (of knowledge conversion) is triggered by meaningful "dialogue or collective reflection", in which using appropriate metaphors or analogy helps team members to articulate hidden tacit knowledge that is otherwise hard to communicate' (Nonaka and Takeuchi, 1995, p71).

Collective reflection involves the types of learning we discussed earlier. Citing Mezirow (1991), Raelin (1997) defines two types of reflection. The first we could align with double-loop learning, the second with triple-loop:

Process reflection *is an examination of how we go about problem solving with a view toward the procedures and assumptions in use. Process reflection also takes into account how we think about a given situation*

Premise reflection *goes into a final step of questioning the very presuppositions attending to the problem to begin with. In premise reflection, we question the very questions we have been asking in order to challenge our fundamental beliefs*

Raelin, 1997, p567

We suggest that this type of reflection and learning is often dependent on creating an appropriate context as well as having a catalyst who provides the conditions for exceptional learning.

In the following section we introduce a company named TECHNO[1] in which we discovered exceptional learning sustained by JO,[1] its founder, whom we have identified as the catalyst with a mentoring style of management. Emphasis is laid on the context of design review, which is central to the early stages of new product development at TECHNO.

INTRODUCING TECHNO

Founded in 1986, TECHNO is a spin-off of a European university research centre. The company develops new equipment for advanced medical imaging, radiotherapy, ionization and sterilization. TECHNO is a world leader in its activities. Most of the early product developments (from 1986 to 1994) were based on scientific principles and technical solutions enabling the development of medium-sized advanced equipment, at a cost-effective price for the first time. This 'revolutionary' concept, created by JO, has been progressively refined and enriched, leading to new products and applications. It must be stressed that only few people in the world are able to develop 'new generations' of equipment. The company profited from pioneer advantages and competitive leadership, creating new fields of applications and new markets. Listed on the stock market in 1998, TECHNO acquired several competitors in Europe and North America, strengthening its leadership in industrial applications.

The authors have known JO, founder and R&D leader within TECHNO, for a number of years. In our 'source research', dialogue appeared as an important issue in interpersonal learning. Several collaborators at TECHNO mentioned the role played by JO in the knowledge creation and learning processes during the early stages of new product development. More recent encounters with JO underpin our illustration of the relationship that sustained a mentoring approach to knowledge creation (Borredon and Ingham, 2002). We also returned to TECHNO for a final interview with JO, and it is this interview that has added inspiration to most of this chapter. (The research methodology is briefly presented at the end of this chapter under 'Appendix: methodology'.)

A MENTORING STYLE OF MANAGEMENT

Apart from founding the company, JO was its chairman and executive director until very recently when he realized that to stay in this role while the company expanded would mean taking on responsibility for over 1000 employees. His interest being in people, he considered he could only have a personal managerial relationship with 150 individuals.

1   The names TECHNO and JO are fictitious, and replace the real names of the company and its director for copyright purposes.

I saw that I had reached my limit! I preferred to step down an echelon and work with 150 people (the maximum you can know sufficiently well) to integrate these groups and to maintain personal inter-action than to manage what would have become "files on people". So I intentionally handed over to someone else and now I head R&D although I do not see myself as "head" of anyone. I am part of a team of developers.

With a passion for learning and taking on new challenges, JO is renowned worldwide as a scientific leader in the field of imagined new product concepts. His personal 'vision' of new technological developments and potential applications dominate the first stage of the process. He is especially dedicated to a TECHNO context for design development known as the design review (DR). The way JO runs DRs suggested to us that he was not only setting up a very specific context for transfer of tacit knowledge but also a situation for the types of review we discussed earlier in relation to difficulties associated with double-loop learning, or inbuilt routines that prevent deeper learning from taking place.

The rule within TECHNO is that no design reaches production stage without being 're-viewed'. This consists of a designer explaining his innovation, and of his colleagues and JO seeking and finding fault with the design through imagining hindering factors that could impede effective completion or production.

Design reviews are considered an essential context for creativity and for broadening potential. As each idea is presented, and questioned, new ideas are stimulated. These ideas are not always connected.

Designers do not come to a DR with half a solution, expecting someone else to come up with the other half. Each idea or each challenge, each fault found stimulates a better idea or complements and works towards completing the designer's picture of what is needed.

The DR is the context for knowledge exchange and an essential key to creativity and knowledge creation. Everyone knows that they will be subjected to JO's critiques, like it or not! However, no one wants others to criticize their design but JO insists that progress comes about through demolishing and rebuilding ideas which, he claims, are stimulated through collaboration as well as opposition. But the process is painful and sometimes resented.

It's not 'natural' as no one likes their working designs criticized by others. I have discovered that people do not like to share their ideas early on in the process because the objective of the exercise is to find fault. The most human response is to delay the DR for as long as possible in order to have checked out all possible weaknesses in the design oneself. The problem is that the longer we leave the DR, the more there is to unravel before the design is oriented in the right direction.

But there is one rule that cannot be broken at TECHNO, namely that production cannot start without the DR. Here JO's relationship with his team is critical. His role is to ensure that the 'role play' is worked out in full. The designer's role is to present the design and convince others that it is feasible. The others' role is to imagine everything that could have been omitted, as well as likely hindrances. In other words, to ensure there are no thinking routines, no certainty, no assumptions that the design will work but, on the contrary, to sufficiently unravel the process in order to reconstruct it on a more solid and creative foundation.

Failure is seen as part of this process as long as mistakes are learnt from. JO considers that creativity in design is not possible without a degree of 'failure', and he himself ensures that his mistakes are the first to surface.

If we cannot afford to make mistakes, we cannot afford development! I like talking about my worst mistakes! No one can beat me in the number of mistakes they have made. I tell them it is 1000 times better to have 10 ideas demolished. Demolishing 10 ideas and then finding the breakthrough solution is the best way forward.

We have explained that JO sees failure as part of the design process and that demolishing ideas triggers insight. The only unpardonable mistakes are those that are repeated.

He also acknowledges that everyone needs to succeed, excel and feel part of a winning team. He sees that people need conditions which permit extraordinary achievement and that the DR is the opportunity to deal with failure and celebrate success. It is, however, very difficult to get the right degree of challenge into an objective.

Sometimes people achieve remarkable results which are only 60 per cent of the objective we had set. The degree of creativity and innovation is absolutely extraordinary and yet, because there was not 100 per cent achievement, they are disappointed. So we need to balance the degree of challenge. Too much challenge and there is disappointment, too little challenge and we do not get the breakthrough! One of my mistakes is to establish objectives that are too challenging as, even though I have fallen flat on my face, I am usually under the impression that we can always solve any technical problem. So I tend to push the envelope to its limits.

UNDERSTANDING AND MAINTAINING A LEADING TEAM

The manner in which JO maintains pressure and creates a climate that favours creativity is anchored in his own values and needs for a context conducive to maximum innovation. For him, competition is stimulating. He considers he can do better than the market trend, better than a competitor. He needs to know what the competitor is doing; he needs to be invited to appropriate meetings where he can gain access to discussion about design or about client needs.

Mostly ideas are triggered by a problem presented to us by a client. Tetrapak asked us to determine how to sterilize 10 tons of orange juice every hour. This is the type of challenge that comes from market needs, and which stimulates our creativity. Or sometimes we see a competitor present their solution and I immediately think 'we can do this better'. Currently I am interested in nuclear waste disposal, knowing that in Italy competitor teams are investigating this field. I get the initial idea, then I meet with my teams and together we flesh out the design.

Teams consist of peers. There is no leader, as JO views peer groups as being the most effective.

I would love to say that my style of mentorship influences people development. I am not sure if I do, but I see people who are growing, developing, coming up with new ideas and are of very great value. Others develop less. I give the same care to everyone. My experience is that the most efficient organization for development is teams of peers, no real leader in the group, with the combination of a very friendly atmosphere so that people are not afraid that others will use their mistakes to their own advantage. A degree of competitiveness is also vital. The clear barrier to development is a very hierarchical organization where a boss allocates tasks to everyone and where there is a lot of tension. A friendly group which exchanges ideas and which wants to show others what they are able to do, those are the ingredients…

But not everyone in the company shares the same vision of an effective team. JO has to fight for his ideas, and they have an implication for corporate culture and internal promotion. Some consider a boss is needed, while JO claims that authority decisions are not effective within R&D and hierarchy is a barrier to creativity. However, there are obstacles that are more difficult to overcome. R&D achievements are slow in meeting bottom-line expectations. Any innovation takes at least four years to yield results and this is not compatible with those fighting for immediate profit. Within such contexts, risk-takers who can 'fly high' in spite of constraints are needed. Some who were 'too stressed to sleep' did not survive within TECHNO.

It's much more difficult to have a long-term view of management in a publicly held company, subject to strong market pressure, than in a privately held organization. In a way, we did not have these problems when TECHNO was privately held. There was a consensus among the shareholders. Yes, we had to take a long-term view and we were investing in R&D, and yes, it will only bear fruit in four years from now. I have no interest in staying in a company if we are not interested in R&D.

Another difficulty for JO is having others accept that not every member of the team has people or communication skills, and yet still needs not only to find their place within TECHNO but also to evolve within the organization. Most directors consider that promotion depends on the number of people managed. TECHNO must, JO asserts, provide for those who have talent and managerial limitations.

Morris has developed enormously and yet hates and resents DRs. Technically he is excellent, he is able to develop a whole series of machines at TECHNO single-handed. This is one of his exceptional strengths. What he does works. But he dislikes communicating. He develops something remarkable and I cannot get him to present a paper on it at a conference. I know I will not bring him into the team and he will never be a leader. I know people, and my management style is based on human interaction, but there are some situations I cannot change. Flexibility is required and the system needs modifying as people cannot be changed. If we see that DRs are systematically rejected, we need to ask why. We don't always have a solution but we can do things to improve the situation and within R&D authority is not an option.

JO fights for his values. He ensures that his actions speak as loud as his words. He goes to those in difficulty. He considers himself a 'free electron', that is self-stimulating and able to respond to needs wherever they arise. Recently he was called to Sweden where a project was in severe trouble. He spent a week with the team.

Firstly, this demonstrated that we cared about them. Secondly, I could help them see the degree to which they had succeeded. Then, we told all manner of 'war stories', reviewing all manner of disasters which put the present situation into perspective. Apart from working on the design and processes that were at fault, we shared breakfast, lunch and dinners getting to know each other as people. There were those who were completely discouraged but I think that spending time in situ raised morale considerably. It is extremely important to go on site and work together.

JO was not convinced that his presence and working with the team solved the problem. Certainly the team had found a new lease of life and the machine in question was in operation but the client was threatening to cancel the order because of non-respected deadlines. Examples of this sort illustrate the importance of early DRs as well as the openness needed amongst the team when it comes to challenging designs and assumptions.

TOWARDS AN INTERPRETATION

Our case suggests that the search for knowledge creation and 'upper level' organizational learning is strongly supported by the mentor, as 'catalyst'. Some enabling conditions that are consciously or unconsciously developed by the 'mentor' can be identified. They fall into three interrelated categories: personal, contextual and relational.

Personal characteristics lead the mentor to build and strengthen developmental relationships propitious to individual and collective learning and knowledge creation. These processes are sustained and reinforced by the contexts and 'spaces' that are purposely created.

The mentors view themselves as peers within a team. Their authority is primarily based on personal traits (competences, values, behaviour). The mentors endeavour to promote their values and vision, and contribute to creating contexts and 'spaces' that are characterized by an 'atmosphere' conducive to collective creative reflection, which enables and enhances 'upper level' learning. Collective reflection is strongly supported by confronting ideas and promoting dialogue through a process of deconstruction and reconstruction, in which the mentor plays a central role, challenging peers and helping them to question their underlying assumptions.

Nevertheless we think that, in our case, even if they consider themselves as 'peers amongst peers' within the R&D team and behave as such, the 'mentors' *are* the founders, the scientific leaders and some of the top managers of this company. They have the authority and status which enable them to mobilize and leverage the contextual dimensions and the development of relationships favouring and enhancing collective learning and knowledge creation. This can also limit the development of a mentoring style of management insofar as some team members seem to prefer hierarchical relationships.

Our case suggests that the development of contexts and relationships that are conducive to collective organizational learning and knowledge creation does not take place 'naturally'. One of the leader's key roles is to ensure that individuals not only overcome personal reluctance and resistance to attending meetings, but also attend with the conviction that accompanies presenting and sharing ideas and discussing projects. A second challenge consists in helping some members develop the communication skills that are central to the learning processes.

The development of contexts and relations that enhance 'upper level' organizational learning and knowledge creation seems to be characterized by a continuous search for a balance between creating 'tension' and exploring the 'void', both of which are necessary conditions for collective reflection and innovation. 'Tension' enables the team to sustain knowledge creation and innovation processes, and to keep the team at the forefront of technological innovation. The 'void', or the unknown to be revealed, enables dialogue and collective reflection that develop ideas and product concepts that are really new. The leader plays a central role in creating and maintaining this balance. Their status and their position within the hierarchy contribute to creating an organizational 'umbrella', protecting R&D teams from financial market pressures that demand short-term returns.

Our study illustrates some issues that are central to the literature initially discussed. It confirms the role played by a mentoring style of management in supporting dialogue and collective reflection leading to organizational learning and knowledge creation. It shows how important it is to create contexts (both formal and informal) and 'shared space', as a foundation for knowledge creation and to remove barriers that inhibit knowledge-creating behaviours. It suggests that adopting a mentoring style of management depends on personal traits, preferences and capabilities that can be developed.

One limitation is the use of one single case which does not allow any generalization and poses the problem of external validity. A second limitation relates to the methodology. We used data from a very limited number of interviews and focused on the information drawn from our last interview with the 'mentor'. Our intent is to go a step further in this study to better capture and understand the nature of the developmental relationships sustaining organizational learning through interviews with team members.

APPENDIX: METHODOLOGY

The methodology applied in our empirical 'source research' was inspired by principles expressed by Yin (1984) for case study research. This research aimed at understanding the organizational learning processes in R&D projects led by TECHNO. In early 2002 we revisited data from ten interviews drawn from this research, focusing on the role played by JO as a 'transformational leader' (Borredon and Ingham, 2002). Results from this research suggested a 'mentoring style' of management adopted by JO. We then decided to focus on the perception the 'mentor' has of his role. We conducted one semi-structured interview in July 2002. This interview was recorded and fully transcribed. We then developed our interpretation in the light of the literature.

11 The mentor as storyteller

MARGARET PARKIN

THE ROLE OF THE STORYTELLER

For those of you who think of the storyteller as the colourful character that entertains at children's parties, you may not immediately see a link between that and the role of a mentor, but the connection is not a new or a fanciful one. Before the birth of Christ (himself of course a prolific storyteller) the Greek slave Aesop was known for telling his moral tales, whose common-sense wisdom was intended to instruct others in how to live a good and wholesome life. In the ancient Middle East, the Sufis encouraged their protégés to meditate on specially chosen teaching tales that they believed would help them to access a higher wisdom. And indeed, Greek legend has it that Odysseus, prior to setting off on his journey to fight the Trojan War, entrusted his young son, Telemachus, to the care of a wise and trusted friend, Mentor (who also happened to be one of the many manifestations of Athene, the goddess of wisdom).

To further explore the connection between the two professions, we need to go back in history to examine the original role of the storyteller. Far from being a frivolous and childish pastime, storytelling, prior to the invention of the written word, was the main means of passing on information and knowledge from one person to another, or from one tribe to another, or one village to another, just as these days we might rely on the media to keep us informed of world affairs, or in business we might choose to put more faith in what a trusted mentor tells us rather than believe the more formal and 'official' communication channels.

During this time, people became reliant on storytellers, and, as their power and influence became apparent, the profession itself gained in respect and admiration. But along with the prominence came the acceptance of responsibility, and in some cultures, the storytellers, prior to being allowed to practise their art, were actually required to take a solemn vow, in which they declared that any information they passed on to others would fulfil the criteria of being *accurate, interesting and memorable* – a vow which some communicators within organizations these days might find it hard to accomplish.

STORYTELLING AND THE TRANSFER OF CULTURE

The simple passing on of topical information wasn't the only function performed by the original storytellers. In cultures throughout the world, they have had an important role to play in building communities and preserving and sharing historical data. In ancient times, tribes would gather round their campfires at night to tell stories of their heroic deeds and accomplishments. The telling of these stories would then be passed on from one to another (no doubt with a liberal helping of exaggeration and embroidery that is the essence of a good story) and would gradually spread to more and more people within the community. Eventually everyone would be talking a shared language that came to represent the tribe's cultural values and history, which in turn helped them to make sense of their world and their part in it.

In the same way, a business mentor – through their actions and stories told about their actions – can become an embodiment of an organization's values and culture, and can play a vital role in helping to ensure the continuity of these standards from one generation to the next. How often do we witness, with the demise of a particularly charismatic figurehead in an organization, the death of what it was the company once stood for, or, at the very least, confusion for some time over it?

If a mentee is surrounded by company stories that are told positively and enthusiastically, in line with good storytelling traditions, and if, most importantly, they are congruent with the general organizational behaviour that they may witness, then their effects can be far more powerful and believable than any corporate video, newsletter or handbook that you might employ.

In my first book, *Tales for Trainers*, (Parkin, 1998) there is an example of this powerful principle. The chief executive of a large retailing organization in the UK had a rule that all managers, when visiting a store, should park their cars in an area furthest away from the building, the reason for this being two-fold: first, he strongly believed that the parking spaces nearest the store should be for the use of customers as they were the most important people to the organization, and second, parking in this way gave the manager a valuable 'customer's eye view' of the car park. The rule was put to the test when one day the CEO arrived at a particular store when it started to rain very heavily. Rather than compromise his own standards, he still parked in his usual place and ran – a distance of at least 200 yards – to the store. Not surprisingly, he was completely drenched on reaching the building, and the staff, whilst trying to suppress their laughter, had to find him some suitable alternative clothing. Even though, for a while, he might have been perceived as a figure of fun, this CEO more importantly became known as a man of integrity and someone who stood by his own principles.

However, if stories such as these are *not* compatible with organizational behaviour, then both storyteller and story lose all credibility and the whole thing becomes meaningless rhetoric. In addition, there is more likelihood of the mentee inventing their own stories about the company – usually with not quite so positive a spin!

STORYTELLING AND LEARNING

The original storytellers were also involved in education and in the transfer of skills and knowledge. In communities the world over there has always been a tradition of the old educating the young. In our modern-day organizations, we can still witness this transfer of cumulative wisdom, when those people whom anthropologist Peg Neuhauser (1993) refers to as 'the tribal elders' (highly respected or senior members of the organization) are called upon to act as 'master' to the apprentice, or to share their memories as part of an induction or orientation programme. Every organization has its own set of rules and procedures – we couldn't survive without them – but most organizations also have another 'under the counter' version, entitled 'The way we *really* do things round here' and it can be confusing – particularly for a new or inexperienced employee – to know when it is appropriate to follow which set of rules. This is where mentoring can be a valuable tool, particularly if carried out by a tribal elder who has many years' experience, and many relevant stories to tell. Warren Bennis (1996) says:

> Stories are more memorable and interesting than policy manuals and they seem to 'empower.' Tell a story and people will stop sleeping through your meetings.

Bennis, 1996

However, the emphasis here has to be placed on the word 'relevant'. Nancy Mellon (1992), professional storyteller in the United States, says that your 'intention is crucial' if you are telling a story as an illustrative part of a mentoring exercise. You must always aim to have the highest intention on behalf of your listener. In other words, only use a story that you think will 'fit' with the person for whom it is intended, in terms of content, style, message and so on, and make sure that it matches their values and desired outcomes. There is nothing worse than a mentor who *thinks* they are a good storyteller (and we've all met some!) regaling the mentee with *their* favourite story – which has no bearing whatsoever on the situation at hand. This just gives the mentee the feeling of being manipulated and insulted, and in addition is one of the quickest ways for the relationship between mentor and mentee to deteriorate.

STORYTELLING AND PROBLEM-SOLVING

In some ancient Eastern cultures, storytelling was also used as a gentle, yet powerful form of therapy. Patients wrestling with a problem or suffering from some sort of melancholia could expect the doctor to 'prescribe' a traditional tale, myth or fairy story which bore some similarity to their own dilemma, and on which they were instructed to meditate. It was believed that contemplation of the story would provide the patient with a metaphor, that is, a different perspective to consider, and could often offer clarity on the problem that they were facing. In his book *The Uses of Enchantment*, Bruno Bettelheim (1991) says:

> The figures and events of fairy tales also personify and illustrate inner conflicts, but they suggest ever so subtly how these conflicts may be solved, and what the next steps in the development toward a higher humanity might be.

Bettelheim, 1991

Stories used for problem-solving can often offer some comfort for the listener by introducing a 'helper', 'guide' or other protective person. The helper can take many symbolic forms – a fairy godmother, a guardian angel, a Buddha – who always appears at just the right moment, in order to help the hero/heroine on their journey. And indeed, just the notion of the possibility of a 'happy every after' conclusion that is the feature of many fairy tales, can give us a sense of hope and optimism for our own lives.

This notion of using stories as a powerful tool for transition has been a widely held view in the therapeutic world for some time, and its application is now being seen as more acceptable in the business world. The metaphorical element of a story can help people to 'reframe' their own situation, to see that there might be another way of approaching it and to help them towards effecting positive change in their lives. Modern-day mentors are sometimes referred to as 'transitional figures' – helping their protégés towards a mutually acceptable goal, or guiding them on a continuous journey in their organizational life.

The basic structure of most stories – sometimes referred to as the 'story map' – follows this line of transition. The philosopher Aristotle was quoted as saying that a good story encompassed 'the successful change from one status quo to another...' The characters in most stories (real or imaginary) encounter some sort of problem, conflict or challenge (the dissonance) which they deal with, either successfully or unsuccessfully, thereby achieving a resolution of some sort. Nigel Watts (1996) describes this format as a series of points or milestones on a journey:

- the status quo – where we join the hero/heroine
- the trigger – something happens which means the status quo cannot continue
- the quest – the response to the challenge
- the surprise – what really slaps us in the face
- the critical choice – the dilemma
- the climax – the choice we make
- the reversal – the change that results from the choice we make
- the resolution – if the reversal is sustained.

The stages of a story can provide a useful metaphor for a mentee in terms of their own organizational 'journey', particularly if the journey is one that involves a challenge or problem, such as a change of job, a promotion, setting new goals or a change in personal circumstances. If the dissonance in the story is seen to be similar to the one that the mentee is personally dealing with, then the message of the story takes on more significance.

Even a very short story can follow the same 'journey' format. In my second book, *Tales for Coaching,* (Parkin, 2001) there is a humorous tale about two caterpillars who, whilst sitting together on a cabbage leaf, suddenly hear a loud swishing noise, and, looking up, see a beautiful butterfly flying overhead. The first caterpillar looks at the other, shakes his head and says, 'You'll never get me up in one of those things'. The tale itself is only four lines long, but, when used along with appropriate 'trigger' questions, has promoted some of the longest and most profound discussions with listeners, and is a wonderful vehicle for dealing with the notion of change – and particularly the *inevitability* of change.

HOW DO STORIES WORK?

The original storytellers discovered, through trial and error, that the best way to help people make sense of information and commit it to memory, was to create vivid and fantastic images in your mind and weave the information into them – in fact, the more fantastic the image, the easier it would be to remember. What the original storytellers were doing instinctively has since been confirmed by contemporary brain research; that learning and memory work best when:

- the information is seen as part of a *context or bigger picture*
- where there is *novelty and interest* generated
- where *emotions* are involved.

LEARNING THROUGH CONTEXT OR THE BIGGER PICTURE

The neocortex is the part of the brain that deals with our intellectual processes such as thinking and talking, and its primary function is to search out meaning, context and patterns in the world. Stories themselves can contain universally recognizable patterns, symbols and templates – 'once upon a time', 'happy ever after…' and the 'story map' structure mentioned above, which can help us to build coherence out of seemingly random information. A skilful mentor can make appropriate use of story and visual imagery to help the protégé make sense of the patterns or templates that exist within an organization, and particularly to appreciate where they fit into the broader context.

LEARNING THROUGH NOVELTY AND INTEREST

It may almost seem like a contradiction to the last heading, but learning and memory can also be enhanced when information is presented in a novel, out-of-the-ordinary way, that *doesn't* fit with the established patterns and templates in our brains. This is one way in which metaphors can work so powerfully in our minds. A metaphor, the literal definition of which is to 'transfer meaning', is a representation of one experience in terms of another similar experience. It can help us to understand, to make sense of, or at least to think through a possibly complex concept. A metaphor can be anything from a word or short phrase – 'life's a bowl of cherries'; 'work is a merry-go-round' – to a complete story, which is often described as an 'extended metaphor'.

Listening to a metaphor serves as a 'pattern interrupt' in our mind, that is, it jolts us out of our logical, habitual thinking, and helps us to view things more creatively. In a learning context, it can also bypass our natural resistance to change; if a mentee perceives that they are being told what to do by their mentor, then there is always a danger that the defensive barriers will come up. But being offered possible options and solutions through the medium of a metaphor is more acceptable and non-threatening, and there is less perceived pressure to accept the advice being offered.

For a metaphor to work best, there has to be just enough distance or tension between the two comparative subjects known as the 'topic' (for example, 'life') and the 'vehicle' ('bowl of cherries') for the listener to be able to make a connection. If they are too close in nature they will appear over-obvious and clichéd; if too far away they will appear obtuse, and neither will have the desired effect on the thinking of the listener. The mentor must choose and introduce metaphors carefully – 'what sort of journey are you on?'; 'if your job were an act in the circus, what might it be?'; 'if your team were playing a team sport, what would it be?' – to be most effective. If introduced skilfully, these metaphors can then be carried on in subsequent mentoring sessions, for example, 'whereabouts on the journey are you now?'; 'what heroes or villains have you met on the way?'; 'are you still juggling?!' and in some cases be extended – 'what would happen if you changed direction?' which pushes the relationship on to another level.

LEARNING WHERE EMOTIONS ARE INVOLVED

Because the emotional centre of the brain (the limbic system) is situated close to the part responsible for long-term memory storage, we all learn and remember more easily when our emotions have been aroused. A well-told story can trigger positive feelings of curiosity, surprise or excitement, or negative feelings of sadness, shock or anger, far more than, say, a column of figures or other sequential lists and reports.

Humour is an emotion that deserves a special mention because of its particularly powerful effects. When we laugh, our brains are stimulated to produce catecholamine, an alertness hormone, which in turn brings about the release of endorphins, the body's own natural painkiller. This chemical can also act as a kind of memory fixative in relation to information being taken into the brain; in other words, we remember more easily if we associate the information with humour. This works particularly well if a key learning point is *followed* by a humorous story, rather than the other way round.

Appropriate humour can be incorporated into a mentoring relationship, although the emphasis has to be on the word *appropriate*, in other words, the humour should be shared and enjoyed by both parties equally, and not at the expense of one over the other. People enjoying a funny story and laughing together is a great way to defuse tension, and can also help to build a sense of community and sometimes even a shared language between the collaborators.

The power of the story also lies in the fact that, while our conscious minds are relaxed and absorbed, the unconscious mind is free to take in the moral or message that the story contains. This absorption in a story can also produce the effect which psychologist Mihaly Csikszentmihalyi (1990) calls 'flow'. This is the feeling you might have when you're so engrossed in an activity that you lose all notion of time, space and self, and just become one with the activity. This state is the *optimum state* for learning to take place.

Original research carried out by Roger Sperry in the 1960s into the functions of the two brain hemispheres also provides us with insight into the value of storytelling in unconscious learning (Sperry, 1968). We tend to associate the left hemisphere with functions such as language, logic and sequence, and the right hemisphere with functions such as music, pictures and daydreaming, although in reality, it's more complicated than that, and it would be wrong to try and draw strict demarcation lines between the two. Hearing a story appeals to both left and right hemispheres of the brain equally – the left processing the words sequentially and analytically, and the right dealing with visualization and pattern recognition. This means that the left side reduces its usual level of dominance over the right, allowing a greater degree of creativity, freedom and openness. The more that mentors can utilize this knowledge with their protégés, the more they will encourage them to access both hemispheres of the brain, and consequently develop a more rounded approach.

FINDING STORIES

As mentioned above, *purpose* and *intention* in choosing and telling a story are crucial, and the worst thing a mentor can do is to take the 'one story fits all' approach to storytelling with their protégés. The world is full of stories, in books, in newspapers, on television, and now enhanced by the Internet, and it is simply unnecessary to take a one-dimensional approach. Mentors should become accustomed to tuning their brains into the 'story wavelength' and keeping their minds open to the possibility of useful material, such as the following.

PERSONAL EXPERIENCES

It is worth reflecting on and assessing your own personal experiences for their 'story potential', although as mentioned earlier it is important to ensure their relevance to a given situation. The following checklist may be useful:

- What happened in the situation?
- Who was involved? Did they remind you of anyone? In what way?
- Why did the event strike you as significant?
- What lesson(s) did you learn from the incident, and what underlying principles or patterns of behaviour were there?
- What parallel could you draw between this and the business world?
- Which protégé might benefit from hearing this story, and why?
- What change might the story bring about in this person?
- Is it appropriate and suitable for the ethics and values of this individual or organization?
- Does it convey a positive and constructive message?

It is when you reflect on a story in this way, and discover the *underlying lessons and principles*, that you can decide if the material is relevant and 'transferable', in other words – is it worth retelling to other people in the hope that they can glean the same or similar lesson to you? It is the underlying principle that should be important here; the story is merely an illustrative vehicle.

For example, a colleague of mine describes a relationship with a mentee of his who is a very proficient horsewoman. On his own admission he knows nothing about horses, but he is a very keen and experienced golfer. If he chooses to incorporate some of his own personal golfing tales to illustrate a particular point in their mentoring sessions, the commonality is the *level of expertise* that they both share in the two separate sports, not the sport itself.

When you're using your 'story filters' to dredge through your own personal history, don't just choose success stories to retell. Mentors who only tell superhuman-type stories about themselves can very easily alienate themselves from their protégés; rather than being seen as inspirational, they are seen as unattainable, and are not easy to relate to or indeed learn from. Experience shows that people find more readily endearing a person who also tells stories of their own failures, mistakes, weaknesses and vulnerabilities.

FILMS AND TELEVISION

Here again, be clear as to why you are discussing a film or television programme with your mentee; this is not just about having a chat! Choose positive or at least constructive tales to discuss in a mentoring session; the majority of stories featured on news programmes tend to focus on the sensational and very often negative aspects of life. Stories should be there to uplift or, at the very least, to make people think. Choose films with a strong storyline, and those with a useful and relevant pattern or analogy that you can match to your protégé's situation.

FABLES

Although they were written thousands of years ago, the moral tales of storytellers like Aesop and La Fontaine are still relevant, and just as fresh and 'punchy' today as they were then. Be aware of how many common phrases and metaphors used in your mentoring sessions can claim their origins from fables – 'the tortoise and the hare' (a lesson in time management, personal organization and the dangers of complacency), 'the fox and the sour grapes' (a way of rationalizing failure), 'the boy who cried wolf' (the dangers of exaggeration and lying) and so on. Fables can be particularly powerful if introduced *after* a discussion around a difficult situation, to serve as a summary and to bring about closure. A friend of mine regularly counsels her young son through difficult situations at school by consulting her book of fables, and saying, 'Let's see what Aesop has to say about this', thereby encouraging the development of concepts and rules for application the next time he is faced with a challenge.

FOLK AND FAIRY TALES

Those of you who have children will no doubt appreciate the vast number of stories that exist in this category from all cultures around the world. As well as their entertainment value, many fairy tales hide a learning message that can be both contemporary, (for example, 'The Ugly Duckling' is a classic tale of how to deal with low self-esteem) and complex (for example, 'The Sleeping Beauty' can offer the listener a way of dealing with and confronting a 'sleeping' or dormant aspect within themselves that they have been avoiding). In some cases, the mere mention of some of these well-known tales is enough to trigger a response from the mentee; in other cases, it might be suggested that they reread the original tale prior to a discussion with their mentor.

MYTHS AND LEGENDS

Many of our everyday sayings have been extracted from this rich source of ancient stories – for example, 'Pandora's box', 'Achilles' heel', 'the Midas touch' (Bulfinch, 1979) – and they can all form a powerful type of shorthand language that can be shared with others to describe certain events or problem scenarios. Myths and legends were originally created to help listeners make sense of the world around them and they can serve the same purpose today if incorporated into a mentoring relationship.

THE INTERNET

There are a growing number of storytelling organizations and enthusiasts who have websites on the Internet, mainly, it would appear, in the UK, the US and Australia. Some useful websites are:

- www.sfs.org.uk – Society for Storytelling (UK)
- www.trainingoptionsuk.com – Margaret Parkin (UK)
- www.storydynamics.com – Doug Lipman (US)
- www.thestorynet.com – Kat Koppett (US)

USING STORYTELLING IN THE MENTORING RELATIONSHIP

For mentors and their mentees, there are two sides to the storytelling coin, and both can be of great value. First, as mentors, we can utilize the full range of story and metaphor with our mentees as a tool to help the process of transition and change. Second, we need to encourage and listen to the stories that they have to tell us about themselves, and in particular the way in which they tell them, i.e. the type of metaphorical language that they use. People tend to use metaphor (consciously or unconsciously) particularly when they feel some emotion – excitement, anger or happiness – about the topic they are speaking on. The danger is that some people can get on a track of telling the same (very often negative) story endlessly about themselves, which in turn can become a self-fulfilling prophecy. A skilful mentor can help the mentee to analyse and 're-author' the story, and subsequently change their beliefs about themselves.

Storytelling, although often described by some as the most potent form of communication, is also a non-invasive tool for learning and change. A prescriptive or probing approach to mentoring very often just breeds resistance in the recipient; whereas it is much easier to respond to the gentle power of a story – simply because there is nothing to resist.

12 Variation in mentoring outcomes: an effect of personality factors?

TRULS ENGSTROM

Questions about the impact of personality on mentoring effectiveness have been raised by academic researchers (Allen et al., 2000; Eby *et al.*, 2000; Tokar *et al.*, 1998; Turban and Dougherty, 1994) and practitioners (Lee *et al.*, 1999), but few studies have so far tried to answer this call. The argument is relevant to the extent that the observed differences in mentoring effectiveness might be explained by personality factors in the participants involved in the mentoring dyad. Ragins *et al.* (2000) showed that mentoring relationships vary in quality, and can even be dysfunctional. In their qualitative study, Eby *et al.* (2000) found negative experiences in 84 of 240 mentoring relationships, and most frequently reported was a general mismatch within the dyad, including distancing and manipulative behaviour, which constituted 75 per cent of the total number of bad experiences. Ragins *et al.* (2000) found that satisfaction with the relationship accounted for more of the variance in job and career attitudes than the type of mentor or even the presence of a mentoring relationship.

Personality is composed of a variety of dispositions to behave in certain ways, in which people differ, and these individual differences may be organized hierarchically. If the mentor–protégé relationship is 'as fragile as any personal relationships one enters into' (Scandura, 1998, p464), discrepancies in personality structures within the mentoring dyad could really put the relationship under stress. We do acknowledge that the controversy between personality and situation as determinants of behaviour is not completely solved (Furnham, 1992). However, from an interactionalist's perspective it may be argued that this controversy is somewhat misleading when applied to social behaviour. The social situations in which individuals find themselves are determined, at least in part, by the personalities of the interacting individuals. No one really doubts that there is evidence of personal inconsistency and situational variability in social interaction, although the amount of variance in behavioural variables that are accounted for by personality factors may be low (Eysenck and Eysenck, 1985; Pervin, 1984).

Some research studies have focused on the question of whether personality factors will influence the likelihood of entering into a mentoring relationship. For instance, Kalbfleisch and Davies (1993) found a direct and indirect relationship between high self-esteem and good communication skills and participation in mentoring. Allen *et al.* (1997) reported that an internal locus of control and upward striving (conceptually related to conscientiousness) correlated positively with an urge to mentor. These same personality attributes were unrelated to perceived barriers to mentor relationships. Altruism and positive affectivity were positively related to the motivation to mentor (Aryee *et al.*, 1996). Scandura and Ragins (1993) reported that a combination of extraversion, openness, conscientiousness and low neuroticism (masculinity) was related to having had a mentor. Relatively high levels of agreeableness and conscientiousness (androgyny) were predictors of receipt of psychosocial support and career development assistance even when controlling for gender. They conclude that there is a relation between personality and receptiveness to mentoring.

Turban and Dougherty (1994) showed that protégés influenced the amount of mentoring they received by initiating relationships with mentors. An internal locus of control, high self-monitoring and emotional stability enhanced initiation, which mediated the relationship between personality characteristics and the mentoring received. These results suggest the important role of personality (in this case the locus of control, extraversion and lower neuroticism) in employees' efforts to obtain mentoring and (in conjunction with the work of Scandura and Ragins (1993)) the role it may play in the receipt of mentoring (Tokar *et al.*, 1998). Finally, in a study of quality of peer and supervisor relationships as perceived by 100 protégés and non-protégés, Fagenson (1994) generated correlation data on how needs for autonomy, power and achievement (representing extraversion, conscientiousness and low agreeableness) relate to the perceived quality of mentoring received. Her data indicated no relation between protégés' personalities and their perceptions of the quality of mentoring received. From the limited literature in this area, then, personality seems more salient in determining who becomes a protégé than how a protégé reacts to the relationship.

The present study investigates the relationships between the perceived success of the mentoring dyad and the personality of the participants. First, what are the relationships between the dyad's perceived success and the personality of the mentor and protégé respectively? Second, what are the relationships between the perceived success of the mentor and the protégé's personality, and between the perceived success of the protégé and the mentor's personality? Finally, what are the correlations between similar personality traits and perceived success in the dyad? These questions follow the model of dysfunctional mentoring and outcomes proposed by Scandura (1998).

A FIVE-FACTOR MODEL OF PERSONALITY

Systematic efforts to organize a taxonomy of personality began as a response to McDoughall's (1936) suggestion that a five-factor model (FFM) would be appropriate. Although other models have been proposed, for example, Catell's 16-factor model, a convergence of views on the structure of personality traits has led to the five-factor model (Barrick and Mount, 1991; Norman, 1963; McCrae and Costa, 1985). According to Tokar *et al.* (1998), research on the 'big five' personality factor model has demonstrated that the FFM has robustness, generalizability and comprehensiveness to an extent that it 'provides a useful preliminary organizational framework for most, if not all, nontrivial personality features' (p117). The FFM can be traced back to Allport and Odbert's classic work in the 1930s (Allport and Odbert, 1936) and also encompasses Murray's (1938) taxonomy of psychological needs (Costa and McCrae, 1988), Jung's (1971) psychological types (McCrae and Costa, 1989) and Eysenck's (1947) two-factor model (McCrae and Costa, 1985). It had been 'sleeping' for almost 50 years until Costa and McCrae used it to make order out of the chaos of different personality traits. The present study is based upon Engevik's (1992) version of the FFM inventory. The model is still controversial, however, and in the context of organizational psychology it may be argued that other concepts than those included in the FFM are important predictors of job performance constructs (Block, 1995; Schneider and Hough, 1995).

The FFM contains the following dimensions:

- extraversion
- emotional stability
- agreeableness
- conscientiousness
- openness to experience.

EXTRAVERSION

While 'coping' is personality in action under stress (Bolder, 1990), it also represents broader categories of behaviour when adapting to demands in general (Costa *et al.*, 1996). Individuals high on 'extraversion' are likely to be cheerful, active, assertive, energetic, enthusiastic, talkative and outgoing; have a great sense of humour; and prefer social interaction. They are also likely to create large networks for support and learning. Under stress, extraversion is associated with rational action, restraints, substitution and positive thinking. The extreme 'introverts' are likely to show the opposite type of behaviour. Clearly, great differences on this dimension may pose high demands on both members of the mentoring dyad. Similarity should be expected to relate to satisfaction with the mentoring process, and extraverts should be expected to be generally more pleased with their learning and development.

EMOTIONAL STABILITY

'Emotional instability' or 'neuroticism' denotes a tendency to display anxiety, self-pity, tension and worry; react with strong emotional outbursts; and also be rather touchy. Under stress, the neurotic personality is likely to display ineffective coping mechanisms like hostility, self-blame, escapist fantasy, withdrawal and indecisiveness, thus taxing rather heavily their social network, but without having the ability to use it for constructive solutions of the problems causing stress. Differences in the degree of emotional stability are likely to make interaction within the mentoring dyad difficult. Co-operation with an individual high in neuroticism is likely to cause agitation and disturbance. Time will be wasted by the emotionally unstable, and use of the social network will not be optimal. Due to their lower ability to cope with stress, the protégé is less likely to be recommended by the mentor to take the lead in demanding situations allowing positive self-promotion. Higher neuroticism should therefore be related to less satisfaction with the outcomes of the mentoring relationship.

AGREEABLENESS

'Agreeableness' covers the tendency to be appreciative, forgiving, kind, generous, sympathetic and trusting. Almost self-evident, these behavioural tendencies are likely to influence the outcomes of the mentor–protégé relationship. This should apply both when it comes to discrepancies between the actors in the dyad, and when relating the individuals' scores on this dimension to satisfaction with the outcomes of the process.

CONSCIENTIOUSNESS

'Conscientiousness' denotes tendencies to be efficient, organized, reliable, responsible, and thorough. It is also associated with perseverance and personal growth, and negatively associated with passive and ineffective responses. Under stress, the individual low in conscientiousness seem to be unwilling to deal effectively with the situation, preferring to make jokes, excuses or feckless efforts instead of tackling the problem head on. Discrepancies on this dimension should cause frustration to both mentor and protégé. Low individual scores on this dimension should relate negatively to satisfaction with the outcomes of the mentoring process, both within and between each of the parties.

OPENNESS TO EXPERIENCE

'Openness to experience' covers the tendency to be artistic, curious, imaginative, insightful, original as well as interested in a wide range of situations and activities. To rethink problems from different perspectives, seek new information and try novel solutions is typical behaviour for this group. Under stress, the 'open personality' is likely to display a sense of humour, but no faith. This may be a double-edged sword in a mentor–protégé relationship. On the one hand, openness must be displayed for the sake of optimal learning, but, at the same time, openness may contribute to distractions and slow down the developmental processes expected to occur within the dyad. Thus prediction of the value of this behavioural tendency is far more difficult. In general, however, it seems reasonable to assume that individual differences along this dimension should be important in mentor–protégé relationships.

SUCCESS FACTORS AS A RESULT OF THE DYAD

An impressive range of organizational benefits from mentor–protégé relationships have been identified (Alleman, 1989). For the purposes of this study we focused on the success factors described for mentors and protégés. These two groups created the success categories used to define total success within the mentoring dyad. After reviewing the literature, we discovered eight areas of benefit for the protégé and four thoroughly described areas of benefit for the mentor. This led us to develop and eight-point list for the protégé and a four-point list for the mentor, which we have conflated into the eight-point list below.

1   *Career development:* Mentoring is important for career development, both for mentors and protégés (Kram, 1985a). From the mentor's point of view, the mentoring role is an important development component of their career (Kram, 1985) and life (Levinson *et al.*, 1978). Mentoring enhances the remuneration, promotions and pay satisfaction of the employees who receive it (Dreher and Ash, 1990; Dreher and Cox, 1996; Scandura, 1992; Whitely *et al.*, 1991; Whitely and Coetsier, 1993). For protégés, mentoring relationships are related to organizational advancement, career development and career satisfaction (Fagenson, 1988, 1989; Roche, 1979; Scandura, 1992; Whitely *et al.*, 1991).

   The mentor often becomes the living proof of potential success and of what can be achieved. If the mentor assists appropriately they can help the protégé realize their career goals (Clutterbuck, 1985; Franzén and Jonsson, 1993) and create rapid advancement opportunities (Rosenbach, 1993). The fact that protégés help the mentor with their job, and serve as a source of organizational information and intelligence, often results in the mentor becoming a trusted adviser (Rosenbach, 1993). As a result of this the mentor can increase their own possibilities of promotion by letting the protégé become their successor (Clutterbuck, 1985).

2   *Personal development:* The protégé is developed both personally and professionally (Franzén and Jonsson, 1993). A mentor benefits from the protégé's energy and enthusiasm, and gets new perspectives and ideas that contribute to their own development (Clutterbuck, 1985; Burke and McKeen, 1990). In addition, hard evidence shows that veterans in life and health insurance seem to increase their sales when mentoring.

3   *Learning:* Relationships play a central part in learning, and individuals from every career stage benefit from alliances, only some of which may approximate to traditional mentoring (Kram and Bragar, 1992). We also know that mentors can provide protégés with more focused learning, enabling them to study the managerial and leadership techniques of successful people in real-life conditions (Rosenbach, 1993). The mentor makes productive use of their own knowledge and skills in middle age, and learns in ways that otherwise would not be possible for them (Burke and McKeen, 1990). Thus the mentor learns from the relationship (Clutterbuck, 1985), and becomes a better leader (Hultman and Sobel, 1994). The process especially introduces the mentor to new knowledge about the different levels of the organization (Franzén and Jonsson, 1993).

4   *Motivation:* Knowing the mentor is available and believes in the protégé's abilities is motivating in itself (Hultman and Sobel, 1994). To shape a young promising co-worker can be motivating, challenging and stimulating, especially if the mentor's own career has reached a permanent or temporary plateau (Clutterbuck, 1985). The successful protégé gives the mentor a sense of pride at contributing to the organization (Rosenbach, 1993), and respect from other colleagues (Burke and McKeen, 1990). Finally, it has been suggested that mature men have reached that time in life when they derive satisfaction in serving altruistically (Levinson *et al.*, 1978; Sheehy, 1976).

5   *Professional network:* The mentor introduces the protégé to senior staff by including them in their projects (Clutterbuck, 1985; Franzén and Jonsson, 1993). The introduction often results in improved network ability (Rosenbach, 1993).

6   *Social network:* Protégés can also break into executive social networks, which could have taken much longer without the mentor's support (Rosenbach, 1993).

7   *Status enhancement within the company.* The protégé learns from and is encouraged by the mentor as their role model, and can advance into more senior roles within the company (Clutterbuck, 2001).

8   *Status enhancement outside the company:* The protégé achieves a higher profile through their mentor (Clutterbuck, 1985).

HYPOTHESES

Hypotheses were formulated for the relationship between personality factors and the success factors (that is, career development, personal development, learning, motivation, network and status).

INTRA-INDIVIDUAL HYPOTHESES

The first set of hypotheses is concerned only with the protégés, and built upon an expectation that personality factors would influence their perception of the outcome of the mentoring dyad. This set focused on the relationships between the protégés' five personality scores and their perception of success as measured against the eight criteria outlined above (PP).

- H_0 – There is no correlation between the protégés' personality scores and the protégés' perceived success in the dyad.
- H_1 – There is a correlation between the protégés' personality scores and the protégés' perceived success in the dyad.

Parallel to this, a second set of hypotheses was concerned only with the mentors, and built upon an expectation that personality factors would influence perception of the outcome of the mentoring dyad. This set focused on the relationships between the mentors' five personality scores and their perception of success as measured against the relevant four criteria outlined above (MM).

- H_0 – There is no correlation between the mentors' personality scores and the mentors' perceived success in the dyad.
- H_1 – There is a correlation between the mentors' personality scores and the mentors' perceived success in the dyad.

INTER-INDIVIDUAL HYPOTHESES

The third set of hypotheses was concerned with the relationship between the mentors' personality profile and the protégés' perception of success. This set of hypotheses was built upon an expectation that the mentors' personality factors would be so important that they would by themselves determine how the protégés would perceive the outcome of the mentoring dyad. This set focused on the relationships between the mentors' five personality scores and the protégés' perception of success as measured against the eight criteria outlined above (MP).

- H_0 – There is no correlation between the mentors' personality scores and the protégés' perceived success in the dyad.
- H_1 – There is a correlation between the mentors' personality scores and the protégés' perceived success in the dyad.

The fourth set of hypotheses was concerned with the relationship between the protégés' personality profile and the mentors' perception of success. This set of hypotheses was built upon an expectation that the protégés' personality factors would be so important that they would by themselves determine how the mentors would perceive the outcome of the mentoring dyad. This set focused on the relationships between the protégés' five personality scores and the mentors' perceived success as measured against the relevant four criteria outlined above (PM).

- H_0 – There is no correlation between the protégés' personality scores and the mentors' perceived success in the dyad.
- H_1 – There is a correlation between the protégés' personality scores and the mentors' perceived success in the dyad.

DISCREPANCY BETWEEN THE PARTICIPANTS

Built upon the expectation that mentor–protégé similarities in personality profiles would enhance the effect of the relationship from the protégés' point of view, this fifth set of hypotheses covered the relationship between each of the five personality discrepancy scores and the protégés' perception of success as measured against the eight criteria outlined above (DP):

- H_0 – There is no correlation between mentor–protégé discrepancies in personality scores and the protégés' perceived success in the dyad.
- H_1 – There is a correlation between mentor–protégé discrepancies in personality scores and the protégés' perceived success in the dyad.

Likewise, a sixth set of hypotheses built upon the expectation that mentor–protégé similarities in personality profiles would enhance the effect of the relationship on the mentors' side. This final set of hypotheses covered the relationship between each of the five personality discrepancy scores and the mentors' perception of success as measured against the relevant four criteria outlined above (DM):

- H_0 – There is no correlation between mentor–protégé discrepancies in personality scores and the mentors' perceived success in the dyad.
- H_1 – There is a correlation between mentor–protégé discrepancies in personality scores and the mentors' perceived success in the dyad.

RESEARCH DESIGN AND METHODOLOGY

Thirty mentoring dyads from a large multinational company in the process industry were studied. The company's programme had been going on for over six years and was formalized for the first year. If the dyad wished to continue beyond this period it would be in an informal setting. The participants in this study had fulfilled the training, and the mentoring relations had been going on for a minimum of nine months. The scope of the programme can be described as focusing on the vocational dimension, while psychosocial support also forms part of the scheme.

In order to test the hypotheses presented earlier a questionnaire, divided into four parts was developed:

1   questions about perceived success
2   the FFM model of personality
3   career-related questions
4   demographic questions.

MEASUREMENT OF PERCEIVED SUCCESS

Based on the literature's reported benefits of the dyad, a seven-point itemized rating scale (Likert type) was used to assess each respondent's degree of satisfaction with the individual attributes.

Personality

The test used to investigate the 'big five' personality factors originated in the FFM. The version used is modified and culturally adapted by Engevik (1992). The analyses are based upon standardized ipsative personality scores (ipsative scores are those that are obtained from multiple-choice questionnaires) (Engevik, 1994). Ipsative scores have better validity than T scores, and therefore ipsative scores are normally the best predictors for the purposes of personality evaluation. However, the ipsative scores can under special circumstances (low variation) give highly misleading results (Engevik, 1992). The respondent grades themself on a seven-point semantic differential scale.

Career satisfaction

Career-related questions were framed using an inventory adapted from Whitely *et al.* (1991).

METHOD OF ANALYSIS

The research model was a set of six main hypotheses for the personality perspective, which were grouped together two by two and analysed on the basis of three subsets of research models.

The first model analysed the individual groups separately without considering the other group. The second model analysed one group's perception of success relation with the other group's personality profile. The third model analysed the discrepancy scores' relative to perceived success for each group in turn. In order to measure the third model a discrepancy score was calculated. The discrepancy score is the absolute value of the difference between the personality values. The personality scores for each of the five personality factors are standardized for mentors and protégés respectively. The values of the scale start at 0 (no discrepancy), and each unit equals one standard deviation.

The data were analysed by SPSS v.10.0. The original success scores were recoded into sum scores of 'dyad success' and 'career success'. Introductory tests were performed in order to find any systematic bias between the two groups – mentors and protégés – and their relationship with personality. In addition, tests were performed for variables thought to influence personality. Educational levels were coded from 1 for high school to 7 for PhD following the local educational system. Finally, each respondent identified their gender (0 = woman, 1 = man), and their age.

We wanted to examine the correlation between the success variables and the personality profiles, and found it reasonable to believe that the correlation should be linear if present. Therefore we used Pearson and McBravis's correlation for linearity to test the hypotheses.

In order to specify the strength of any confirmed correlation, we used simple regression to find the slope α and explained variation R^2.

RESULTS

A large number of correlations were tested with a 5 per cent significance level. Although few significant relationships were found, they clustered in a way that makes it possible to draw some interesting conclusions. Personality factors are related to perceived success in mentor–protégé relationships, as are age discrepancy and gender constellation to a certain extent. Alphas for the FFM factors are 0.90 for agreeableness, 0.88 for extraversion, 0.89 for conscientiousness, 0.92 for emotional stability and finally 0.91 for openness to experience (Engevik, 1993).

PROTÉGÉ'S PERSONALITY AND PROTÉGÉ'S PERCEPTION OF SUCCESS (PP)

P's openness to experience scores were correlated with P's perception of status within the company ($r = -0.48$), with P's perception of status outside the company ($r = -0.39$) and with P's perception of social network ($r = -0.44$). P's extraversion score was correlated with P's perceived learning ($r = -0.39$).

The conclusion of these findings is that P's perceived status within the company, P's perceived status outside the company and P's perceived social network as a result of the dyad are larger when the protégé themself is high on openness to experience.

MENTOR'S PERSONALITY AND MENTOR'S PERCEPTION OF SUCCESS (MM)

M's scores for agreeableness were correlated with M's overall perception of success ($r = -0.40$), with M's perceived motivation ($r = -0.45$) and with M's perceived career attainment ($r = -0.38$).

The conclusion of these findings is that M's overall perception of success, M's perceived motivation and M's perceived career attainment as a result of the dyad are larger when the mentor themself is high on agreeableness.

MENTOR'S PERSONALITY AND PROTÉGÉ'S PERCEPTION OF SUCCESS (MP)

M's scores for agreeableness were correlated with P's perceived learning ($r = 0.46$), and M's score for conscientiousness were correlated with P's perceived career attainment ($r = 0.37$).

PROTÉGÉ PERSONALITY AND MENTOR'S PERCEPTION OF SUCCESS (PM)

P's conscientiousness scores were correlated with M's overall perception of success ($r = -0.54$), with M's perceived career attainment ($r = -0.37$), with M's perceived personal development ($r = -0.56$), with M's perceived learning ($r = -0.50$) and with M's perceived motivation ($r = -0.40$).

The conclusion of these findings is that the mentor's overall perception of success, perceived career attainment, perceived personal development, perceived learning and perceived motivation as a result of the dyad are high when the protégé scores high on the personality dimension conscientiousness.

DISCREPANCY SCORES AND PROTÉGÉ'S PERCEPTION OF SUCCESS (DP)

The extraversion discrepancy scores were correlatedwith P's perceived career ($r = 0.39$), and with P's perceived motivation ($r = 0.36$).

When the discrepancy is large, the protégé perceives less motivation and less career attainment as a result of the dyad.

The conclusion of these findings is that in order for the protégé to perceive successful career development and motivation as a result of the dyad, both mentor and protégé should have the personality variable extraversion in equal measure ('birds of a feather flock together').

The conscientiousness discrepancy scores were correlated with P's overall success (r = −0.41), with P's perceived personal development (r = −0.39), with status within the company (r = −0.38), with status outside the company (r = −0.41), with social network (r = −0.38) and with professional network (r = −0.39).

When the discrepancy is large, the protégé perceives more personal development, status within the company, status outside the company, social network and professional network as a result of the dyad.

The conclusion of these findings is that in order for the protégé to perceive success, personal development, status within the company, status outside the company, social network and professional network as a result of the dyad, mentor and protégé should have different amounts of the personality variable conscientiousness ('birds who disagree stay in one tree').

DISCREPANCY SCORES AND MENTOR'S PERCEPTION OF SUCCESS (DM)

The discrepancy scores for agreeableness were correlated with M's overall perception of success (r = 0.36) and with M's perceived motivation (r = 0.37).

When the discrepancy is large, the mentor perceives less success and less motivation as a result of the dyad.

The conclusion of these findings is that in order for the mentor to perceive success and high motivation in the dyad, both mentor and protégé should have the personality variable agreeableness in equal measure ('birds of a feather flock together').

DISCUSSION AND CONCLUSION

EXTRAVERSION

Extraversion is the personality dimension with the strongest correlation with perceived success as result of the dyad. The results tell us that the protégé perceives more success as a result of the dyad if their mentor has a similar amount of the personality variable extraversion. These results can be related to other results which show that persons with high self-esteem and high communication competence are more likely to participate in mentoring (Kalbfleisch and Davis, 1993), as *high* self-esteem and a *high* level of extraversion are basically the same dimension of personality (Barrick and Mount, 1991). We can conclude that extravert persons are more likely to participate in a mentoring relationship. However, individuals that are low on extraversion (introverts) will, if they get a chance, benefit just as much from a mentoring relationship.

AGREEABLENESS

Agreeableness is the personality dimension with the second strongest correlation with perceived success as a result of the dyad. The result shows that the mentor perceives more success if their protégé has a similar amount of the personality variable agreeableness. At the same time, the mentor perceives overall success if they themself is high on agreeableness. In other words, it is important to match individuals with equal levels of agreeableness in order to achieve a successful relationship.

CONSCIENTIOUSNESS

Third in strength in relation to perceived success as a result of the dyad is conscientiousness. The results indicate that the protégé perceives more success if the discrepancy in conscientiousness between mentor and protégé is high. At the same time the mentor perceives a higher level of success if the protégé is high on agreeableness. In other words, in order to get a high perception of success, for both participants, as a result of the dyad the mentor should be low and the protégé should be high on conscientiousness.

EMOTIONAL STABILITY AND OPENNESS TO EXPERIENCE

These two dimensions are the most difficult to interpret. The correlations indicate that the protégé perceives a higher degree of success if they themself score high on openness to experience, and if the mentor scores high on emotional stability. The correlations found only show the personality dimensions from one of the participant's point of view. This makes it difficult to draw direct conclusions. However, the individual correlations are strong and should be remembered. It should be noted that protégés high on emotional stability have been shown to enhance initiation of mentoring (Turban and Dougherty, 1994), so there might be a link between a mentor's and a protégé's level of emotional stability. The dimension must be further investigated in order to state any clear relationship.

This research has argued for the relevance of personality factors as a useful tool in creating mentor–protégé relationships. The focus has been the importance of knowing the relationship between personality and perceived success as a result of the mentoring dyad.

First, this study reveals theoretical support for the notion that both mentors and protégés have some basic success determinants for the mentoring construct. These success variables will influence the participants' overall perception of success.

Second, theory suggests that the relevance of personality factors should be further researched. Based on theory, an instrument was developed to conduct an analysis of the possible correlation between personality and perceived success as a result of the dyad.

Finally, using the correlation test, T test and regression analysis, linear relations were shown to exist between personality variables and perceived success. The relations were found between all personality factors and both the mentor and the protégé, and the study showed that clustered significance was especially strong between the personality dimensions extraversion and agreeableness.

We strongly believe that the findings presented are representative and that the traits are important in mentoring relations. However, situational factors must be taken into consideration because the observed relationships in the present finding are only moderately strong.

FINDINGS IN RELATION WITH EARLIER RESEARCH

The present findings support those of Kalbfleisch and Davis (1993) and reflect a new dimension to the importance of extraversion traits in mentoring. The findings further open a wider understanding of the findings of Turban and Dougherty (1994). As these are the only solid empirical studies on the relationship between mentoring and personality, the present study paves the way for further research on the area.

PRACTICAL CONSEQUENCES

As a consequence of this research, we would recommend that compatibility in personality is taken into consideration as a variable when mentor–protégé relationships are created. This is most relevant in a formally arranged mentor relationship, but even in an informal arrangement an active human resource department can probably use these findings. For example, will knowledge about different traits' impact on perceived success help creating successful dyads? By advising mentors and protégés on what traits they should look for in a future mentor relationship, it might be possible to act proactively instead of reactively in the actual process.

FUTURE RESEARCH

Future research should focus on the possible interaction between personality and situational factors to determine the optimal strategies for dyad development. A study should be developed that takes both the personality and the situation into consideration simultaneously. Another important refinement would be to replicate this study with a new sample group. Replication is important because of the low number of dyads included.

13 Virtual mentoring

PROFESSOR ELLEN FAGENSON-ELAND and
RACHEL YAN LU

> *A tree as big around as you can reach starts with a small seed; a thousand-mile journey starts with one small step.*
>
> *Lao-Tse (1998)*

Mentoring is a special type of 'love' relationship that forms between a mentor and their protégé (Levinson *et al.*, 1978). Mentoring was first investigated in the United States in the 1970s (Levinson *et al.*, 1978). In the 1980s, the United Kingdom became involved in this discussion and the European School of Mentoring was established (Clutterbuck, 1991; Parsloe and Wray, 2000).

While face-to-face mentoring is the most common form of mentoring, a new type of mentoring called 'virtual mentoring', 'e-mentoring' or 'online mentoring' has emerged. This special type of mentoring is computer-mediated rather than conducted face to face (Ensher *et al.*, 2002). Its rise has been attributed to the development of computer technology and the easy access and availability of the Internet (Hake, 1999). Virtual mentoring has been growing quite rapidly and various virtual mentoring programmes have been created in the United States, for example, Youth Trust, Ask the Employer, K-12 Educational Programs, university-sponsored programmes and National Mentornet.

A virtual mentoring relationship was established between the two authors of this chapter. When Professor Ellen Fagenson-Eland was asked to contribute to this book she requested the director of the European Mentoring and Coaching Council, Dr David Clutterbuck, to recommend a student to work with her. Dr Clutterbuck recommended Rachel Yan Lu, a doctoral student at the Catholic University of Leuven, Belgium. Due to the geographical distance between the two authors and the more extensive academic experience of Professor Eland, Ms Lu became the virtual protégé of Professor Eland for the purposes of writing this chapter. Our virtual relationship, which started on 26 February 2002 and ended when this chapter was completed, is explored in this chapter.

While virtual mentoring is becoming more popular in practice, research on this latest form of mentoring has not kept pace (Ensher *et al.*, 2002; Hamilton and Scandura, 2003). There are many questions that can be posed about virtual mentoring. For example, one might ask what is the nature of virtual mentoring? What are the conditions that encourage virtual mentoring? What are the functions that are provided in a virtual mentoring relationship? What are the advantages and disadvantages of virtual mentoring compared with face-to-face mentoring? What competences should virtual mentors possess? What are the challenges faced by e-mentors? In this chapter we will formulate answers to these questions using the e-mentoring literature and our e-mentoring experience. It should be noted that while the business and management literatures have been relatively silent on this topic, the education literature has more actively addressed e-mentoring issues and will be applied appropriately in this chapter.

DEFINITIONS OF VIRTUAL MENTORING

The form of mentoring that is based upon electronic communication is called e-mentoring, telementoring, cybermentoring or virtual mentoring. These words will be used interchangeably in the rest of the chapter.

Virtual mentoring has been defined as:

> *the use of e-mail or computer conferencing systems to support a mentoring relationship when a face-to-face relationship would be impractical*

O'Neill et al., 1996, p39

> *a computer-mediated relationship between a senior individual who is the mentor for the lesser skilled protégé, with the goal of developing the protégé in a way that helps him or her succeed*

Single and Muller, 2001

> *a computer mediated, mutually beneficial relationship between a mentor and a protégé which provides learning, advising, encouraging, promoting, and modelling, that is often boundaryless, egalitarian, and qualitatively different than traditional face-to-face mentoring.*

Bierema and Merriam, 2002, p24

The virtual relationship between a mentor and a mentee is maintained mainly by e-mail accompanied by Internet resources relevant to both parties. In a virtual mentoring relationship, both the mentor and the mentee cross boundaries of age, race, culture and other diversities, to share information.

THE NATURE OF VIRTUAL MENTORING AND CONDITIONS THAT PROMOTE E-MENTORING

In order for virtual mentoring relationships to flourish, mentors and protégés need access to a computer and the Internet. Virtual mentoring relies on e-mail interactions and Internet resources, and consequently requires computer literacy. People who do not know how to type or use e-mail systems are unlikely to consider e-mail interaction as a rich instrument and are unlikely to seek relevant information via the Internet (Rudy, 1996; Harrington, 1999).

The nature of virtual mentoring can be described as an asynchronous, text-based means for communicating with dispersed groups (Harrington, 1999). The time gap between sending a message and receiving feedback is the most noted asynchronous aspect of e-mail (Harrington, 1999). E-mail interactions are based on written text, which is a less enriched communication mechanism than face-to-face interaction. However, according to Harrington (1999), with sufficient time, effort and attention devoted to e-mail communications, it is indeed possible to compose text filled with social meaning.

BENEFITS OF VIRTUAL MENTORING

Virtual mentoring, being a dynamic, two-way reciprocal relationship, benefits both mentors and protégés (www.cob.mnsu.edu). As in face-to-face mentoring relationships, virtual mentors offer advice and provide both professional and personal support to mentees, or what Kram and others have deemed 'psychosocial support' and 'career guidance' (Kram, 1985a; Ragins and McFarlin, 1990; Scandura, 1992). While face-to-face mentoring is normally based on one-to-one relationships, e-mentoring offers a great opportunity for a group of people to communicate and share information with a mentor (Harrington, 1999). An organization's listserv, for example, is a mechanism through which e-mentoring of a group of individuals can occur. Discussions with external worldwide specialists and mentors via the Internet can enhance 'global citizenship' and learning.

Below are typical comments made by students about e-mentoring in one of the e-mentoring programmes organized by Youth Trust, an organization that provides work internships for students (www.youthtrust.org.):

> 'I think the programme has helped me learn how to use computers more. I also think the friendship between us is fun.'
> 'It is cool to have someone else to ask questions of and to get their opinion on different things. It's also neat to have someone give you advice who has probably had more experience than I have.'
> 'My mentor has been another friend to write to. I can write to her about my problems and stuff that I can't talk about with my parents.'

E-mentoring, when included as part of the curriculum, can enhance students' progress and improve their schoolwork. E-mentoring can help students obtain valuable information about the workplace and careers. Below are typical comments made by teachers about how their students benefited from Youth Trust's e-mentoring programme:

> 'Students in e-mentoring relationships enhanced their technology-related skills.'
> 'E-mentored students created positive relationships with professional adults.'
> 'E-mentored students improved their letter-writing skills.'

However, while Youth Trust teachers and students focused on how e-mentoring benefits mentees, e-mentoring benefits mentors as well. Serving as a mentor is a rewarding experience for professionals and research has found that virtual mentoring, like face-to-face mentoring, increases professional growth, enhances professional identity and renews a mentor's enthusiasm for their own work (Ackley and Gall, 1992; Wighton, 1993; Levinson *et al.*, 1978; Luna and Cullen, 1995). Moreover, protégés, whether they are face-to-face protégés or e-protégés, can offer fresh ideas and innovative methods to their mentors, who may experience career advancement as a result of the information they gain from the relationship. Face-to-face protégés and e-protégés who recognize their mentor's value can make their mentors feel respected and needed, and can provide a boost to their self-confidence (Levinson *et al.*, 1978). Since mentoring contributes to the growth of a student or a younger employee, all kinds of mentors can obtain satisfaction from helping a young person blossom. Here are some typical comments from e-mentors working in the Youth Trust programme:

> *'I can't imagine a better way to meet our [company's] objectives…friendship, motivation, career exploration…than a programme like this.'*
>
> *'I have found it somewhat difficult to communicate with a student I hadn't met and who seems to have had a growing-up experience that is vastly different from what mine was. It has been a learning experience for me.'*
>
> *'I look at my involvement in the e-mentoring programme as a greater definition of my success as much as anything I've done in the business arena.'*

MENTORING FUNCTIONS

According to Kram (1985a), traditional mentoring functions centre around two rubrics: career/professional functions and psychosocial/personal functions. Career functions are devoted to helping the protégé learn the ropes of the organization and to secure advancement. Psychosocial functions develop the protégé's feeling of competence and a sense of self-identity which assists them in a professional role (Kram, 1988). There are five career functions and four psychosocial functions (Table 13.1).

Table 13.1   Mentoring functions (adapted from Kram, 1988, and Luna and Cullen, 1995)

Career/professional functions	Psychosocial/personal functions
Sponsorship: opens doors and makes connections for the protégé to help them advance in their career.	*Role modelling:* the mentor demonstrates valued behaviours, attitudes and skills to help the protégé feel competent and confident, and to establish a clear professional identity.
Exposure and visibility: creates opportunities for the protégé to demonstrate competence, such as including a protégé in important meetings to enhance their visibility.	*Acceptance and confirmation:* provides ongoing support, respect and admiration to strengthen the protégé's self-confidence and self-image.
Coaching: provides relevant feedback to improve the protégé's performance and potential.	*Counselling:* provides a helpful and confidential forum for exploring personal and professional dilemmas. The mentor needs to have excellent listening skills and can establish rapport that allows both individuals to address important concerns and promote trust.
Protection: provides support to the protégé for different situations and assumes responsibility for mistakes that are beyond the protégé's control.	*Friendship:* mutual caring and intimacy that continues beyond daily work tasks and involves the sharing of experiences outside the immediate work setting.
Challenging assignments: assignments are delegated that stretch the protégé's current knowledge and skills to help them advance.	

MENTORING FUNCTIONS IN FACE-TO-FACE AND VIRTUAL MENTORING RELATIONSHIPS

According to Kram (1985a) mentors employ the *sponsorship* function more than any other mentoring function. Sponsorship helps organizational newcomers build their reputation and become known. Sponsorship also helps protégés obtain promotions and desirable sideways moves. While both face-to-face mentoring and virtual mentoring can fulfil this function, e-mentors are likely to have less impact as sponsors than face-to-face mentors. In face-to-face mentoring, mentors meet with organizational powerholders to discuss the protégé's career. In virtual mentoring relationships, online mentors converse with organizational powerholders through text, and learn as much about the protégé's work situation as they can from afar. However, they are unable to exchange verbal or non-verbal gestures, or to establish a rapport, with the key organizational players. Instead, they need to rely on their own established reputation to enhance the protégé's reputation.

Exposure and visibility is a key mentoring function. Face-to-face mentors typically provide protégés with opportunities to prove themselves in front of key organizational members (Kram, 1988). E-mentors have great difficulty providing this function since, by definition, visibility is a visual phenomenon to a great extent. However, e-mentors can make their protégés more visible by assigning and announcing important protégé responsibilities online, with frequent complimentary progress reports posted.

The mentoring function of *coaching* is dedicated to helping a protégé accomplish work objectives (Kram, 1985a). When a mentor coaches a protégé, they pass on wisdom, knowledge and their point of view. Face-to-face mentors may be able to accomplish this function more easily than virtual mentors since face-to-face mentors are able to conduct verbal exchanges with their protégés and can rely on non-verbal cues. E-mentors, in contrast, exclusively coach their protégés through the written word over the Internet. However, both online and face-to-face mentors can coach their protégés by providing prompt feedback and suggestions to protégés to help improve their performance.

Protection can support and further individual advancement by reducing risks that may threaten the reputation of a protégé (Kram, 1988). Mentors take responsibility for mistakes made by mentees. While face-to-face mentors can arrange meetings with key individuals to shield their protégés from harm, this is not an option for e-mentors. Virtual mentors can provide protection for their protégés by sending out e-mails supporting their protégés when they are at risk or need to be defended.

Challenging work assignments provide learning opportunities, and equip the individual with the necessary technical and managerial skills to take advantage of these opportunities (Kram, 1985a). Good mentors are also goal-oriented and enable their mentees to reach new or higher levels of mastery. Both face-to-face mentors and e-mentors can fulfil this function. For instance, e-mentors can provide protégés with challenging materials online to read and tasks to fulfil. However, e-mentors will never really know their protégés' potential since they have never met them and must instead rely on the protégé's assessment of their own potential and competence. This makes the definition of *challenging* more difficult for e-mentors to determine.

Psychosocial functions are important in enhancing individuals' sense of competence, confidence, identity and effectiveness in their work roles (Kram, 1988).

Role modelling is the most frequently reported psychosocial function used in face-to-face mentoring relationships (Kram, 1985a). Consciously or unconsciously, a protégé finds in the mentor's attitudes, values and behaviours a particular image that they can imitate and create. In virtual mentoring relationships the behaviours and attitudes are not quite as visible as they are in face-to-face relationships. Protégés can 'feel' the attitudes of their online mentors, but they do not have an opportunity to actually watch and/or interact with them. Since protégés may not fully understand their environment, they need to see examples of how rules are adhered to and how relationships are initiated and maintained. Additionally, since protégés may need to learn how to operate a particular piece of equipment or machinery, e-mentoring may not be as effective as face-to-face mentoring, where a demonstration can be performed. Role modelling seems necessary to the mastery of some practical work-related skills. This function may be beyond the capacity of virtual mentors. Protégés in e-mentoring relationships may need to be more categorical when asking for detailed information about operations than protégés in face-to-face relationships. Still, written instructions, tutorials, books and videoconferencing can be used as substitutes for role modelling (Hamilton and Scandura, 2003).

Acceptance and confirmation is a function that provides psychological nurturing through positive feedback on performance, mutual liking, respect and trust (Kram, 1985a). A junior person receives support and encouragement, and develops a sense of competence, when seeking acceptance and confirmation from their mentor. While this function is comparatively easy for face-to-face mentors to provide, virtual mentors can provide ongoing support and encouragement to their protégés by writing politely and respectfully to them. It is clearly a challenge to develop mutual liking and trust when contact occurs only through the use of a computer.

Counselling is a psychological function that allows a protégé to explore personal issues with their mentor that may interfere with a positive feeling about themself in the organization (Kram, 1988). Sharing and exploring these concerns with a trusted mentor is helpful to career advancement. While face-to-face mentors can meet with their protégés in private to discuss their problems, online mentors must provide counselling over the Internet. Due to the potential distribution of e-mail correspondence beyond those intended to receive it, a protégé might hesitate to discuss their personal problems with their e-mentor. Nevertheless, in the last few years, some psychotherapists have been providing online counselling to patients (Binik *et al.*, 1997). By sharing orally, people can communicate with and understand each other through gestures, facial expressions and body language. These cues and signs in face-to-face communication are invisible in e-communications, thus making the function of counselling more difficult to deliver for e-mentors.

The psychosocial mentoring function of *friendship* results from mutual liking, understanding and enjoyable informal sharing about one's work and family (Kram, 1985a). This function allows the protégé to feel like a peer of the mentor, which, in turn, enables them to interact more comfortably with others in positions of authority. Friendship can more readily develop in face-to-face relationships than in virtual relationships. Eye contact and non-verbal behaviours such as handshakes and hugs help friendships flourish among individuals who are close to one another. Virtual mentors and protégés are less likely to be able to informally share experiences if they have never met one another. According to our own experience in writing this chapter, it was difficult to develop rapport and friendship when online communication was the only avenue available to get to know one another.

Trust is an important component of mentor–protégé relationships that permeates the delivery of almost every mentoring function. It may also be the most obvious obstacle to an effective virtual mentoring relationship. What is trust? 'Trust is a psychological state that manifests itself in behaviours towards others, is based on the expectations made upon behaviours of these others, and on the perceived motives and intentions in situations entailing risk for work relationships with those others' (Costa, 2000, p3). In this definition, trust is viewed as an attitude held by an individual in relation to another individual or a group of individuals. It is not easy to establish trusting relationships in face-to-face mentoring relationships and it is much more difficult to establish trust in a virtual relationship when the two parties have never met and behaviours are invisible. For example, when Professor Eland asked Ms Lu if she would be interested in writing this chapter, Ms Lu replied immediately to Professor Eland and described her high level of interest and willingness to participate in and commit to this project. However, this single e-mail did not provide Professor Eland with sufficient confidence that Ms Lu could be trusted to keep her promises and fulfil her obligations. Ms Lu tried to reassure Professor Eland of her interest and commitment in another e-mail. Two months after those e-mail correspondences were exchanged (after sending 14 e-mails to each other with many breaks in between these communications), trust was not yet completely built up. For instance, in considering Ms Lu's other competing demands, as reported by Ms Lu to Professor Eland, Professor Eland feared that the promised text written by Ms Lu would not be sent to her as scheduled. This kind of doubt is less likely to arise between face-to-face mentors and protégés because they know each other, have frequent discussions and can arrange to meet one another if a problem arises. Therefore, trust is key to an effective virtual mentoring relationship. When Ms Lu sent the promised material to Professor Eland on time, Professor Eland was able to trust Ms Lu to a much greater extent. When requested material from Ms Lu was not received in a timely fashion by Professor Eland, Professor Eland's trust waned. Is there any way for online mentors and mentees to establish trust when they have never met one another? In our opinion, open and sincere sharing, detailed and elaborate explanations, timely responses and deliverables are crucial strategies for establishing online trust.

In summary, virtual mentoring can potentially provide most of the functions that face-to-face mentoring provides. If a mentor is willing to help a protégé online, if mentors and protégés are committed to communicating frequently with one another, and if they trust one another enough to share professional as well as personal information and concerns, then, effective mentoring can take place online.

ADVANTAGES OF VIRTUAL MENTORING OVER TRADITIONAL MENTORING

What are the benefits of virtual mentoring over traditional mentoring (Bierema and Merriam, 2002)? According to Muller (2000) online mentoring presents a cost-effective opportunity that transcends the constraints of time, synchronous communication and geography. Bierema and Merriam (2002) contend that virtual mentoring's boundarylessness and egalitarian characteristics are its greatest strengths.

Face-to-face mentoring requires both mentor and mentee to be available at the same time, which is a great inconvenience to both parties. Normally, a mentor has their own heavy workload in addition to the task of mentoring protégés. It is therefore difficult for a mentor to always be available when the mentee needs help. As a result, face-to-face mentees must wait for their mentors to schedule time to meet with them. In contrast, in virtual mentoring relationships, both parties communicate at a convenient time. In our own example, Ms Lu did not experience the same time availability problem with Professor Eland as she did with her on-site doctoral dissertation mentors at her university. However, Professor Eland, as an associate editor of *The Academy of Management Executive*, was available online every day to receive paper submissions as well as Ms Lu's e-mails.

Not only does a virtual mentoring relationship provide greater time flexibility over traditional mentoring, it also can occur independent of geography. The mentor and the mentee can be hundreds or thousands of miles away from one another, communicating easily via e-mail. This allows people from remote areas to participate in virtual mentoring activities. Via the Internet, an Asian mentor may have a European protégé, or an African mentee may have an American mentor. Ms Lu, a Chinese mentee, and Professor Eland, her virtual mentor from the United States, communicated via e-mail, although they never held face-to-face meetings.

Virtual mentoring has the potential to cross barriers of age, social status and hierarchical relationships that are sometimes obstacles in traditional mentoring alliances. For example, traditional mentoring occurs quite frequently between younger employees and older, more powerful, senior employees (Kram, 1985a). Hierarchical status and visual cues are reduced over e-mail, making it easier for disparate age and status groups to converse (Sproull and Kiesler, 1986).

Virtual mentoring also diminishes misunderstandings that can arise due to cultural and racial differences. Stereotypes in face-to-face mentoring relationships become invisible in a virtual forum, allowing mentoring to be the focus of the relationship (Bierema and Merriam, 2002).

Historically, women and individuals with disabilities have been considered 'risky' protégés as compared to white males (Dreher and Cox, 1996). This has made it difficult for these groups to find voluntary mentors (Hansman, 1998; Murrel *et al.*, 1999). However, virtual relationships, which occur through an internet communication system, make gender and/or disability relatively invisible. This has prompted several e-mentoring programmes to be used as retention strategies for women in science and engineering (Muller, 2000). For example, the University of Washington's Do-it e-mentoring programme helps people with disabilities in their academic pursuits and professional careers (Bierema and Merriam, 2002). Moreover, virtual mentoring relationships also help heterogeneous mentor–mentee pairs avoid cross-gender misunderstandings (Kram, 1988). These diverse pairs can share their experiences freely and discuss relevant information with one another over the Internet without meeting publicly or privately or being scrutinized unnecessarily.

E-mentoring can become one of several management development tools featured alongside knowledge-based systems (Martinson, 1997; Harrington, 1999). E-mentoring offers a cheap and easily accessible means to support learning.

Furthermore, because of the 'relatively self-absorbed' nature of e-mail (Sproull and Kiesler, 1986, p1497), protégés in virtual relationships have freedom and space to reflect upon and assess their progress. That is, protégés can become self-aware and feel self-confident without interruption, since they need not consider the immediate reactions of their mentors. Ang and Cummings (1994) found that a mentee's willingness to provide feedback in a virtual relationship increases when it is not delivered face-to-face. Virtual communications are a particular advantage for introverted mentees who are freed from the pressures of face-to-face communications that occur in traditional mentoring relationships. According to a study by Hubschman (1996), introverts in virtual mentoring groups had higher achievement scores than introverts in non-virtual mentoring groups.

In short, virtual mentoring has the potential to overcome a variety of barriers that are present and visible in face-to-face relationships. Virtual mentoring relationships offer egalitarian opportunities to a diverse set of individuals.

DISADVANTAGES OF VIRTUAL MENTORING

Compared with face-to-face mentoring, virtual mentoring has some specific limitations (Harrington, 1999; Hansen, 2000; Bierema and Merriam, 2002).

First, mentors and mentees need to have access to computers, have a knowledge of computer technology and be literate in software communication systems. In reality, however, not all professionals own computers (Harrington, 1999) nor do they have sufficient computer literacy (Bierema and Merriam, 2002). Moreover, professionals of the 'older generation' who learned work-related knowledge and skills from an experienced individual face to face, may find it difficult to feel comfortable using the new technology (Bierema and Merriam, 2002).

Second, individuals who are 'fortunate enough' to have access to a computer and to be computer-literate may not be able to find or recruit the right mentor to assist their development (Bierema and Merriam, 2002). This is because they may not know experts who are willing to be committed to virtual relationships. 'Having to ask for a mentor is more difficult than asking for a date,' stated a founder and president of an innovative new Web-based programme. Furthermore, it is especially difficult to match individuals in virtual relationships when the motivation, personal interests and level of commitment of both parties is unknown. Individuals who lack established reputations and credentials may find it particularly difficult to secure a virtual mentoring partner. This is because one's accomplishments and background 'on paper' are all that potential mentors and protégés have to determine whether or not they should enter into a virtual mentoring relationship with one another.

Third, the communication between a mentor and a mentee in a virtual relationship is text-based and does not provide face-to-face intimacy and spontaneity (Harrington, 1999; Hansen, 2000; O'Brien, 2002; Bierema and Merriam, 2002). As a result, it is difficult to establish trust and confidence between mentors and mentees, particularly when both parties have never met one another (Bierema and Merriam, 2002, p221). Moreover, virtual communication does not pick up non-verbal cues, such as intonation and body language, which provide hints and indications of emotional reactions (Harrington, 1999). Furthermore, text-based virtual communication is neither confidential nor secure (Harrington, 1999). Thus individuals may not feel confident that their e-mails are being read solely by the parties designated to review them. Business e-mail is more likely to be read than private e-mail, leading some practitioners to suggest that personal e-mail rather than company e-mail should be used in e-mentoring relationships.

Fourth, another disadvantage of virtual mentoring relationships relates to their asynchronous feedback element. That is, immediate feedback may not be provided – a message that is sent by one party might be responded to after a great deal of time has transpired. Such asynchronous communication might be discouraging to both the mentee and the mentor.

The mentee might lose self-confidence when they are in a troublesome situation and do not receive immediate help from their virtual mentor. The mentor might lose enthusiasm and interest when there is no immediate reaction from the mentee, and may believe that there is little return for their investment of time and energy. Such untimely responses may result in miscommunications and misinterpretations and, in the long run, the commitment of the other party in the virtual relationship may be doubted (Bierema and Merriam, 2002).

Finally, conducting negotiations, providing explanations and exchanging subjective views via e-mail is not as effective as performing these activities in face-to-face meetings (Hansen, 2000). For example, explanations of problems in e-mentoring relationships may not be as clear as in face-to-face demonstrations. Furthermore, explanations and feedback provided by mentors are not always understood by their virtual mentees (Harrington, 1999). As a complementary tool, the mentor may offer Internet resources to the mentee for self-directed learning. However, surfing the Internet is very time-consuming and the time invested may not yield significant benefits for the mentee (Hansen, 2000). For the mentor, sowing a great deal but reaping a small harvest may result in disappointment.

Having discussed the advantages and limitations of virtual mentoring, we need to find out how to leverage the advantages and avoid the disadvantages inherent in these types of relationships. We also need to determine which mentor competences are needed to maintain a healthy and productive virtual mentoring relationship.

ESTABLISHING GOOD VIRTUAL MENTORING RELATIONSHIPS AND NEEDED MENTOR COMPETENCES

What competences do virtual mentors need in order to sustain effective mentoring relationships? Based upon the discussion presented thus far there are some specific competences that seem most critical for virtual mentors to possess. They are:

- computer literacy
- computer accessibility
- Internet access
- computer software and hardware skills
- excellent written communication skills
- the ability to communicate trust, friendship, openness and emotion through text
- an established reputation
- online availability
- the ability to maintain the confidentiality of computer messages
- time to communicate frequently
- the ability to understand communication without visual cues, gestures or voice tones
- leadership skills
- comfort in seeking and providing written feedback online.

REFLECTIONS UPON THE CHALLENGES TO VIRTUAL MENTORING

Having discussed a number of issues related to virtual relationships, we need to reflect upon the challenges presented by this non-traditional form of mentoring.

First, according to media-richness theory, e-mail is a poor choice for complex exchanges that involve serving as a role model, providing explanations or conducting negotiations (Harrington, 1999). Given these limitations, we question whether:

1 telephone-based communications should be used to complement e-mentoring communications and/or whether
2 face-to-face meetings should be required for virtual relationships in which complex learning occurs, or simply whether
3 e-mentoring should be considered an ancillary tool which is used to assist in the conduct of face-to-face mentoring relationships.

Second, we discussed earlier how virtual mentoring could overcome disparities resulting from demographic, cultural and other differences by providing mentoring opportunities for all types of individuals. However, can virtual mentoring surmount language barriers? For example, if an Italian-speaking individual seeks an online mentor, must the mentor also speak Italian? Clearly, an English-speaking person who is not familiar with Italian will have great difficulty providing online mentoring support. However, there are software programs that serve as 'interpreters', allowing speakers of diverse languages to communicate.

Third, if virtual mentoring helps develop 'global citizenship', can its benefits extend to individuals who live in the poorer regions of the world? It would seem that there is little sense contemplating virtual mentoring connections which require a computer and Internet access for people who do not possess the basic necessities to survive.

Moreover, virtual mentoring raises many questions for researchers and practitioners to consider. For example:

- What is the role of the telephone and fax machine in e-mentoring relationships?
- What is the nature of learning in virtual situations?
- How do virtual mentoring relationships develop?
- Are there specific stages that characterize the evolution of virtual mentoring relationships?
- What contributes to quality feedback in an e-mentor's response to their protégé?
- How should members of virtual dyads be matched?
- How can e-mentoring be introduced in organizations to enhance employee development?
- What are the contextual factors in organizations that influence the effectiveness of virtual mentoring relationships?
- How does e-mentoring differ for one-to-one versus one-to-group virtual mentoring relationships?
- What advantages and disadvantages do combined mentoring systems have compared to relationships that are solely conducted face to face or virtually?

In conclusion, we note that e-mentoring has been widely used to facilitate learning and development in this technologically driven era. Its success challenges traditional learning and teaching models, and encourages support for distance learning. Virtual mentoring also provides access to mentors on a global scale. However, many challenges to virtual mentoring remain, prompting the need for more in-depth, systematic research to be conducted.

On a final note, we would like to point out that our virtual mentoring relationship was successful in that we were able to complete the chapter to the satisfaction of the book's editors. While we were not always able to agree or communicate clearly with one another due to native language differences, scheduling problems and the limitations of e-mail, the virtual relationship benefited both of its partners. Without the use of e-mail communication, the mentoring relationship between Ms Lu and Professor Eland would never have occurred. The reader can judge whether this would have been unfortunate. We think so.

14 When mentoring goes wrong...

DR BOB GARVEY

This chapter is based on a range of source material from my own research and the research of others, my own direct practical experience and the practical experience of others, and the mentoring literature. Thanks to all those who have been generous enough to share their stories and advice; your contributions to this chapter make all the difference. Where appropriate, participants' confidentiality has been maintained.

Mentoring is a growing phenomenon on both sides of the Atlantic. It is increasing, employed in a range of contexts, and examples of mentoring may be found in the public and private sectors, in large and small businesses, in social sectors and not-for-profit. It is used for a variety of purposes including to:

- develop managers
- support induction
- 'fast-track' people into senior positions
- support change
- gain long-term unemployed people employment
- reduce crime
- increase school attendance
- support anti-bullying policies in schools
- improve performance in whatever context it is employed
- improve skills
- transfer knowledge
- support equal opportunities policies and diversity.

This list, although incomplete, raises many issues and questions about how mentoring is understood and perceived by those who engage in its practice. It is fair to assume that most people who engage or wish to engage in mentoring activity expect a successful outcome and there is much evidence of just this (see, for example, Wilson and Elman, 1990; Garvey, 1995a).

However, there is scope for mentoring to go wrong (see for example Antal, 1993; Hurley and Fagenson-Eland, 1996; Carden, 1990; Garvey, 1995b) and this chapter explores these issues and questions, and offers some practical suggestions as to how these might be resolved.

BACKGROUND

Since earliest times, mentoring has had a place as a key element of human intellectual and emotional development. In the last 10 years, the use of mentoring has gained momentum throughout industry, commerce and the public services (Clutterbuck, 1991; Garvey, 1999). As a result of this rapid and almost systematic application of the process, the meaning of mentoring has become confused. There is debate among practitioners and academics as to its true and distinctive nature. Some search for a clear definition of the concept and, in a world of increasing complexity, simplicity has appeal. However, it is probably more appropriate to offer a rich and 'thick description' (Geertz, 1971) of mentoring to highlight its complexity rather than attempt to simplify.

What do I mean by 'mentoring?' This is an important question because any judgements you may make as a reader of this chapter need to be made against a common perspective or a shared understanding. I have found myself working with groups of potential mentors and talking about my perspective on mentoring, only to find that what I call mentoring, they call something else! This is not to say that the description of mentoring offered here is definitive, or that there is an expectation that you, the reader, will agree with my description, but what follows is a personal description of mentoring and is offered here as a reference point.

There are four main elements to mentoring. First, mentoring is a relationship between two people, with learning and development as its core purpose. Second, it involves certain human qualities and attributes such as trust, commitment and emotional engagement. Often, in successful mentoring partnerships, the pair respect and like each other. Third, it includes the use of certain skills such as listening, questioning, challenging and supporting. Fourth, central to mentoring is 'the mentee's dream' (Caruso, 1996); that is to say, mentoring is primarily for the mentee. The concept is therefore fundamentally associated with a desire to progress, learn, understand and achieve. It is often employed where a transition is needed. For example, a new job, a promotion, a new stage of life, setting up a business, facing retirement, moving from unemployment to employment, effecting a reorganization or other change.

Mentoring can take many forms (see Garvey, 1999) depending on the following:

- the perspective the organization or the organizers take on the purpose of mentoring
- the culture and structures of the social setting
- the style and the role adopted by key players as 'normal' within the social setting
- the power and control orientation of the social setting
- the perspective the organization or organizers take on knowledge, creativity and innovation
- the views participants take on learning and development
- the time and cost
- the training and follow-up support for mentors and mentees
- the motivations of the participants.

Clearly, the form mentoring takes within a social setting influences its potential for success or failure. Mentoring has both the potential to be genuinely supportive and helpful to people and to be abusive and manipulative (Carden, 1990). In part, this is because it is such an ordinary and natural human activity, and difficulties in relationships are part of the human condition.

In addition, genuine practical and structural difficulties contribute to the success or failure of mentoring and, on occasions, mentoring is subject to social and cultural pressures.

This chapter is about the challenges of the 'downsides' of mentoring.

WHEN MENTORING GOES WRONG

There are three broad areas in which mentoring may go wrong:

- practical or logistical issues
- relationship issues
- scheme and organization issues.

PRACTICAL OR LOGISTICAL ISSUES

TIME

Time in the context of mentoring is a complex issue. Those who participate in mentoring regularly raise issues relating to time. The significance given to these issues and the meanings ascribed to them are many and varied but, generally, time-related issues are commonly associated with failing mentoring relationships.

The central issues commonly expressed in the literature are:

- both mentor and mentee need to commit time to their relationship
- mentors need time to develop their skills
- mentoring relationships take time to develop
- mentees take time to learn, change and develop.

Time commitment

In a survey (Garvey, 1995a) of 84 potential mentors, 63 per cent said that the biggest concern was 'time commitment' when asked how they felt about taking on the role of mentor.

The impact of this concern is manifest in the following extract from a participating mentee:

> *I recently asked for an appointment to see him [my mentor] before Christmas and his secretary said, 'No appointments are available until the New Year'.*

This example comes from the NHS but my experience suggests that a 'time-pressure culture' has emerged in many other work situations.

Clutterbuck (1998) in a study of 22 mentors noted that 10 per cent of participants in the research cited time problems as a reason for failure in the relationship.

One contributor to this chapter who was mentoring a university student said:

> *Basically, she couldn't manage to fit in the time for mentoring with all the other activities she was doing. I gave her several opportunities to meet. She said she wanted to meet but we finished the relationship after two meetings, several phone calls and some e-mails.*

Changed or broken mentoring appointments, not meeting for weeks on end, or agreeing to mentor and then not meeting at all are possible signs of:

- lack of commitment to mentoring on the part of one or both parties
- a problem of time management from one or both parties
- no clear need or recognition of a need for mentoring
- lack of mutual agenda-building, or ground rules at the early stages of the relationship
- a time-pressure culture.

In a time-pressure culture (Garvey, 1995a) individuals often discuss the long hours that they work almost competitively in the belief that the person who works the longest hours is the 'best' employee. This situation is of concern as putting in long hours often leads to poor performance brought on by tiredness and stress. People in time-pressure cultures may have difficulties in finding the time to develop mentoring relationships.

The practicalities of time management are not difficult. Most people have the knowledge and skills to manage time. They know, for example, the need to prioritize, to allocate time for activities, to work to deadlines and plan when to start an activity. If they do not know these things, they can learn them very quickly but this does not mean that they will apply these skills or knowledge. This suggests that time management is more about attitudes of mind and behaviours than skills or knowledge. Individuals with time-pressure problems can be difficult to deal with because sometimes their environment or the cultural setting creates their problems. If this is the case, the changes in attitude or behaviour from the individual may need to take account of their social context. Individuals need to understand the cultural pressures to behave in certain ways and learn to manage their behaviour within this context. In other situations where the time use issue is not culturally founded, the individual may need a major personal attitudinal change in order to effect a change in behaviour.

Interestingly, in work-based relationships, mentors and mentees often report that the main topic of conversation within mentoring relates to time. Here there is a real opportunity for the mentor to facilitate real changes in time-related attitudes and behaviours through dialogue, support and challenge. Similarly, in other contexts, the mentor is able to do the same. Mentoring partnerships offer the context in which both parties are able to develop a better understanding of their own behaviour with regard to time use.

In these times of fast action and constant change, mentoring is an activity which people seem to need increasingly. However, the pressures to perform at ever increasing levels may put too much pressure on mentoring and squeeze it out. Mentoring offers the opportunity to take time to reflect, to develop ideas and to draw breath – the essential element of high performance. One challenge for mentoring organizations is to allow it to do its work without interference.

Time and mentoring skills

There can be little doubt that mentoring involves the application of certain skills and that training can assist in the acquisition of these skills. But mentoring is not about skills alone, and skills employed without regard to the way in which they are employed and the attitudes behind them can make the mentee feel like they are being 'techniqued' or manipulated. The mentee may feel that the mentor has hijacked their agenda. Sometimes this situation is related to a mentor's power or control orientation. Here the mentor is dominant in the partnership and feels the need to perhaps give advice, make suggestions and control the agenda. Put together, this can lead to the mentee feeling disempowered, and the partnership may break down.

Although a new or inexperienced mentor may be full of good intentions, their enthusiasm to make a difference can sometimes dominate. The skills employed by a mentor need to be grounded in certain other attitudes and personal qualities such as:

- respect
- patience
- an open mind and flexible attitude
- being aware of their own developmental needs.

These are particularly important in the early stages of the relationship, when trust-building is very important.

A contributor to this chapter observed that, in her scheme, relationships often had difficulties after the second or third meeting. Similarly, in schemes within organizations, mentoring managers often rush to offer advice and guidance before the mentee has had time to understand their issues. Egan's (1994) three-stage process can be helpful here (Alred *et al.*, 2002, 33–46). The elements are: 'exploration' – 'understanding' – 'action'. The inexperienced mentor is often very keen to get to the 'action', and consequently there is inadequate 'exploration' and poor 'understanding' from both parties. The result is often that the action is not fully understood or 'owned' by the mentee. This can lead to either action which fails or no action at all on behalf of the mentee (Greenwood Partnership, 2000). In part, this may be due to the mentor focusing too much on the outcome of the relationship and less on the mentoring process and relationship issues. Successful mentoring partnerships often pay attention to the process, skills and the relationship itself by regularly reviewing and evaluating progress together.

It is also possible for the action-oriented mentor to devalue thier own skills. In a recent workshop session with young managers who were thinking about mentoring, one of the participants said after a practical session, 'I didn't do anything, I just listened!' Here the 'just listening' was seen as inconsequential and lacking in action. In my view, listening is probably the most important action a mentor can take.

Another solution is to design any mentor training to focus on the process as a priority and the skills element as secondary. In this way, time is devoted to understanding the importance and significance of each of Egan's stages and the skills employed at each stage. This can lead to the participants realizing that listening is the most important aspect of a mentoring relationship.

Another idea to help avoid mentoring problems of this sort may be found in ongoing review meetings for mentors. Research (Garvey, 1998) has shown that mentors value events where they can discuss mentoring issues with each other and gain support from others involved in the scheme. Often the mentor's requirement in such meetings is for further skills practice.

An additional solution is to develop mentor supervision (Barrett, 2002). This is rather like a mentor for the mentor! Here the mentor will be linked to another more experienced mentor and they will be able to explore the 'live' mentoring issues together in order to develop improved understanding of the process. In this way mentoring becomes part of the complex network of relationships within an organization.

So far we have focused primarily on the mentor. The mentee obviously contributes to the process and the relationship and it is possible to be a skilled and competent mentee. Reflective thinking skills are important for the mentee but these also need to be grounded in certain attitudes. For example, a competent mentee needs to be:

- committed to their own learning
- flexible in their approach to learning
- honest and open about their own behaviour
- open to feedback
- proactive in the relationship.

All too often people are thrown into mentoring either as a mentor or a mentee with inadequate preparation. Taking time to consider what is required in advance, either in workshop sessions before starting or by the parties discussing these issues and establishing common ground rules, pays dividends later.

Time to develop the relationship

Mentoring relationships change over time. Some writers (see, for example, Kram, 1983) show that the mentoring relationship moves through various stages or phases:

- initiation
- cultivation
- separation
- redefinition.

Others (Holloway and Whyte, 1994) have likened the phases of a mentoring relationship to those of life, as in Table 14.1.

Both these frameworks show that mentoring is not about a quick fix but, rather, a longer-term relationship that endures and changes over time. Being aware of this at the outset is important. All too often mentoring can 'go wrong' if either or both parties think it is about the short term. Time is often both the trust builder and the developer in mentoring.

Table 14.1 Saying goodbye

Life	Mentoring
looking for a partner	gaining commitment
going out together	getting involved
courting	getting together
engagement	getting to know each other
marriage	working together
growing together, developing a history	learning together
parting	review and evaluation

Mentees take time to learn, change and develop

An individual's holistic development is generally acquired through a combination of one-to-one social learning processes, wider social interactions and reflection over time. This often happens informally rather than through the formal delivery of discrete pieces of knowledge or skills in the form of 'content', although some skills-based things are learned in this way. Sometimes, a mentor may need to 'coach' the mentee in specific skills areas or around specific issues in the short term, but this is part of the mentor's skill set rather than the only aspect.

One of the commonly reported benefits of mentoring is 'satisfaction at seeing someone else develop and change'. Mentors who are generous with their time know this and recognize that it may take a few years for someone to really change and develop. The experienced mentor is patient and stays 'with' the process even when the going gets tough. Learning is not always an easy process and the mentor can provide crucial support for the mentee at times of crisis. Failure to do this can leave a mentee feeling let down.

RELATIONSHIP ISSUES

It is often suggested (Rogers, 1961; Bennetts, 1996; Polyani, 1958) that certain conditions need to be in place for people to learn and develop. Bennetts (1996), in her research, suggests that the conditions under which mentoring relationships flourish are 'the same as those in a good counselling relationship' (p3). Rogers (1961), drawing on the counselling tradition, talks of the 'core conditions for learning', which include: empathy, genuineness, unconditional, positive regard and ability to communicate all these to others (p281). All these 'conditions' need to be in place over time for learning to develop. Due to the often intense and sometimes emotional nature of mentoring relationships, these conditions take on particular significance. A mentoring relationship without these core conditions is inevitably under pressure.

DIMENSIONS, BOUNDARIES AND ASSUMPTIONS

Sometimes mentoring relationships may flounder if the participants fail to develop any sense of the dimensions, boundaries or assumptions held within the partnership. It can be helpful to think about the mentoring relationship in terms of dimensions, as in Figure 14.1.

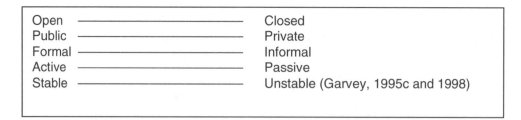

Open	————————	Closed
Public	————————	Private
Formal	————————	Informal
Active	————————	Passive
Stable	————————	Unstable (Garvey, 1995c and 1998)

Figure 14.1   Relationship dimensions

These dimensions are continuums and can be used to describe and discuss the relationship in order to establish ground rules or to evaluate progress or change in the relationship over time.

The *open/closed* dimension represents the content of the mentoring relationship. At the *open* end, anything can be discussed; personal, emotional, work-related and so on. At the *closed* end, there may be an agreement to focus on certain topics. Both parties may negotiate the extent to which they feel comfortable with the content aspects of the partnership. This may change over time.

The *public/private* dimension relates mainly to schemes within organizations. The issue is: who knows about the mentoring? If it is *private* it may lead to relationship difficulties later, as *private* mentoring within an organization can lead to speculation and innuendo. It is often 'safer' for the mentoring to be in the *public* domain to avoid speculation and rumour (the consequences of which are discussed later in this chapter).

The *formal/informal* dimension relates to the operation of the partnership. In the *formal* dimension, the participants will agree times and places to meet in advance and 'time manage' the relationship. In the *informal* dimension, the operational arrangements are more relaxed. This can sometimes lead to difficulties when the contacts are either too frequent and at inconvenient times or the contacts in this more relaxed dimension can become too infrequent.

The *active/passive* dimension is about activity. Who is responsible for taking action? An active partnership is one where both parties take some sort of action as a result of the mentoring discussions. This may take many forms from, in the case of a mentor, an intervention on a mentee's behalf or, in the case of the mentee, a change in behaviour or activity. It may be possible that one party is more active than the other. *Active* can also mean that contact is regular. A *passive* mentoring relationship is one where there is little action taken by either party as a result of mentoring discussions. Contacts between the parties may also have lapsed. It may be possible to have a mentoring partnership in which one party is *passive* and the other *active*. Sometimes difficulties may arise in the *passive* dimension if the mentor feels inactive and therefore ineffective – 'I'm not doing anything.' Frustration can also come here if the mentee becomes *passive*.

The *stable/unstable* dimension is about trust-building, consistency and confidence. A *stable* partnership is one in which the behaviour of both parties has an element of security and predictability. An understood consistency and regularity provide a feeling of stability. This may also be linked to a feeling of commitment, and the element of trust is of great importance in this dimension. An *unstable* relationship is unpredictable and insecure. This dimension is a manifestation of some of the negative aspects of mentoring which result from the human condition. People can sometimes be moody and unpredictable because of their own agendas and issues (Gladstone, 1988). Trust may be lacking and the commitment may be questionable (Garvey, 1995c).

As a consequence of the uniqueness of mentoring relationships, each specific pair may feature different combinations of the dimensions. Theoretically, it may be possible that certain combinations of the dimensions are present in a mentoring relationship that are absent from other types of relationship. It is possible for mentor and mentee to view the relationship's dimensions differently. It is also possible that some of these dimensions must be perceived by both parties simultaneously for the relationship to be an effective one. Research (Garvey, 1995c, 1998) shows that successful mentoring relationships move backwards and forwards along the continua over time but that often dimensions down the left-hand side (held by both parties at the same time) of Figure 14.1 offer the most potential for success in organizational schemes. These are achieved by using the dimensions framework as the basis for regular discussion and review of the relationship between mentor and mentee.

Further insights into paired relationships or dyads may be gained from Georg Simmel's work (1950). He observed that the dyadic relationship is unique for a number of reasons. The 'secret' held between *two* people is the maximum number needed for the security of the secret. This secrecy between two would seem to be a fundamental aspect of the dyad and contributes to trust-building. In addition, the element of confidentiality must be of prime concern in the mentor relationship. The 'secrecy' in this sense (rather than conspiratorially) places a mutual dependency on the relationship. If a third party is introduced, the social structure fundamentally alters. If one party drops out of the relationship of three, the group can still exist in the remaining two. In a dyad, if one drops out the 'group' is obviously at an end.

The issues of dependency and the termination of the relationship can be powerful forces within the pair. There is always the potential for either greater dependency or a lack of trust evolving. Simmel (1950) likens the risk of termination of a dyad to the threat of death. He suggests that 'the fact that we shall die is a quality inherent in life from the beginning...we are, from birth on, beings that will die' (p124). This impending end is something that may affect the mentor relationship dramatically. It could bring the pair closer together and thus they become more dependent on each other. Alternatively, trust may be put under strain as the potential ending draws nearer.

Further, some people may become concerned at the notion of dependency within mentoring. This is a natural concern but it is not necessarily a negative one. Obviously, it is important for both parties to be able to 'let go' or change the nature of their partnership. But sometimes dependency is an active and positive choice, and sometimes it is beneficial. A participant in this chapter who has a physical disability said, 'To look a dependency through the eyes of a disabled person is very different to an able-bodied person. Dependency is a good and positive choice for me and my mentor.' This implies that dependency can be a temporary state and an active choice. The issue is if it becomes a destructive, controlling or dominating dependency; then there is a problem.

Simmel (1950) also mentions the concept of 'triviality' in relation to the dyad. This may be created by the 'sentimentalism and elegiac problems' identified by Simmel but it may equally be rooted in the initial mutual expectations in the relationship failing to materialize in practice. Further, the regularity and frequency of similar experiences within the relationship may create a sense of triviality, a closing-down of the content. The value of the 'content' of a mentoring relationship can be measured by its rarity, its uniqueness to the parties involved. In dyadic relationships which 'do not result in higher units, the tone of triviality frequently becomes desperate and fatal' (Simmel, 1950, p126).

The risk of triviality entering the mentor partnership is great and if, in a formal system, the relationship is to work effectively, vigilance is needed to reduce this risk by the parties keeping in touch with and monitoring their relationship.

Levinson (1978) tells us that most mentoring relationships last for two to three years. He observes that at times the relationship 'comes to a natural end and, after a cooling-off period, the pair form a warm but modest friendship' (p100). Bennetts (1995) does not support this view and has identified cases where mentoring relationships develop into life-long friendships or love relationships.

Kram (1983) goes some way to supporting the Levinson view and describes the 'cooling-off period' as one of the phases in the relationship. However, the relationship, if it is an intense one, may terminate with 'strong conflict' (Levinson, 1978), and although the meaningful elements remain with the mentee, the mentor may be left to mourn and go through the classic stages of grieving.

The dyad also has the potential for great intimacy. (Simmel is not referring to sexual intimacy here, although Bennetts (1995) suggests that this may be a possibility in the mentoring relationship. This point is more fully discussed later.) However, generally the relationship, based on interdependence, does not 'grow beyond its elements' (Simmel, 1950, p126). Simmel suggests that the dyad often develops this friendship quality as the relationship has, by its nature, an inbuilt tendency for intimacy and mutual dependence. This is not due to the 'content' (the things the individuals discuss) of the relationship but rather the unique shared quality of the relationship – as Simmel puts it, 'an all or nothing' relationship. This intimacy of friendship exists 'if the 'internal' side of the relation, is felt to be essential; if its whole affective structure is based on what each of the two participants give or show only to the one other person and to nobody else' (Simmel, 1950, p126). It is this exclusive and essentially 'secret' or private nature of the mentoring relationship that often creates a strong, stable friendship (Chao and O'Leary, 1990; Hunt and Michael, 1983; Shapiro *et al.*, 1978). But, as previously discussed, this strength may cause eventual emotional difficulties for both the mentor and mentee as the relationship ends (Levinson, 1978).

SEXUAL INTIMACY

Mainiero (1989) argues that if the relationship is to be mutually beneficial, it is essential that the relationship is close. Hurley and Fagenson-Eland (1996) identify three types of intimacy or closeness in work-related cross-gender mentoring relationships:

- non-sexual psychological intimate relationships
- office romances (sexually intimate relationships)
- sexual harassment.

These are viewed as points along a continuum of extremes. Nieva and Gutek (1981) suggest that the issue of sexuality and intimacy is best understood in the context of 'sex role spillover' (Hurley and Fagenson-Eland, 1996, p43). In the case of male mentors who feel uncomfortable with women in the workforce, they suggest that the male will base his perceptions of females on the female role with which he is most familiar in other aspects of his life. According to Hurley and Fagenson-Eland (1996), the type of relationship which emerges within cross-gender mentoring is likely to be dependent on the male mentor's perspective. This raises the issue of the use and abuse of power in the mentoring relationship. This point is discussed later.

Hurley and Fagenson-Eland (1996) characterize non-sexual intimacy as involving 'mutual closeness, affection, trust, respect, commitment, and self-disclosure' (p43). They describe these relationships as 'non-sexual, psychologically intimate relationships' (p43). She suggests that these relationships sometimes have the potential to be misconstrued in the workplace by 'jealous co-worker(s)'.

Levinson (1978) observed this in his research and accounted for it by implying that the root cause is deep-seated sexism – 'to regard her as attractive but not gifted, as a gifted women whose sexual attractiveness interferes with her work and friendship, as an intelligent but impersonal pseudo-male or as a charming little girl who cannot be taken seriously' (p98). Chao and O'Leary (1990) together with Ragins (1989) suggest that some co-workers perceive intimate sexual relationships in cross-gender mentoring even if none exist. Bowen (1985) reports that some female mentees are subject to sexual innuendo and speculative rumour within the organization. Hurley and Fagenson-Eland (1996) believe this is a result of these 'jealous co-workers' who view mentoring as being linked to favouritism and career success. It is here that the *public/private* dimension becomes important and the argument for formal organizational schemes is strengthened.

In a cross-gender study that looked at sexuality in the workplace (Lobel *et al.*, 1994), '968 of 1,044 respondents reported non-sexual, psychologically intimate relationships with opposite gender co-workers' (Hurley and Fagenson-Eland, 1996, p43). This suggests that non-sexual relationships are the more common form of cross-gender relationship in the workplace.

However, cross-gender mentoring relationships do have the potential for becoming sexually active partnerships and can develop into office romances. Clawson and Kram (1984) suggest that sexual activity is the result of the heightened emotional state and sheer intensity of the relationship. In my UK study of mentoring (Garvey, 1998), out of the 500 or more participants there was only one reported case of this type of relationship developing. I suggest that the potential may be present but generally, in the UK, this is not great.

There are mixed views as to the benefits or negative effects of the office romance. Some (Bureau of National Affairs, 1988; Lobel *et al.*, 1994) suggest that there may be positive effects on the participants' career progression but others conclude the opposite (Ford and McLaughlin, 1987; Mainiero, 1989; Powell, 1986).

Ending such sexual relationships causes the biggest problems as there is the potential for the break-up to slide into sexual harassment (Bordwin, 1994; Lobel *et al.*, 1994; Mainiero, 1989). This adds another layer to the problems associated with ending a mentoring relationship identified by Levinson (1978) and discussed above.

Sexual harassment, as the most extreme example of intimacy in cross-gender mentoring, is clearly the most damaging and offensive point on the continuum. Hurley and Fagenson-Eland (1996) identify two main types of harassment at work. One is where there is a 'quid pro quo sexual harassment' (p45). This is where there is the offer of preferment or other like benefit in return for an acceptance of a sexual advance. The other type is a 'hostile or offensive working environment' (p45). This is very often related to power and status in a hierarchical relationship. Clearly, hierarchy is often associated with mentor relationships (Chao and O'Leary, 1990; Vertz, 1985). This is discussed later in this chapter.

Sexuality in mentoring is not restricted to opposite-sex relationships. Levinson (1978) states that 'mentoring is best understood as a form of love relationship' (p100) and as such 'it is a difficult one to terminate' (p100). In her research into the 'loving' aspect of mentoring, Bennetts (1995) found that 'the word "love" was used in an holistic way; for some it was used as a part of their spiritual philosophy; but for others it was a mixture of both. This included a strong emotional attraction, which led to being "in love". Some individuals handled that aspect of the relationship by remaining silent and never mentioning it to their mentors or learners, and some individuals made it explicit and the relationship became sexual' (p11). However, in every case the relationship was conducted with integrity and was not based on the abuse of power. She also noted that 'it would be too simplistic to think that these were ordinary romances. They were described in the same way for both opposite and same sex partners, regardless of their previous chosen sexuality' (p11).

Torrance (1984) supports this finding – 'Those who organise and foster mentor programs should also recognize that the mentor relationship may in time become one of friendship, teacher, competitor, lover or father figure. If the relationship is a deep and caring one (and this seems to be a major characteristic of a genuine mentor relationship), any of these relationships may evolve. However, because of the caring nature, the outcomes are not likely to be harmful. However, this may be a necessary risk' (p55).

SCHEME AND ORGANIZATION ISSUES

PURPOSE AND SCOPE

In 1985, Kathy Kram suggested a framework for developing a mentoring scheme (Kram, 1985b). This had four main stages:

- defining objectives and scope
- diagnosis
- implementation
- evaluating.

Defining objectives and scope

It is very important to have a clear sense of whom mentoring is for and in what circumstances. Experience shows that these issues are best addressed collectively and through dialogue with various interested parties and stakeholders. Confusion around the scheme's scope and objectives at the start can lead to failure and resentment.

Diagnosis

It is important to have a good understanding of the organizational factors which both contribute to the success of mentoring and to its failure. Those involved with mentoring need to be aware of both these elements and to develop strategies to deal with them.

A feasibility study is often a good starting point. This needs to investigate the factors within the organization or social context that will support mentoring and the factors that might not. The feasibility study also needs to identify where there is some current mentoring activity and the extent to which mentoring is understood. In many cases it is likely that people will be mentoring in a particular context, regardless of whether there is a scheme or not! Some of those involved may not refer to the activity as mentoring but they will be aware of the importance of developmental relationships. It is with these people that a mentoring scheme has the best opportunity for survival. Mentoring is normal and quite natural, and any scheme needs to have a strong voluntary element.

Implementation

Research (Garvey, 1998) has shown that many people in organizations are very tired of initiatives. New initiatives are often viewed as gimmicks, as management game-playing or as short-lived. Mentoring therefore needs to be introduced slowly and in the mentoring way. Because mentoring is natural and organic, it is often best to try to nurture it in an organization from a position of strength. Working with a small group of volunteer enthusiasts is a good place to start. Gentle publicity for mentoring, support meetings and support materials help to keep it going. My research has shown that implementing a scheme in this natural and organic way enables mentoring to grow securely and quickly. One organization of 2500 staff started with just 12 enthusiastic mentoring pairs and within a year the total had risen to 85 mentoring pairs. This was achieved through very low-key marketing activity, support (in the form of training, ongoing mentor support and support materials such as books and videos) and word of mouth. Forcing people to mentor is often the recipe for failure and problems.

Measurement and evaluation

A further consideration is the desire to measure mentoring. In many social settings, there is a strong and understandable desire to prove that mentoring is working. The public sector is often driven by value-for-money considerations. In social mentoring schemes, there may be a very strong desire to reduce crime, increase employment and achieve better educational results. In private sector organizations, there is a strong desire for efficiency, high performance and profitability. However, measurement can also become a controlling device which may distort activities like mentoring and give the impression that mentoring is about social control. One of the great minds of the twentieth century, Albert Einstein, said, 'Not everything that counts can be counted. And not everything that can be counted counts.' What is key to mentoring evaluation is the appropriateness of the measuring instrument. Sometimes the desire to count means that what 'counts' is missed. It can be like trying to measure the temperature of a room with a ruler! Obviously, this is wholly inappropriate.

So, what can be measured numerically in mentoring? The list is not very long:

1 the number of people participating
2 the duration of relationships
3 the number of people who have received training and support
4 the cost of training and support.

This type of data is useful and gives clues about the extent of mentoring within a particular setting but it only gives a partial picture. Other performance descriptions such as:

- increased sales figures
- reduced crime
- reduced reoffending
- improved numbers in employment
- better bottom line

(to mention a few) are more important but can only be attributed to mentoring by association. Therefore, qualitative indicators such as:

- improved motivation and commitment
- faster learning and sharper thinking
- improved enthusiasm and relationships
- increased ideas flow and improved understanding of issues
- improved stress management
- change/development achieved more easily
- greater confidence and autonomy (Garvey, 1995a; Wilson and Elman, 1990)

contribute to our understanding of mentoring as a natural and very human activity.

Mentoring, it could be argued, is fundamentally linked to the human 'generativity' (Erikson, 1965) motive and is therefore essential for human progress in any context. Generativity is the desire to influence the next generation. This is sometimes manifest in parent–child types of relationship and is linked to a motivation to mentor.

So multiple methods, both numerical and descriptive, of measuring or evaluating mentoring offer the most potential for understanding the impact or effects of mentoring in various contexts. The challenge to any organization wishing to encourage mentoring within a scheme is to:

- accept it as a legitimate activity
- support it with time and other resources
- measure what you can and listen to what people say.

It is important to be aware of what really counts!

Although Kram's (1985) framework has proved helpful, it does not necessarily guarantee a successful scheme (see Garvey, 1995b). An organization could spend considerable time working with this framework but still end up with a failing scheme. This may be due to a range of other issues such as culture and management style, the importance of knowledge within the workplace and sometimes simple personality clashes or other dysfunctional behaviour.

POWER, STATUS AND HIERARCHY

The issue of power in the mentoring relationship is often associated with gender (Brown, 1993). It is also associated with position and status. Work in the US indicates that many mentees (66 per cent of those studied) view the mentor as offering the key or passport to future career advancement (Burke, 1984). This is very much a US perspective on mentoring where sponsorship is seen as a prime motive for mentoring partnerships at work. In such a climate of competitiveness among one's peers, individuals, desperate for advancement, may engage in a range of unsavoury behaviours.

Studies in the US (Brown, 1993; Fagenson, 1989; Ragins, 1989; Burke, 1984; Landau, 1993; Gutek, 1985; Reynolds, 1993) all point to mentees and mentors, both male and female having fears and concerns over sexual harassment. And yet the US experience is that harassment is quite generally widespread but not exclusively in the context of mentoring. The underpinning motivation for mentoring at work in the US, together with wider social pressures, may be a cause of these problems.

In the UK, the emphasis in mentoring is more on learning and development. Arguably, the potential for status abuse in mentoring may be less in the UK as the dominant thinking about mentoring is clearly different. This is not to say that the potential does not exist in mentoring; clearly it does. This issue cannot be ignored as it plays a part in our understanding of mentoring.

Research (Alred *et al.*, 1996) shows that often when someone is invited to become a mentor their initial response is to feel flattered. This is a natural response to such a request – it can be confirming of one's position and status – but here lies the potential risk. If being a mentor is viewed as only confirmation of, say, one's ability or status, there are clear difficulties for the partnership ahead. The mentor may cast themself in a superior role to the mentee, and the 'core condition' of unconditional positive regard (Rogers, 1961) is strained.

The research (Garvey, 1998) from one UK public sector organization which introduced mentoring showed that there was no problem in finding volunteers to become mentors but there was a grave shortage of potential mentees. Many of these volunteers were well intentioned and had much potential to be very good mentors. However, the strong hierarchy and status orientation which characterized the organization meant that becoming a mentor was primarily confirmation of their status. Often many of these volunteers were motivated by the desire to, as many respondents say, 'put something back' into the organization. This is a common motivation and, on the surface, one which seems reasonable but in this particular context it was more about the potential mentor's insecurity in the face of reorganization and change than about 'putting something back'. In some ways the 'putting back' can represent a form of arrogance on behalf of the potential mentor. It is about 'them' and their contribution rather than the mentee's development.

The lack of potential mentees coming forward was perhaps a sign that the mentees had fears and concerns about the motivations of the mentors. Consequently, they sought developmental support outside the mentoring scheme. Mentoring was working in the 'shadows' (Egan, 1993). Mentoring does occur naturally outside a formal scheme, and sometimes this is as effective and legitimate as the formal process (Ragins and Cotton, 1999).

In another organization a mentor said – 'mentoring enables me to spread my influence around the organization, it gives me allies'. Although this may be true and could be seen as positive for the mentor, it is also about establishing a political power base rather than a developmental alliance for the mentee. Again, Rogers' (1961) core conditions of learning are challenged when mentoring is not an act of a generous spirit. Mentoring with ulterior motives is morally dubious. Wood (1970), in commenting on Kantian moral philosophy, suggests that people must be treated as 'ends in themselves' rather than as 'means to an end' for the activity to be morally robust. Mentoring which is about political power and status views the mentee as a means to an end, and is therefore morally wrong.

McClelland and Burnham (1976) do not see the application of 'socialized power' as something necessarily associated with 'dictatorial behaviour', but as 'a desire to have an impact, to be strong and influential' (p235). This type of power, which they associate with the 'good manager', is not focused on the individual and 'personal aggrandizement' (p235) but is aimed 'toward the institution which he or she serves' (p235). McClelland and Burnham suggest that the successful manager is one who is able to use 'socialized power' for the benefit of the organization. Power may be described in terms of the attributes held by the majority in an organization. This is influenced by the organization's structure and values. Personal power is more associated with the charismatic leader, but this influence is often transitory in nature and short-term. Mentoring activity is usually more long-term than this (Levinson, 1978). Arguably, the 'good mentor' will have the needs of the organization in their mind, the whole picture, as well as a focus of attention on the needs of the individual. Mentoring, focused in this way, creates a unique and special relationship that has worked for centuries for the individual participants.

A further issue is the real and perceived hierarchies within organizations. Mentoring can often be associated with hierarchy. During the 1980s 'a new wave of management thinking developed which questioned much of the received wisdoms' (Ezzamel *et al.*, 1993). These challenges included a review of management structures. This resulted in management layers being eroded so that organizations became 'leaner' and 'fitter'. With this came the demand for different managerial abilities (mentoring being just one of these). However, Ezzamel *et al.* (1993) assert that, despite the change of language, 'the command and control system lives on, concealed beneath the trappings of the facilitate and empower philosophy'. The language of change is very much in place but the realities have not yet fully materialized. The underpinning assumption made from the past was 'father knows best' – in effect, the paternalistic, senior male who dominated those of lesser status. Mentoring has overtones of such historical thinking and this may 'colour' its application. Mentoring, it may be inferred, as a part of the 'new language' could still be dogged by past thinking of power and control within organizations.

THE CULTURE AND MANAGEMENT STYLE

As mentioned in the introduction of this chapter, the form mentoring takes is often influenced by the type of organization or social setting in which it occurs. Clawson (1996, p10), suggests that mentoring forms are influenced by the degree of mutuality and comprehensiveness of the relationship (Figure 14.2). 'True' mentoring is located at the 'mutual interest' point and at the highest point of the 'comprehensiveness' axis. In his vision of the future, Clawson (1996) posits mentoring as facilitating flatter, egalitarian, customer-focused business environments.

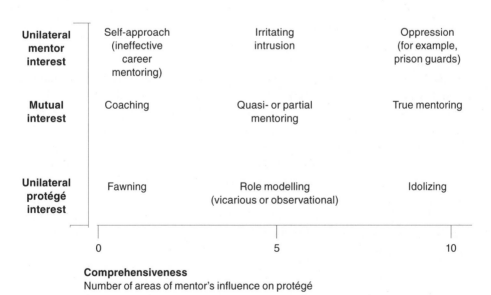

Figure 14.2 The degrees of mutuality and comprehensiveness of the mentoring relationship

If these are the qualities of future business activity where knowledge and learning are vital components, mentoring must start to feature. Mentoring is associated with new organizational forms (Garvey, 1999).

The real danger for mentoring is the tendency for it to be adopted as a strategy for facilitating learning and change without due consideration for the social setting or the cultural context. All too often, mentoring is used as the 'fixer' of problems, a 'fast track to success', a 'cure-all' without due consideration for the wider social, political and economic context. An organization can talk development as much as it likes, but without real commitment to the notion it is just another initiative to squeeze a little more out of people (Garvey, 1995b).

The same is true in social mentoring. It is certainly desirable for governments to set objectives such as reducing youth crime. But to make such an objective the sole driver and evaluation instrument without regard to the people and personalities involved may start to look like social engineering. If the young person feels that the agenda for mentoring lies outside themselves, they will be alienated from mentoring (see the video *New Chances, New Horizons* (1999) for positive insights into social mentoring). Clawson's observations in Figure 14.2 present a real practical and moral challenge for mentoring.

CULTURAL FOCUS

In a very strong 'task'-focused culture the 'people' aspect may be disregarded. (The term 'task'-focused culture is not used here to mean the same as Handy's (1986) or Harrison's (1972) Task Culture. It is used here to mean a focus on the job itself in its technical sense, and is not concerned with the people who do the job.) In some organizations some individuals are motivated by the notion that 'I did it the hard way and so should you' – 'in at the deep end' thinking. Such people are not particularly mentoring-aware and tend to thwart developmental initiatives. If these people mentor, they may have the strong desire to instruct the mentee in 'the old ways' of the organization. Thus developmental progress becomes blocked. This behaviour may not be a conscious attempt to thwart progress but rather a deeply ingrained schema, socially constructed and reinforced.

Having made the above point however, there is evidence to the contrary. In a mentoring scheme known to me, the mentor was a very task-oriented, 'no time for people' type person. He dominated the mentor discussions with advice, and the mentee loved it! The mentee said, 'I listened and took what I wanted and ignored the rest. He was just like my Dad.' I think that this is a very good example of a skilled mentee at work. However, for some organizations this could create a dilemma as to 'who should mentor, and are they mentor material?'

Mentoring is the sort of learning that changes lives, opens eyes, sets new horizons, values the person and is mutual and reciprocal (Carden, 1990). So, while 'in at the deep end' thinking and advice-giving can create problems for mentoring, they can also create opportunities for mentoring. The mentee may be able to play a part in the mentor's development and behavioural change in that the mentee may influence the mentor's thinking just as much as the other way round. Therefore, selecting people to be mentors and mentees needs to be done with consideration of many issues.

Matching and mismatching

In the desire to have successful mentoring relationships, the matching process can become quite technical. The potential participants could complete psychometric, learning style and personality questionnaires. A 'dating agency' approach could be taken. Despite all this effort, there is still no guarantee that the mentoring will 'work'.

Another is to try to create a mentoring organization that is supportive and encouraging of others and then just let the mentoring happen. There is still no guarantee that the mentoring will 'work' in this less controlled environment.

It is my experience that the best way to avoid matching difficulties is first to introduce the idea of 'no fault divorce' as a strong philosophy in mentoring. Mentoring is a human activity and is therefore subject to human frailties. Second, it is important to offer both parties the opportunity to explore what is meant by mentoring before engaging. Third, a strong element of voluntarism is necessary. And it should be recognized that mentoring relationships can take time to develop, and they do change over time.

The Egan (1994) model discussed earlier emphasizes this point. Mentoring cannot be about 'quick fixes' any more than education can be. The lesson from writers such as Dewey (1958), Levinson (1978) and Daloz (1986) is that learning is not a process that can be forced or hurried. Mentoring is a process that is subject to dynamic change through time. The current perception of society and business as a fast-changing, fast-moving environment seems at odds with the mentoring concept. However, there is plenty of evidence that when the conditions are right, mentoring does speed the learning process. But for some the great paradox is that while businesses and social schemes need fast learning environments and fast change, and they introduce mentoring to this end, their cultures, structures and thinking patterns seem unable to support it well enough.

CONCLUSION

Mentoring is a highly complex human interaction and there is much scope for mentoring to 'go wrong'. This chapter has attempted to highlight just some of the reasons. What is of greater importance to anyone interested in successful mentoring in any context is how to avoid the problems and maximize the benefits. This chapter has also suggested ways in which problems could be avoided.

It is important to remember that mentoring is a human relationship and, as such, needs to be treated with integrity and respect. But because it is human there will always be difficulties and challenges to work with. This does not diminish its power for transition, learning and change.

To conclude, a colleague of mine was asked by a company director, 'Does mentoring work?' My colleague replied, 'Does friendship work?' The company director replied, 'Well, it does and it doesn't.' 'Yes,' replied my colleague, 'it's just about the same with mentoring!'

All good things must come to an end: winding up and winding down a mentoring relationship

15

DAVID CLUTTERBUCK and DAVID MEGGINSON

Objection, evasion, happy distrust, pleasure in mockery are signs of health: everything unconditional belongs to pathology

Nietzsche, 1990, p103

One of the least researched and most feared aspects of the mentoring relationship is its ending. In consequence of this, we decided to explore what the literature had to say about the issue and then to gather some qualitative data from experienced mentors and mentoring scheme organizers about endings. We told our informants of a distinction we were making between *winding up* and *winding down* relationships (*winding up* being a proactive approach, with a clearly defined transition, and *winding down* being a gradual drift apart) and asked them to give us data about good and bad experiences of each, and any views that they had on what constitutes good practice in ending mentoring. We sought their responses by e-mail and received 44 usable replies, some of which were from groups of people connected with a particular scheme or organization. We analysed these replies by categories derived from the data itself rather than a priori, and then we clustered the themes. We present this analysis and draw conclusions from this for both practice and for further research. Our analysis suggests that effective mentors most often opt for clarity of ending. It also explores some of the constituent skills in bringing about a satisfactory ending.

THE LITERATURE ON ENDING MENTORING RELATIONSHIPS

The founding authors of modern mentoring, Levinson *et al.* (1978) and Kram (1983), have written extensively about endings. In Levinson *et al.*'s writing a psychodynamic view is taken, drawing on Erikson's view of generativity, which is primarily the concern in establishing and guiding the next generation (Erikson, 1965, p258).

If this need is denied, the older individual is left 'with a pervading sense of stagnation and personal impoverishment' (Erikson, 1965, pp258–9). Levinson *et al.* emphasize that the ambivalent emotions (gratitude *and* resentment) at the end of the mentoring relationship serve a positive function of enabling the parties to separate and move on into new relationships.

Kram (1983, p614) takes a longer view of the evolution of the mentoring relationship. She suggests that there are four phases:

- initiation
- cultivation
- separation
- redefinition.

Interestingly, the last two of these four are both concerned with ending. About these latter phases she talks about:

A *separation* phase, during which time the established nature of the relationship is substantially altered by structural changes in the organizational context and/or by psychological changes within one or both individuals; and a *redefinition* phase, during which time the relationship evolves a new form that is significantly different from the past, or the relationship ends entirely (Kram, 1983).

She sees the separation phase as both quite disruptive and critical to development. (Kram, 1983, pp619–20). The redefinition phase provides the evidence of changes having occurred in both individuals – the senior continues to be a supporter and takes pride in the junior's successive accomplishments; the younger operates independently and on a more equal footing (p621). This works well when the mentor has other outlets for generativity (pp622–3), but can become destructive if the mentee feels undermined/held back or the mentor feels threatened by the mentee's success. Kram concludes by saying that relationships are not 'readily available to all individuals in the early stage of a career because of organizational conditions and/or limited individual capacities to form enhancing relationships' (p623). In other words, there are two determinants of limited success in endings – organizational conditions and the capability of the parties to form satisfactory relationships.

Other descriptions of phases in mentoring include our own four-stage model – establishing rapport, direction-setting, progress-making and moving on (Megginson and Clutterbuck, 1995, pp30–34), and Parker Armitage's five-stage model – build trust/set contract, reframe, transference, transmute, transform (Parker Armitage, 1994). Both Parker Armitage and Kram, with their psychoanalytic perspective, see the penultimate stage as involving disruption and loss, whereas we tend to take a more pragmatic look at the issue, with the challenges of dealing with rupture and loss only occurring at the final stage. Much of the pragmatic literature on mentoring does not even acknowledge this sense of loss. Instead these authors argue that having clear objectives and proper preparation can mitigate any such problems (Conway, 1998; Fowler, 1998) or that moving the mentee out into a network of subsequent support gets round the problem (Caruso, 1996; Enomoto *et al.*, 2000; Higgins and Kram, 2001).

Other authors see endings and, in particular, problems with endings as being caused by structures and processes in organizations or in society at large. One group of such authors sees these causes as being addressable by features of the mentoring scheme. Having a contract (Forret, 1996); talking through potential ending problems (Conway, 1998, p34 ff.); achievement of the objective as in 'making partner' in professional service firms (Ibarra, 2000); or extensive training (Megginson, 2000) offer potential solutions.

Less optimistically, some authors, who see the problems caused by organizations or societal pressures, offer no solutions. The issues they highlight include: the need to address the cycle of delusion, and in particular the invasion and colonization of clients' inner worlds (Piper and

Piper, 2000); the need to increase the communitarian or social exchange value of mentoring in society (Gibb, 1999); the need to research how career stage influences the success of mentoring (Peluchette and Jeanquart, 2000); in case of mergers, the need to focus on informal relationships (Rigsby *et al.*, 1998).

So, a picture is beginning to emerge of approaches to the topic of endings. They can be seen in Table 15.1 below.

Table 15.1 Approaches in the literature to endings in mentoring relationships

Approach to endings	Key issues	Proposals for addressing them
Psychoanalytic – transference used	Psychodynamics are the source of both pain and growth	Psychiatric insight, acting out, working through (Parker Armitage, 1994) A long timescale (Kram, 1983)
Psychoanalytic – dynamics recognized	Psychodynamics create challenges for both parties to circumvent	Create generativity elsewhere for mentor (Kram, 1983) Bondage is misidentification of the seer with the seen (Wilber, 1985) Mentor-centred focus leads to abusive relationships (Bennetts, 1998) Ending is a generative act that leads to despair (Garvey, 1997)
Pragmatic – dynamics recognized	Loss must be recognized and acknowledged	Emotional intelligence (Clutterbuck and Megginson, 1999, pp17–22) Minimize overestimating of mentor's transformational leadership behaviour (Godshalk and Sosik, 2000) Mentor maturity limits possibilities (Megginson, 1998) Focus on the learner's dream (Caruso, 1996) Essentially sad; reflect on own experience of letting go (Whittaker and Cartwright, 1997) Risk of collusion; loss of momentum; line manager pressure (Whittaker and Cartwright, 2000) Manipulating or engineering relationships difficult or impossible (Hale, 2000) Match mentor and mentee focus (English and Sutton, 2000)
Pragmatic – dynamics downplayed	Endings just need to be managed properly	Avoid alternative power structure (Fowler, 1998) Move mentee into a network of relationships (Caruso, 1996; Enomoto *et al.*, 2000) or developmental networks (Higgins and Kram, 2001) Truly dysfunctional relationships will be left by disadvantaged party (Ragins *et al.*, 2000) Time pressure and churn of employees militate against success (Swap *et al.*, 2001) Distrust and prejudice met by active listening (Parsloe and Wray, 2000)

Approach to endings	Key issues	Proposals for addressing them
Organizational – scheme plans	Endings can be managed by features of the scheme	Geography, work schedule, chemistry cause rupture; contract solves problems (Forret, 1996) Premature ending effects mitigated by co-ordinator talking through problems (Conway, 1998) 'Making partner' provides break point (Ibarra, 2000) Extensive training needed (Megginson, 2000)
Organizational – circumstances	Endings will be caused by circumstances in society	Address cycle of delusion, and invasion and colonization of client's inner world (Piper and Piper, 2000) Increase communitarian or social exchange value of mentoring in society (Gibb, 1999) Career stage influences success (Peluchette and Jeanquart, 2000) In case of mergers, focus on informal relationships (Rigsby et al., 1998)

Grouping the types in Table 15.1 we can see three main approaches to the question of endings:

- *Psychodynamic*: where endings are seen to evoke older and unresolved difficulties which must either be *worked through* in the service of growth, or *worked round* in order to function reasonably.
- *Pragmatic*: where designers of schemes or skilled mentors can follow practices which either *eliminate* or at least *mitigate* the effects of any difficulties with endings that either party to the relationship might feel.
- *Organizational*: where the relationship is influenced by the context in which it operates and parties are subject to forces outside themselves (and indeed the scheme of which their relationship may be a part), which *determine the outcome* or *precipitate the ending*.

This framework will be used to analyse the perspectives adopted by our respondents, and, within each perspective, conclusions are drawn about how to respond to the issue of endings.

RESPONDENTS

Our respondents were from a variety of sources; what they had in common was lengthy experience of mentoring or mentoring schemes. Table 15.2 lists the categories of respondent.

As well as the UK respondents, and various unspecified or multi-country international respondents, we also had respondents from Africa – various countries (2); Australia (2); Canada (1); Finland (1); Ireland (1); Switzerland (1); USA (2).

Table 15.2   Categories of respondents to the survey

Sector	Number	Details
Charity	5	2 UK; 3 young people UK
Consultant	12	
Education	4	1 further education; 3 higher education
Government	2	1 UK; 1 Australia
Large business	13	7 global; 1 Finland; 1 Ireland; 4 UK
Professional body	3	3 UK
Religion	1	1 global – church
Unspecified scheme	2	
Small business	1	
Sport	1	

THEMES

We defined *winding up* as the ending of a relationship 'where there is a clear transition between being in the relationship and progressing to self-reliance or a new relationship'. We defined *winding down* as being 'where mentor and mentee gradually drift apart'. We asked respondents to comment on:

- good experiences of winding up/down
- bad experiences of winding up/down
- what constitutes good practice.

So the first stage of data analysis was to order content from the respondents according to its relationship to these categories. Some of the responses claimed that the framework was unhelpful, and these have been noted separately.

COMMENTS ON GOOD EXPERIENCES OF WINDING UP

'Gradual.'

'Leave rescue contact.'

'Jointly agree specific objectives at beginning.'

'Discuss at the outset at what point they envisage the relationship ending.'

'Finish because the formalized period (nine months) is up.'

'Change in mentor's/mentee's circumstances.'

'Welcome keeping in touch.'

'Having a clear style of mentoring means that ending can be a move to a less formal relationship.'

'Moving away.'

'Clear objectives met and so come to a natural end.'

'Time limit for mentor to check progress, set time aside for this.'

'Mentee to lead the discussion.'

'Clear that the "high-level insights" were covered, agreed to change meeting frequency and subject.'

'Calling up or chatting online – act as sounding board to reaffirm earlier exchanges.'

'Setting the scene from the start has enabled me to build a good friendship following the end of the formal relationship.'

'Time frame for the relationship clearly agreed at the outset – can be reviewed/extended.'

'"End point" adds dynamism to the relationship.'

'Negotiating a handover to new mentor.'

'Get the learners to agree that the ending will take place within a session rather than outside one.'

'Even with a "good" ending, I let them know that there is also one session left "in the bank" that they can cash in at any time.'

'Invited to an awards ceremony where the mentee proudly lined up a collection of trophies showing clear progress in methodology and achievement.'

'Develop an ethical, non-encroaching friendship at the end of the formal mentoring process.'

'I was mentor to a chief executive who lost their job. The issues we were discussing were no longer relevant and payment no longer available. The person became depressed and required help in finding alternative employment, they became demanding/aggressive in asking for time. By using the contract and reverting to process we were able to negotiate finding additional and appropriate help and work towards an ending of that relationship and negotiating a new one when they were offered a new post.'

'We are clear from the beginning that it will end (almost starting with "the end in mind").'

'Start to see him every other week instead of weekly.'

'Creating a book using photos and materials from the last year as a "celebration" of our time together; there is also a "graduation" ceremony that we can link into, that will formalize the ending.'

'Talk about endings in general.'

'We check religiously at the end of every session for detailed evidence that the discussion has moved things forward, and regularly discuss how many further sessions are likely to prove helpful.'

'Talk about end of the process at the first session.'

'The commitment is open-ended (though we give an indication of "how long this sort of assignment tends to last").'

'Discuss the hurt with the young person, as the disruptive behaviour that follows has a knock-on effect. If the young person can understand the process then we have found that this has aided a smoother relinquishing of the attachment. The transition process becomes more understandable.'

'Say they will miss the young person but that their achievements stand out.'

'Managed endings are preferable, but if the young person cannot stand the thought of leaving I have known them not to return to the final festivities. We write and invite them to pop back and say hello or goodbye.'

'We have also found group work around endings is useful; mentors and mentees have at times invited a member of the staff to go for tea or something. This helps to facilitate the ending.'

'With a CEO of a railway company, we agreed a year's engagement – and he wanted two! At the end of that, we parted as old friends, both having moved on.'

'Wind-up was a warm handshake to welcome the mentee into membership, meeting the shared expectation of when the relationship would end. The mentor remained an adviser, with an "open door", but in practice there was only limited contact after that.'

'Ended on a good note: the mentor assured me I could make an appointment with her any time and discuss any issue.'

'Contract clear and work within it.'

'Clear parameters, expectations, ground rules established at outset; knowing the duration gave a greater sense of urgency.'

'Worked on ending and wanted to achieve as much as possible in the last three months, so he would be ready to "fly" on his own.'

COMMENTS ON GOOD EXPERIENCES OF WINDING DOWN

'There is a sadness when the relationship ends, even if it continues in another form.'

'Mentee is someone I can test out ideas upon – and she still tests them out on me. Maybe this is a gender thing?!'

'At first mentor did not want to let go and was jealous of my success but the relationship has evolved into friendship and we respect the different strengths that we both have.'

'In informal relationships in business I don't think there is necessarily any end point, nor should there be: the mentor remains as a touchstone/reality check/inspirer even when the frequency of contact lessens.'

'Both content with an informal keep-in-touch relationship.'

'Never felt it ended per se, always felt I could call if I wanted.'

'Employee left but continued to keep in touch by e-mail. I tried to maintain the relationship by providing helpful feedback, questions and ideas. As demands grew for him the exchanges reduced, but there have recently been updates, spurred by a desire to keep me informed, a wish to use me as a reference, and perhaps because he finds my responses useful.'

COMMENTS ON GOOD EXPERIENCES WHICH CANNOT BE CLASSIFIED AS WINDING UP OR DOWN

'Some just seem to keep going and not have a defined end.'

'Ending due to values-related issues.'

'In my experience a mentoring relationship seldom ends.'

'In my own experience, mentoring relationships don't end, they evolve into supportive co-mentoring forms, the relationship of equals able to help and support each other as part of a network.'

'Mentors often find endings difficult; at times I have had to discuss this with the mentor before the ending.'

'The mentee not only developed self-reliance but went on to be a mentor.'

'It hasn't ended – we discussed termination and decided we both benefited and wanted to continue.'

'The relationship and trust turned into a strong bond between us, and now we have become very good friends. She has become a stronger person and more self-reliant and confident, but there were always new issues arising where she still wants to discuss the options.'

COMMENTS ON BAD EXPERIENCES OF WINDING UP

'When mentee's independence is jeopardized by corruption or red tape.'

'Mentors left in limbo.'

'Unwillingness (embarrassment?) on the part of mentees to actively end the relationship.'

'Interference (jumping in) by the mentor when the mentee can't articulate self.'

'When chief executive disapproves of senior managers "wasting time" or "passing on secrets", winding up can be painful and almost traumatic!'

'Not sure it would help to discuss the idea at the outset, maybe once we had become comfortable with each other.'

'My mentor has left/moved/been promoted.'

'Often when a mentor relationship ends it reminds the young person of other "unfinished" traumatic endings. The young person acts out, trying hard to prevent the ending, thus the hurt.'

'Mentee became obsessed with the detail of her development plan. I became resentful and felt undervalued at her constant changing, often at very short notice. I think I was over-accommodating; although I fed back it was not early enough, so I sensed a lack of trust. This meant that I held back, which I think led to a lack of trust. The relationship felt rather brittle; she said she found me rather cool; the ending (for both, I think) was a bit of a relief.'

COMMENTS ON BAD EXPERIENCES OF WINDING DOWN

'Arise from overburdened mentors.'

'Arise from over-ambitious expectations.'

'Becoming over-busy and not finding the time.'

'Lack of common purpose established means no conclusion can be reached.'

'Because of difficulties in fitting in, mentee carried on, but never formally ended, so often seeks me out and I think, "Not again, I really don't want to prop up this person forever." I'd feel I was letting mentee down if I didn't make time for them.'

'Assumptions made by the mentor not checked, assuming high level of intelligence of mentee, owing to his purported understanding.'

'Awkwardness as neither party wanted to make the other feel unwanted.'

'Tend to rather fade out than come to an agreed end.'

'Mentee has resisted moving on and develops a dependency upon the relationship and continues to seek it.'

'Even though one can look back and appreciate the ability to move onward and upward, there is a need for a deliberate ending rather than a drifting away.'

'Blurs into ongoing counselling relationship – this is an insidious process – mentor is at risk of becoming involved in advising and counselling in all areas of personal and professional progress, so dissolution is seen as an affront.'

'Very painful, mentee is close colleague, now uses every excuse to avoid discussion or a "completion" or "closure" or divorce. How it is ending without mutual assent is the problem. There are gender issues here. We have damaged each other in a recent project where he failed to deliver and I got very angry and spoke my mind. I have to wonder how far mentors can be friends when mentoring is at best a temporary engagement between two people and one apparently stops caring… His excuses of "I am too busy to talk" are wearing very thin and my need to talk is getting more urgent. He is telling me in writing not face to face that he does not feel it would be healthy to talk just yet. His inability to engage with trying to sort out the current impasse is becoming fossilized into an unwillingness to even try. When I tried to talk to him he turned deep magenta. I think that he is exercising silence as a means of control. My feeling is that the mentoring relationship broke down when I was in a position to challenge head-on – I suspect that he saw my mentoring as "subservience" to his needs – and that is not how I saw or see it.'

'Competence-based mentoring sounds safer, but when the personal in the relationship folds, even that is under pressure.'

'An uncomfortable end where the mentee leant rather heavily on me and because she was young and female, my wife became irritable about the frequent phone calls… Frequent assurances from me that the relationship was strictly professional did not assuage the anxiety of my wife and in the end I became increasingly cold (and probably unhelpful too) whenever my mentee called. Instead of talking to my mentee and explaining the situation I fudged the issue and eventually she stopped calling and the relationship ended. I met her months afterwards and she was friendly enough and said how I had helped her, but I still avoided the issue, and only apologized that I did not continue the mentoring because I was busy. I hope that I would find a more honest and forthright approach to this problem in the future – three of us lost out.'

'A senior executive said that he would ring to arrange another appointment, and I knew that he wouldn't. We hadn't got on the same wavelength and neither of us had been brave enough to discuss the key issue, which was our relationship and chemistry.'

'The relationship fizzled out – it was meant to be for a finite period but usually ran over and then "petered out"… Both mentor and mentee felt uncomfortable and not sure about a good way of closing.'

'As mentor I felt uncomfortable because I wanted to keep in touch with the successes and felt an ongoing responsibility in the case of the less successful ones. The mentees wanted to keep their options open including continuing access to the mentor – just in case.'

'Faded away; meetings became more difficult to schedule and regular ones were cancelled.'

'I didn't really realize it ended but it dawned on me one day that I hadn't heard from him in a very long time – which also means that I did not contact him either.'

'Due to lack of availability and other issues in our lives we gradually drifted apart.'

'She was so quiet and shy that she always found our meetings awkward; she would never say much or telephone me; I felt as though I was constantly trying to keep things going. At the end of a year I moved and was quite relieved about this.'

'There was no formal structure and it drifted. It was a bit like breaking up, when one party loses interest and does not communicate it.'

'Relationships that peter out and no one really knows what happened.'

'Those we have to guide to ensure they do not get too attached.'

COMMENTS ON BAD EXPERIENCES WHICH CANNOT BE CLASSIFIED AS WINDING UP OR DOWN

'Some young people will avoid this due to feelings that it may evoke.'

'One side or the other disappointed and feels let down (didn't land me the job; insufficiently available; abused trust I placed in you).'

'A third way that mentoring ends is when it is funded by a third party, and may stop suddenly.'

'Mentee was not of a mind to consider the lateral thinking required to change his perspective.'

COMMENTS ON GOOD PRACTICE

'Briefing on how to end well.'

'Get together to review, provide feedback to the partner and celebrate.'

'See each relationship as just one of a series through life.'

'"Without prejudice" agreement from start to let each other out of the relationship if needed.'

'Agree triggers for invoking early discussion about the need for an ending.'

'Ground rules very clearly established right up front.'

'Having a regular schedule through to the end.'

'Co-ordinator ensures parties aware when endings are approaching, and encourages winding down.'

'Inform parties that continuation will be outside support or supervision of the scheme.'

'Initial training on stages, so ending (including approximate date) is kept in mind throughout.'

'Reflect during training about what is important at end – celebrating, support networks, emotions.'

'Reflect on and evaluate the relationship.'

'Discuss formal length at start, set schedule and objectives and work through till achieved.'

'Parties need to be aware of how the relationship is likely to develop.'

'Continually check that expectations of both sides are similar.'

'Good reasons for ending should be part of initial conversations – needs competence in having good conversations.'

'Relationships organized for a certain period so "organized winding up" has no particular social dynamic.'

'Stay objective and use non-prescriptive counselling methods to direct the mentee to appropriate practitioners to assist with personal/self-development as opposed to professional development.'

'Clear understanding of what is expected; focus upon what they intend to achieve in the relationship.'

'Periodic meetings to monitor progress.'

'Put a time frame together to satisfy the objectives.'

'Agreeing up front how to end saves any possible embarrassment further down the line.'

'Meet with the mentee initially to sort out the relationship contract, also talk about the ending process. That way everyone goes in with their eyes open. Set goals and realistic expectations.'

'At the beginning discuss how it might come to an end, and how both parties would like to deal with that, when it happens.'

'Conclude after a year because then other mentees get the opportunity to choose the mentor for themselves – and mentees can become mentors for others.'

'Find a way for mentees to thank and appreciate mentors, usually with a small gift (sometimes straight, sometimes wild, depending upon the culture of the organization).'

'Formal closure meeting and celebration discussing "what went well; was the programme what you expected; advice for future mentees or mentors".'

'Officially conclude the programme and release participants from their formal commitment.'

'A learning contract is essential – once achieved between the learner, the mentor and the line manager, then an assessment and evaluation process can be invoked, including milestones/timetabled reviews.'

'Clearly articulate that mentoring in the professional context relates to work methods and career development, which might extend to attitude and demeanour but never to personal counselling.'

'Discussing the phases of the mentoring process and what is expected of both parties on inception – goals of the relationship, milestones of mentee's professional and career development, boundaries, expectations and rights.'

'Discussion about the next stage is key, mentors and young people who have a positive relationship will happily discuss the next step for both parties.'

'Have an agreed "wind-down process".'

'Marking the end with a special event – a graduation ceremony where mentors and young people celebrate what they have achieved together.'

'Recognizing the relationship's value by talking about the benefits and talking about things that have been learnt.'

'Relationships that end well are planned well; there is no surprise to the ending; there is an agreement at the outset as to what is expected in terms of content and time frame.'

'Reviewing progress and open discussion are important in preparing to end.'

'Clear expectation at the beginning of the contract, covering objectives, times of meeting, contact between meeting, reviews and what to do if either party feels it is changing or not working.'

'Clear, time-bounded objective to review and close the initial relationship as soon as the mentee is showing they have taken personal responsibility for their own development.'

'"Mentoring contract" should include agreement that the mentor and mentee will discuss and plan for the future of the relationship before it winds down or ends.'

'Options should include a realistic acceptance that the relationship, in spite of both parties' best intentions, may in fact end or just peter out.'

'The ideal is that the (non-mentoring) relationship continues as a friendship, or even as a "buddying" relationship.'

'The time-limited nature of the relationship should be clear up front along with the time frame.'

'Agreeing a "win–win" agreement at the start, the final part of which is "consequences" – of success and of the relationship not working. By discussing both outcomes up front, I have never had a challenge with ending any relationship or continuing it for that matter.'

'Have a clear objective or time limit, explained to parties.'

'Monitor the relationships, and intervene in cases of bad wind-down.'

'Mentor training workshop.'

'Review and feedback.'

'Roles and criteria for continuance should be mutually agreed at the outset; scheme issue guidance on these issues.'

'A plan for a wrap-up meeting and evaluation with some "quick options" on how to continue informally.'

'Check regularly to see if both partners are getting something out of it.'

'Discuss duration at first session.'

'Discuss early in the partnership so both parties know what the expectations are.'

'Discuss possible scenarios that would indicate it was time to end; then check in once in a while to see where things stand.'

'Have an understanding of the transition but not until you know more about each other.'

'Scheduled review on a periodic basis.'

'After verbal review, celebration, feedback; leave a brief written evaluation.'

'Always work to a contract which is agreed at the outset; be firm on boundaries.'

'Attend to what is going on in the relationship between us, rather than just ploughing through their development plan. This leads to a more robust relationship and a better ending.'

'Work through a personal development plan; towards the end we review, and mentee drafts the next stage, leaving them with a structure for their own development. This signals the end of one phase and the beginning of the next.'

'Rules set at the beginning about confidentiality, what is expected of both parties and that the relationship ends when the issue has been resolved, unless both agree it should continue for another issue.'

'Have formal closure to enable people to release from formal obligations.'

'A contract should be established.'

'The duration of the relationship is critical – it can be reviewed and extended to suit.'

'From induction remember the relationship has a beginning, middle and end; milestones are time-limited.'

'Most important data in preparing for wind-down is the baseline- or goal- setting written work done at the beginning of the relationship.'

'Review progress a third of the time from the end.'

ANALYSIS

This data set has been provided in a very full state because readers may want to analyse it for their own purposes. However, for the purposes of this chapter our analysis will focus on the approaches to endings. We will examine the three biggest categories from the data set above. It is interesting to note that these are 'comments on good experineces of winding up', 'comments on bad experiences of winding down' and 'comments on good practice'. The latter is not surprising because of the roles of our respondents – many were scheme organizers or professional mentors so not surprisingly their thoughts turn readily to good practice. In total, 27 out of 44 respondents had something substantial to say about this aspect. We were interested to see that 23 had an offering on good experiences of winding up, whereas only 6 had good experiences of winding down. By contrast 19 had bad experiences of winding down and only 7 had bad experiences of winding up. Winding up is seen as coming to a good, clear end, whereas winding down is seen as inconclusive and unresolved. This is interesting, because this was not the only possibility. A case could be made for winding down being an appropriate ending for a relationship designed to foster a gradual weaning and the building of independence on the part of the mentee. Winding up can be seen as violating the closeness and relationship that has been built. The 'minority' categories give some instructive examples of such practices.

Returning to our three main approaches to endings, these are repeated here as a reminder:

- *Psychodynamic*: where endings are seen to evoke older and unresolved difficulties which must either be *worked through* in the service of growth, or *worked round* in order to function reasonably.
- *Pragmatic*: where designers of schemes or skilled mentors can follow practices which either *eliminate* or at least *mitigate* the effects of any difficulties with endings that either party to the relationship might feel.
- *Organizational*: where the relationship is influenced by the context in which it operates and parties are subject to forces outside themselves (and indeed the scheme of which their relationship may be a part), which *determine the outcome* or *precipitate the ending*.

ANALYSIS OF COMMENTS ON GOOD EXPERIENCES OF WINDING UP

Of the 23 respondents with a good story of winding up, we categorized 2 as psychodynamic, 19 as pragmatic and 3 as organizational (one case fell into two categories). The psychodynamic cases emphasize the effect of the end point on the dynamism in the relationship, and the need to work through hurt and a disruptive response leading to relinquishing of attachment. The organizational cases speak of negotiated periods, natural ends and negotiated handovers. Features repeated more than once among the pragmatic accounts include:

- leaving the door open for further contact
- agreed objectives at the start
- an agreed time frame at the start
- starting with 'the end in mind' (Covey)
- sticking to a contract
- meeting clear objectives

- checking progress
- gradual
- a good ending in session
- an awards ceremony acknowledging transition.

ANALYSIS OF COMMENTS ON BAD EXPERIENCES OF WINDING DOWN

In the bad experiences there seem to be more examples of people (8) calling upon psychodynamic interpretations than in the good experiences. It is unclear whether this is because psychodynamic interpretations engender bad experiences or whether bad experiences leave us reaching for our psychopathology textbooks. We feel a strong respect, however, for the psychodynamic perspective, because those holding it seem to look deeper into what is going on than the somewhat brusque approach often adopted by the pragmatists.

The concerns of the psychodynamic cases include:

- dependency on the part of the mentee or mutual learning partner
- unwillingness to face making the other feel unwanted
- dissolution seen as an affront
- gender dynamics led male mentee to see female mentor as subservient – she wasn't
- male mentor's wife suspicious of female mentee's dependency
- 'breaking up is hard to do'
- addressing over-attachment.

These contrast quite sharply with those of the 13 pragmatists:

- over-burdened mentors
- over-ambitious expectations
- lack of common purpose, mentor kept it going
- assumptions not checked, lack of bravery in facing relationship issues
- fading out, and not discussing it.

Fading out without discussion was the most frequently cited negative experience.

There was only one organizational case. This focused on availability.

ANALYSIS OF COMMENTS ON GOOD PRACTICE

The 27 cases that commented on good practice were nearly all pragmatic in approach. All, except three, did not seem to countenance the possibly of failure. These two suggested that provision for failure should be made.

Pragmatic guidance includes:

- brief on how to end well
- discuss length and schedule
- explain stages in relationship either at start or once relationship established
- set relationship/learning contract
- agree limits of relationship
- explain ending process

- set objectives
- allow for failure and easy exit
- agree triggers that evoke an ending discussion
- advise parties of approaching end
- check if objectives are shared
- periodic review and reflection on relationship – attend to what is going on
- agree when objectives are achieved
- roles and criteria for continuation agreed
- final review – provide feedback and review/celebrate achievements and learning
- provide means for mentee to thank mentor
- see relationship as just one of a series
- discuss next stage in mentee's development
- advise that continuation is outside scheme.

SOME CONCLUSIONS ON MENTOR SKILLS AND COMPETENCES IN RELATIONSHIP CLOSURE

Our data do not indicate that there is only one way to bring a mentoring relationship to a successful ending. However, they do suggest that the mentor needs to:

- *prepare the mentee for the fact that endings can and probably will occur, as the relationship fulfils its purpose*. Many of the respondents referred to the importance of agreeing expectations at the start, setting a formal end date (even if that is subsequently postponed) and preparing the mentee mentally for the break. One talks of a 'realistic expectation that winding up or winding down may occur – and acceptance of both as possibilities'. Another says that having a formal end point 'adds dynamism to the relationship'.
- *recognize when a relationship is maturing* (especially when there is not an externally imposed 'sell-by' date). This requires sensitivity on the part of the mentor to the changes within the mentee and the quality and quantity of the learning exchange. However, these factors on their own may not be evidence enough that it is time to disengage. Relationships, in our field experience, often go through patches of low activity as the mentee concentrates on other issues or falls between peaks of learning need. Moreover, relationships that lack sufficient mutual challenge may peter out before they achieve their potential – and this is down to the competence of both parties in maintaining motivation and interest. Intuition, observation and open dialogue provide the clues as to which stage the relationship has reached. Some relevant quotes from our study: 'If I sense a lack of energy on the part of the mentee, I bring it into the open'; 'Preparation for the end is easier, if the mentor is truly listening'; 'A progression of new issues may keep the relationship going'.
- *review the relationship regularly.* In this way, the 'maturity review' is less daunting for both parties. The mentor can also use this opportunity to reflect, learn and improve their practice for future relationships. One respondent talks of having a 'formal discussion to signal the end of formal and beginning of informal mentoring'.

If there is a need to close down the formal relationship, the mentor should have the skills to:

- *assist the mentee to accept and embrace the ending process.* Recognizing the benefits of an empowered ending may help manage the process of grieving, in some cases.
- *develop a clear, mutual understanding of what has been achieved and how the relationship should now evolve.* One mentor shares with each mentee at the end a log of the progress that has been made. Other respondents talk about moving into 'supportive co-mentoring'; of 'leaving the mentee with a continuing structure for their own development' and 'the need to identify support networks for the mentee once the relationship has ended'.
- *make the ending point clear.* Some mentoring pairs symbolize the transition, with a celebratory meal, or even just a card. (Examples we have encountered elsewhere include giving each other a 'diploma' and floating paper boats down the river – each holding a candle – as a kind of Viking funeral for the relationship.)

THE ENDING OF A CHAPTER...

There can be no 'correct' way of dealing with endings. It depends upon the perspective that you take to the issue. These views are not competing – a feature of management thinking that has exasperated 'guru' researchers among others (Huckzynski, 1993) – they are incommensurable. Within each approach to endings there is no uniformity of perspective. How the dynamics recognized within the approach are addressed is again a contentious issue. However, there comes a point of subdivision, where a coherent story can emerge. At this level of analysis there is a community of practice (Lave and Wenger, 1991) that can create an agreed story about how to address the issue of endings. These agreed stories, while not approximating to 'the truth' about endings in mentoring, do represent 'a truth' about the phenomenon. These truths are levers for determining good practice within specified communities of practice, and serve not only to guide the perplexed, but also to create the reality that they serve.

16 What have we learned from this book?

GILL LANE and DAVID CLUTTERBUCK

What lessons can we learn from the different perspectives covered within this book? The chapters have shown a range of research projects that together look at the complex issue of the skills and competences that make for effective mentoring. It is not designed to be the final word, more an introduction to the arena of mentor competence and an invitation to others to continue the research – both empirical and practical – into the more detailed competence aspects.

Nor do we seek to amalgamate all the topics covered. It has been impossible to draw up a single table of key competences for effective mentors from the pages of this very diverse text. Although what emerges is recognition that the writers have approached the topic from a number of differing angles, it has been possible to capture the key themes in a generic model of mentoring competence (Figure 16.1).

THE UNIFYING MODEL

Each author has shown key competences which they consider relate to mentoring effectiveness. In simple terms the 'doing' type competences – the functions which mentors perform – emphasize the managing of the relationship and the transfer of knowledge from the mentor to the mentee. Mentors have to take into account the context and adapt the approaches to suit each individual. The 'doing' type competences are balanced by the 'being' type competences. These recognize the personal characteristics that make for effective mentoring and much of the mentor's background experience in career, in people management and in helping others to develop comes into play with the experience they offer to the mentee. An awareness of the ethics within which mentoring takes place is paramount.

HOW DOES THE MODEL RELATE TO THE KEY COMPETENCES OUTLINED IN THE CHAPTERS?

Each chapter provides an indication of the main competences that its author considers to be the key to mentor effectiveness, and we can see how they fit into the generic model.

Within Lane's literature review (Chapter 1) both the 'doing' type competences and the 'being' type competences are found in abundance. It is easy to spot the different ones. 'Doing'

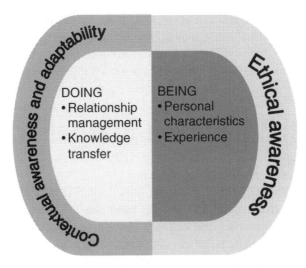

Figure 16.1 A generic model of mentoring competence

type competences include helping and supporting functions; acting as guide, tutor, coach and confidant; giving advice and direction; and so the list continues. Given the number mentioned in that chapter it would be inappropriate to take up this last chapter to record them all. Lane's mention of 'being' type competences from the literature is a shorter list, including such attributes as being trustworthy, commanding respect, being non-judgemental and being empathetic, to mention but a few. Suffice to say that the literature on mentoring is full of the nuances of the two main competence areas as depicted in the generic model. Clutterbuck brings this model into his process of mentoring, with specific competences for each of his five phases of mentoring (Chapter 4).

Lane's mix of functional competence (the 'doing' type) and personal competence (the 'being' type) within her research (Chapter 5) underpins the generic model. From acting as a sounding board within the 'doing' type competences to being empathetic within the 'being' type competences, we have the split of competences as depicted within the generic model. As her research depicted a fairly even ratio of basic 'doing' competences to 'being' competences, we have shown the generic model as a model of two equally sized halves.

In Engstrom and Lankau's work on personality factors and mentoring outcomes (Chapter 12) the authors give a key place to good communication skills within the 'doing' type arena along with the mentor making use of their own knowledge. They give many examples of other 'doing' type competences such as high self-esteem, internal locus of control, altruism plus a high degree of extraversion and emotional stability.

The stages of the mentoring relationship bring into focus the need for differing competences, as Clutterbuck outlines with the building of rapport on the 'doing' side of the model and the setting of direction on the 'being' side. The function of challenging within the progression stage is equally matched by the characteristic of understanding, and so we can see examples of the differing competences displayed in the generic model coming through at each stage of the mentoring process.

Borredon and Ingham again endorse the generic model by quoting examples of the competence of responding to mentees' needs amongst the 'doing' type competences, plus confronting assumptions, along with many others (Chapter 10). Courage is their key 'being' competence underpinning all the functional approaches. They also mention the importance of building and strengthening relationships, a key component of the 'doing' side of the model.

A new model of mentoring, integrating concepts drawn from attachment theory, was proposed by Scandura and Pelligrini (Chapter 7), who recognize that individuals seek stability and security within relationships, thus endorsing the 'being' type competences of the model. Functional mentoring – the 'doing' side of the model – was most likely to occur within the 'interdependence (secure attachment)' concept.

Darwin's study (Chapter 3), where mentees were invited to describe the attributes of a significant person who had helped them develop, gives rise to the listing of a host of 'being' type competences fitting with the generic model, where experience is the key to the maturity behind the myriad characteristics Darwin outlines. We have to acknowledge that she also provides us with a list of the 'being' type competences that are – in her terms – volatile but from which mentees learn how not to operate! Darwin gives us a specific reference to differing emphasis based on gender difference which the generic model at present does not capture.

Coaching psychology requires the key 'doing' competences such as facilitating purposeful change and the 'being' type competences such as psychological-mindedness, plus self-regulation and reflection. Grant (Chapter 9) endorses the generic model by referring to the contextual and adaptability elements where mentors should manage change within their mentees by working differently with them at the different stages of the mentees' change process, duly allowing for individuality.

Garvey (Chapter 14) brings us an endorsement of the ethical argument around mentoring, with reference to gender issues, which fit with the 'being' side of the generic model. He endorses the 'doing' side with reference to relationship management, along with many competences on both sides of the model. He tells us that differing pressures arose in the differing contexts giving strength to the contextual awareness element of the model. 'Doing' type competences include not pushing your own agenda as a mentor and not dominating the discussion. 'Being' type characteristics include empathy, along with genuineness and having a flexible attitude.

Winding up a relationship as a positive proactive approach, compared to winding down as a reactive negative approach, from Clutterbuck and Megginson demonstrates the active functional 'doing' type competences (Chapter 15). These include, amongst other functional approaches, recognizing that the relationship is coming to an end, providing feedback and celebrating.

Megginson and Stokes (Chapter 8) tell us that a framework for building mentor competence would best be an amalgam of skills, business case development and the mentor consciously seeking their own direction but including the contextual aspect. This fits well with the generic model, and we read of such competences as building rapport within the 'doing' arena and the ability to suspend judgement within the 'being' arena. Consciousness is a key 'being' type competence that they mention.

The generic model shows ethical awareness, and Gibb provides this with his chapter on moral issues (Chapter 2). Gibb also refers to contextual awareness, and provides a number of examples of 'doing' type functions such as participation in political games, along with a smaller number of 'being' type competences such as awareness of power sources.

The storytelling approach is a delight and one which hopefully every mentor can identify with, fitting again into the generic model, although most emphasis is placed on 'doing' type competences within the contextual framework and the need for adaptability (Chapter 11). These competences include being able to break down parts of the story to help the mentee to see how similar situations can help, along with other functional approaches. The key 'being' type competence is that of being willing to expose one's own weaknesses and mistakes.

Whilst the generic model captures mentor competence, Clutterbuck reminds us that it 'takes two to tango' (Chapter 6). His comments on mentee competences include reference to 'doing' competences such as engaging in constructive dialogue, although this also translates into the 'being' competence of being willing to engage in that dialogue. Capturing the mentor's interest is included in the list of 'doing' competences together with examining one's own motives and drives. Being willing to take the initiative plus being self-motivated, self-reliant and appreciative are just some of the personal characteristics or 'being' type competences that Clutterbuck suggests the mentee requires.

Virtual mentoring, researched by Ferguson and Yan Lu (Chapter 13), places the contextual awareness aspect of the generic model into greater focus. The contextual awareness and adaptability become more noted and apparent. What is interesting for the links with the model is that the 'doing' type competences tell us the pitfalls of the virtual methodology. There is less impact as a sponsor, there is a need to protect only by supportive images, it is harder to coach, there is a need to give prompt feedback and it is difficult to develop rapport. The 'being' type competences show that in the virtual approach the mentor lacks visibility and the opportunity to be a sufficient role model whilst having to be able to communicate trust and openness.

The generic model gives us the important recognition split between 'doing' and 'being' type competences that abound in this book. It allows the context and need for adaptability to be evident and provides us with the ethical dimension.

Some implications and emergent questions are clear.

IMPLICATIONS FOR PROFESSIONAL MENTORS

For those working as professional mentors, whether in-company or externally contracted, the mix of competences that will help to make them more effective as mentors does matter. It is pointless putting time and energy into a mentoring relationship if it ends up being ineffective for the mentee.

If mentors are to be effective, they need to be able to adjust their approach to meet the differing situations within which their mentees operate, so bringing a tailored approach that is individual to the needs of that mentee in their particular circumstances. Given the situation-specific context of mentoring, the mentor needs to use different competences but also to bring a different emphasis dependent on the mentee's need at that time.

The mix of differing competences as shown in this book shows that mentors need to be conversant with a wide range of functional competences and have most if not all the relevant personal competences.

With the global dimension and improvements in technology, mentors need to be able to adjust their methodology according to whether they are practising virtual or face-to-face mentoring, or indeed a mixture of both methods.

Mentees have expectations of a mentoring relationship and mentors need to show greater sensitivity to what methods and techniques works best and when to use these, taking into account the differences between their individual mentees.

The mentor can use the detail from the various research approaches to hone their skills in relation to functional and behavioural approaches. They also need to include skills relevant to the moral issues, the storytelling approach and the mentee needs, and to consider what skills are not applicable in a mentoring capacity. The skills required of a virtual mentor should not be overlooked with the increasing role of that methodology.

Consideration should be given to ongoing self-development by the mentor attempting to keep up to date with advances coming out of such research as contained within this text, together with other ongoing research into any aspect of mentoring. This requires the mentor to remain widely read and to actively seek details of advances in the field, which will inevitably bring with it a raised awareness of mentor and mentee competences. Perhaps the mentor can be encouraged to do their own self-assessment against emerging effective competence measures?

Finally, the mentor needs to adequately prepare mentees for their involvement in the mentoring relationship, and that may include helping the mentee to develop appropriate mentee competence.

Mentors can ask themselves how they can continue to improve their own performance in helping their mentees develop.

IMPLICATIONS FOR MENTEES

Mentees should be encouraged to consider what range of mentee competences they possess, so that they can adequately prepare for their involvement in the mentoring relationship, be ready for it and work at it, rather than letting it happen 'to' them! Given that most mentees attending any training events in respect of potential mentoring are usually told what to expect from their mentor, rather than what they themselves should personally contribute, mentors may need to help them prepare more thoroughly.

In addition, mentees need some knowledge and understanding of mentor and mentee competences, together with the stages of mentoring and the contextual and situational aspects. All these will allow them to more easily judge what is right for them, and their development, at any one time.

Mentees can ask themselves the following questions:

- What do I know about mentoring generally?
- What do I know about mentoring competence in particular?
- What do I expect of a mentor?
- What does my mentor expect of me?
- What do I expect of myself as a mentee?
- What differing aspects of context and my individual situation affect the mentoring that I may expect?
- What can I learn about learning?
- How can I become a more effective mentee?
- What can I learn from my mentor that will make me an effective mentor in turn?

IMPLICATIONS FOR ACADEMICS

Academics interested in mentoring, from any viewpoint, look for a solid base of research. This text brings them a range of research from a number of countries and from a wide range of perspectives, and may thus influence any future research agenda.

There is a need for more research to go into the deeper competence levels such as those that are psychological, situational, time-phased and contextual. Whilst this text gives research examples of some contextual and situational competences, there is more that can be researched into these specifics. In addition, the underpinning detailed competences need further exploration. The development of instruments for assessment and self-assessment would be a natural progression.

MENTOR COMPETENCE VERSUS MENTEE COMPETENCE

Mentoring is a consensual, interactive and independent activity, where both parties can influence the process and the outcomes by their behaviour and their attitudes. The emphasis in the research literature on skills and characteristics of the mentor has created a very biased picture of the relationship dynamics. To some extent, this is the result of an implicit assumption, primarily in US-generated research, that the skills and behaviours of the mentor are more important than those of the mentee – an assumption for which we can find no substantive evidence.

The interaction between mentor and mentee implies a second order of competence – a mutual competence that encompasses the ability to get the best out of the relationship and each other. The quality of the relationship depends, we propose, on how well mentor and mentee synchronize the behaviours.

One way we have considered of measuring this mutual competence concerns the depth to which the process of dialogue reaches. We have identified seven potential layers of dialogue, as follows:

- *Social dialogue* is about developing friendship and providing support/encouragement.
- *Technical dialogue* meets the mentee's needs for learning about work processes, policies and systems.
- *Tactical dialogue* helps the mentee work out practical ways of dealing with issues in their work or personal life (for example, managing time or dealing with a difficult colleague).
- *Strategic dialogue* takes the broader perspective, helping the mentee to put problems, opportunities and ambitions into context (for example, putting together a career development plan) and envision what they want to achieve through the relationship and through their own endeavours.
- *Dialogue for self-insight* enables the mentee to understand their own drives, ambitions, fears and thinking patterns, and is a critical precursor to...
- *Dialogue for behavioural change*, which allows the mentee to meld insight, strategy and tactics into a coherent programme of personal adaptation.
- *Integrative dialogue* helps the mentee develop a clearer sense of who they are, what they contribute and how they fit in. It enables the mentee to gain a clearer sense of self and the world around them; to develop greater balance in their life; and to resolve inner conflict. It explores personal meaning and a holistic approach to living.

While these are not seven steps to mentoring heaven, they do represent an increasing depth of reflection on the part of the mentee and a corresponding need for skills on the part of both parties. A single mentoring session might delve into several layers. In general, establishing dialogue at the social level assists dialogue at the technical level; technical dialogue can evolve into strategic; and so on up the ladder.

The exploration of this mutual competence, along with an increased understanding of how it is influenced by context, is in our view a research priority.

SUMMARY

So the generic level of competence is accepted in part, although it seems all-encompassing. The unifying model – the generic model of mentor competence presented earlier in this chapter – allows for the distinction between the 'doing' type competences and the 'being' type competences, set within the contextual and ethical frameworks in which mentors find themselves operating. There is no doubt that a more detailed contextual framework is called for.

The dominant theme of the book is the vast breadth of ways of understanding mentoring and what makes it work in differing circumstances. It is a powerful intervention because it is so complex but begs for greater knowledge by mentors and by mentees of the differing competence requirements to meet differing situations. Academics can help so far but the research requires practical case study investigation to make sense of the individuality of the situational dimension.

Bibliography

Ackley, B and Gall, MD (1992) Skills, strategies and outcomes of successful mentor teachers. Paper presented at the Annual Meeting of the American Educational Research Association (San Francisco, CA, April 20–24).

Ainsworth, MDS (1989) Attachments beyond infancy. *American Psychologist*, **44**: 709–716.

Ainsworth, MDS (1991) Attachments and other affectional bonds across the life cycle. In Parkes, CM, Hinde, JS and Marris, P (eds) *Attachment across the Life Cycle*. London: Routledge.

Ainsworth, MDS, Blehar, MC, Waters, E and Wall, S (1978) *Patterns of Attachment: A psychological study of the strange situation*. Hillsdale, NJ: Erlbaum.

Alleman, E (1982) Mentoring Relationships in Organisations: Behaviours, Personality Characteristics and Interpersonal Perceptions. Unpublished PhD Thesis: University of Akron, Ohio, USA.

Alleman, E (1989) Two planned mentoring programs that worked. *Mentoring International*, **3**: 6–12.

Alleman, E, Cochran, J, Doverspike, J and Newman I (1984) Enriching mentoring relationships. *The Personnel and Guidance Journal*, **62**(6): 329–32.

Allen, TD, Poteet, ML and Russell, JEA (2000) Protégé selection by mentors: what makes the difference? *Journal of Organizational Behavior*, **21**: 271–82.

Allen, TD, Poteet, ML, Russell, JEA and Dobbins, GH (1997) A field study of factors related to supervisors' willingness to mentor others. *Journal of Vocational Behavior*, **50**: 1–22.

Allport, GW and Odbert, HS (1936) Trait names: a psycho-lexical study. *Psychological Monographs*, **47**(211).

Almaas, AH (1986) *Essence: The diamond approach to inner realization*. York Beach, ME: Samuel Weiser Inc.

Alred, G, Garvey, B and Smith, R (1996) First person mentoring. *Career Development International*, **1**(5): 10–14.

Alred, G, Garvey, B and Smith, R (2002) *The Mentoring Pocket Book*. Alresford, Hampshire: Management Pocket Books.

Ambler, S (1994) Mentor ups success rate. *Computing Canada*, **20**(25): 48.

Ang, S and Cummings, LL (1994) Panel analysis of feedback-seeking patterns in face-to-face, computer-mediated, and computer-generated communication environments. *Perceptual and Motor Skills*, **79**(1): 67.

Antal, A (1993) Odysseus' legacy to management development: mentoring. *European Management Journal*, **11**(4): 448–54.

Argyris, C (1991) Teaching smart people to learn. *Harvard Business Review,* **May–June**: 99–109.

Argyris, C (1993) *Knowledge for Action*. San Francisco: Jossey-Bass Inc.

Argyris, C and Schön, DA (1978) *Organisational Learning: A theory of action perspective*. USA: Addison-Wesley.

Arnold, J (1997) *Managing Careers into the 21st Century*. London: Paul Chapman Publishing Limited.

Arnold, V and Davidson, MJ (1990) Adopt a mentor: the new way ahead for women managers? *Women in Management Preview and Abstracts*, **5**(1): 10–18.

Aryee, S, Chay, YW and Chew, J (1996a) The motivation to mentor among managerial employees: an interactionist approach. *Group and Organization Management*, **21**: 261–77.

Aryee, S, Wyatt, T and Stone, RJ (1996b) Early career outcomes of graduate employees: the effect of mentoring and ingratiation. *Journal of Management Studies*, **33**(1): 95–118.

Ashford, SJ and Black, JS (1996) Proactivity during organizational entry: the role of desire for control. *Journal of Applied Psychology*, **81**(2): 199–214.

Baird, J (1993) in Caldwell, BJ and Carter, EMA (eds) A personal perspective on mentoring *The Return of the Mentor: Strategies for workplace learning*. London: Falmer Press.

Baker-Miller, J (1991) The development of women's sense of self. In Jordan, JV, Kaplan, AG, Baker-Miller, J, Striver, IP and Surrey, JL (eds) *Women's Growth in Connection*. New York: Guilford Press, 11–27.

Bandura, A (1982) Self-efficacy mechanism in human agency. *American Psychologist*, **37**(2): 122–47.

Bargh, JA and Gollwitzer, PM (eds) (1996) *The Psychology of Action: Linking motivation and cognition to behavior.* New York: Guilford Press.

Bar-On, R and Handley, R (1999) *Optimizing People*. New Braunfels, TX: Pro-Philes Press.

Barnett, BG (1995) Developing reflection and expertise: can mentors make the difference? *Journal of Educational Administration*, **35**(5): 45–59.

Barrett, R (2002) Mentor supervision and development: exploration of lived experience. *Career Development International,* **7**(5): 279–83.

Barrick, MR and Mount, MK (1991) The big five personality dimensions and job performance: a meta analysis. *Personnel Psychology,* **44**: 1–25.

Barry, WR (1995) Total cost: total return. *Cost Engineering,* **37**(6): 4.

Bartholomew, K and Horowitz, LM (1991) Attachment styles among young adults: a test of a four-category model *Journal of Personality and Social Psychology,* **61**(2): 226–44.

Bartunek, JM and Kram, KE (1997) A group mentoring journey into the department chair role. *Journal of Management Inquiry,* **4**. Database: *Business Source Premier* 1–15.

Bateson, G (1971) *Steps to an Ecology of Mind.* Toronto: Ballentine Books.

Baugh, SG, Lankau, MJ and Scandura, TA (1996) An investigation of the effects of protégé gender on responses to mentoring. *Journal of Vocational Behavior,* **49**: 309–23.

Baugh, SG and Scandura, TA (1999) The effect of multiple mentors on protégé attitudes toward the work setting. *Journal of Social Behavior and Personality,* **14**: 503–22.

Bennett, R (1992) Developing people for real: some issues and approaches. *Journal of European and Industrial Training,* **16**(5): 3–9.

Bennetts, C (1995) Interpersonal aspects of informal mentor/learner relationships: a research perspective. Paper in proceedings of the European Mentoring Centre Conference.

Bennetts, C (1996) Mentor/Learner Relationships: A Research Perspective. Proceedings of "Making it Happen". Institute of Personnel and Development. Regional Conference, Torquay, pp. 7–14.

Bennetts, C (1998) Traditional mentor relationships: care, communication, creativity. Proceedings of the 5th European Mentoring Conference, AMED, Sheffield Business School.

Bennis, W (1989) *On becoming a leader.* New York: Addison-Wesley.

Bennis, W (1996) The leader as storyteller. *Harvard Business Review,* **74**(1) (Jan/Feb): 154–61.

Berman, WH and Sperling, MB (1994) The structure and function of adult attachment. In Sperling, MB and Berman, WH (eds) *Attachment in Adults: Clinical and developmental perspectives.* New York: Guilford Press.

Bettelheim, B (1991) *The Uses of Enchantment: The meaning and importance of fairy tales.* London: Penguin.

Bierema, LL and Merriam, SB (2002) E-mentoring: using computer mediated communication to enhance the mentoring process. *Innovative Higher Education,* **26**(3): 211–27.

Binik, YM, Cantor, J, Ochs, E and Meana, M (1997) From the couch to the keyboard: psychotherapy in cyberspace. In Kiesler, S (ed.) *Culture of the Internet.* Mahwah, NJ: Lawrence Erlbaum, 71–102.

Blase, J and Blase, J (2002) The micropolitics of instructional supervision: a call for research. *Educational Administration Quarterly,* **38**(1): 6–44.

Block, J (1995) A contrarian view of the five-factor approach to personality description. *Psychological Bulletin,* **117**(2) (March).

Blustein, DL, Prezioso, MS and Schultheiss, DP (1995) Attachment theory and career development: current status and future directions. *The Counseling Psychologist,* **23**(3): 416–32.

Bohm, D *On Dialogue.* David Bohm Seminars, Ojai.

Bolder, N (1990) Coping as a personality process: a prospective study. *Journal of Personality and Social Psychology,* **59**: 525–37.

Bordwin, M (1994) Containing Cupid's arrow. *Small Business Reports,* **19**(7), 53–8.

Borredon, L and Ingham, M (2002) Mentoring, dialogue and knowledge creation: the case of new product concepts at TECHNO. Paper at the 9th workshop on managerial and organisational cognition, Brussels (proceedings).

Bowen, DD (1985) Were men meant to mentor women? *Training and Development Journal,* **36**: 30–34.

Bowlby, J (1979) *The Making and Breaking of Affectional Bonds.* New York: Routledge.

Bowlby, J (1988) *A Secure Base: Parent–child attachment and healthy human development.* London: Routledge.

Boyatzis, RE (1982) *The Competent Manager.* New York: Wiley.

Bridges, W (1986) Managing organizational transitions. *Organizational Dynamics,* **15**(1): 24–33.

Briere, NM and Vallerand, RJ (1990) Effect of private self-consciousness and success outcome on causal dimensions. *Journal of Social Psychology,* **130**(3): 325–32.

Brown, CD (1993) Male/female mentoring: turning potential risks into rewards. *IEEE Transactions on Professional Communication,* **36**(4): 197–201.

Bulfinch, T (1979) *Myths of Greece and Rome.* New York: Viking Penguin Inc.

Bullis, C and Bach, BW (1989) Are mentoring relationships helping organisations? An exploration of developing mentee–mentor–organizational identifications using turning point analysis. *Communication Quarterly,* **37**: 199–213.

Bureau of National Affairs (1988) *Corporate Affairs: Nepotism, office romance, and sexual harassment.* Washington, DC: Bureau of National Affairs.

Burke, RJ (1984) Mentors in organizations. *Group Organization Studies*, **9**: 353–72.

Burke, RJ and McKeen, CA (1990) Mentoring in organizations: implications for women. *Journal of Business Ethics*, **9**: 317–32.

Burns, D (1989) *The Feeling Good Handbook*. London: Penguin.

Bush, A and Coleman, M (1995) Professional development for heads: the role of mentoring. *Journal of Educational Administration*, **33**(5): 60–73.

Caldwell, BJ and Carter, EMA (eds) (1993) *The Return of the Mentor: Strategies for workplace learning*. London: Falmer Press.

Campbell, J (1993) *The Hero with a Thousand Faces*. London: Fontana Press.

Candib, LB (1994) Reconsidering power in the clinical relationship. In Stringer, E and Milligan, M (eds) *The Empathic Practitioner*. New Brunswick, HJ: Rutgers University, 135–56.

Carden, AD (1990) Mentoring and adult career development: the evolution of a theory. *The Counselling Psychologist*, **18**(2): 275–99.

Carter, S (1994) *An Essential Guide to Mentoring*. Corby: IOM Foundation.

Carter, S and Lewis, G (1994) *The Four Bases of Mentoring: Perspectives on the selection and training of mentors*. Presentation to the Research Methodology Conference at Sheffield Business School 1994.

Caruso, R (1992) *Mentoring and the Business Environment: Asset or liability?* Aldershot: Dartmouth Publishing.

Caruso, R (1996) Who does mentoring: the pursuit of the dream. *Proceedings of the 3rd European Mentoring Conference*. Sheffield Hallam University.

Carver, CS (1996) Cognitive interference and the structure of behavior. In Sarason, IG and Pierce, GR (eds) *Cognitive Interference: Theories, methods, and findings*. The LEA series in personality and clinical psychology. Mahwah, NJ: Lawrence Erlbaum Associates, 25–45.

Carver, CS and Scheier, MF (1998) *On the Self-regulation of Behavior*. Cambridge University Press.

Chao, GT and O'Leary, AM (1990) How others see same and cross-gender mentoring. *Mentoring International*, **4**(3): 3–12.

Chesney, MA, Thurston, RC and Thomas, KA (2001) Creating social and public health environments to sustain behavior change: lessons from obesity research. In Schneiderman, N and Speers, MA (eds), *Integrating Behavioral and Social Sciences with Public Health*. Washington, DC: American Psychological Association.

Church, AH (1997) Managerial self-awareness in high-performing individuals in organizations. *Journal of Applied Psychology*, **82**(2): 281–92.

Clawson, JG (1985) Is mentoring necessary? *Training and Development Journal*, **39**(4): 36–9.

Clawson, JG (1996) Mentoring in the information age. *Leadership and Organization Development Journal*, **17**(3): 6–15.

Clawson, JG and Kram, KE (1984) Managing cross-gender mentoring. *Business Horizons*, **May–June**: 22–32.

Clutterbuck, D (1985) *Everyone Needs a Mentor: How to foster talent within the organisation*. London: Institute of Personnel Management.

Clutterbuck, D (1991) *Everyone Needs a Mentor*. (2e). London: Chartered Institute of Personnel and Development (IPD).

Clutterbuck, D (1998) *Learning Alliances: Tapping into talent*. London: Institute of Personnel and Development.

Clutterbuck, D (1999) *New Chances, New Horizons*. Video available from EMCC library www.mentoringcentre.org or the Greenwood Partnership – www.greenwood-partnership.com.

Clutterbuck D (2001) *Everyone Needs a Mentor: Fostering talent at work* (3e). London: CIPD.

Clutterbuck, D and Megginson, D (1999), *Mentoring Executives and Directors*. Oxford: Butterworth-Heinemann.

Clutterbuck, D and Megginson, D (2001) Winding up and winding down a mentoring relationship. Paper at the 8th European Mentoring Centre Conference, Cambridge.

Clutterbuck, D and Ragins, BR (2002) *Mentoring and Diversity: An international perspective*. Oxford: Butterworth-Heinemann.

Collier, RM (1957) Consciousness as a regulatory field: a theory of psychotherapy. *Journal of Abnormal and Social Psychology*, **55**: 275–82.

Colwell, E (1980) *Storytelling*. London: Bodley Head Ltd.

Conway, C (1995) Mentoring in the mainstream. *Management Development Review*, **8**(4): 27–9.

Conway, C (1998) *Strategies for Mentoring: A blueprint for successful organizational development*. Chichester: Wiley.

Costa, AC (2000) A matter of trust: effects on the performance and effectiveness of teams in organisations. Proefschrift, Katholieke Universiteit Brabant.

Costa, PT Jr and McCrae, RR (1988) From catalogue to classification: Murray's needs and the five-factor model. *Journal of Personality and Social Psychology*, **55**: 258–65.

Costa, PT Jr, Sommerfield, MR and McCrae, RR (1996) Personality and coping: a reconceptualization. In Zeidner, M and Endler, S (eds) *Handbook of Coping*. NY: John Wiley and Sons, Inc., 44–61.

Covalseki, MW, Dirsmith, MA, Heian, J and Samuel, S (1998) The calculated and the avowed: techniques of discipline and struggles over identity in Big Six public accounting firms. *Administrative Science Quarterly*, 43(2): 293–327.

Csikszentmihalyi, M (1990) *Flow: The psychology of optimal experience*. New York: Harper and Row.

Daloz, L (1986) *Effective Teaching and Mentoring: Realising the transformational power of adult learning experiences*. San Francisco: Jossey-Bass.

Daniels, TD and Logan, LL (1983) Communication in women's career development relationships. In Bostrum, RN (ed.) *Communication Yearbook*. Beverley Hills, CA: Sage, volume 7, 532–52.

Darwin, A (2000) Critical reflections on mentoring in work settings. *Adult Educational Quarterly*, 50(3): 197–211.

Davidhizar, R and Eshleman, J (1992) Co-dependency in the workplace. *Hospital Topics*, 70: 15–19.

de Maré, Piper, R, Thomson, S (1991) *Koinonia: From hate, through dialogue, to culture in the large group*. London: Karnac Books.

de Shazer, S (1988) *Clues: Investigating solutions in brief therapy*. New York: Norton and Co.

Dean, MR, Marlott, RW and Fulton, BJ (1983) The effects of self-management training on academic performance. *Teaching of Psychology*, 10: 77–81.

Development Processes Publications Ltd and Swansea College (1994) *Mentoring: The definitive workbook*. Manchester: Development Processes Publications Ltd.

Dewey, J (1958) *Experience and Nature*. New York: Dover Publications.

Doherty, K and Schlenker, BR (1991) Self-consciousness and strategic self-presentation. *Journal of Personality*, 59(1): 1–18.

Downey, M (1999) *Effective Coaching*. London: Orion.

Dreher, GF and Ash, RA (1990) A comparative study of mentoring among men and women in managerial, professional and technical positions. *Journal of Applied Psychology*, 75: 539–46.

Dreher, G and Cox, T (1996) Race, gender and opportunity: a study of compensation attainment and the establishment of mentoring relationships. *Journal of Applied Psychology*, 81: 297–308.

Eaton, J and Brown, D (2002) Coaching for change in Vodaphone. *Career Development International*, 7(5): 284–7.

Eby, LT (1997) Alternative forms in changing organizational environments: a conceptual extension of the mentoring literature. *Journal of Vocational Behavior*, 51: 124–44.

Eby, LT, McManus, SE, Simon, SA and Russell, JEA (2000) The protégé's perspective regarding negative mentoring experiences: the development of a taxonomy. *Journal of Vocational Behavior*, 57: 1–21.

Egan, G, (1993) The shadow side. *Management Today*, **September**: 33–8.

Egan, G (1994) *The Skilled Helper: A problem management approach to helping*. Pacific Grove, CA: Brooks and Cole.

Ellis, A and Harper, RA (1961) *A New Guide to Rational Living*. Englewood Cliffs, NJ: Prentice-Hall.

Engevik, H (1992) *Normative and ipsative approaches in the measurement of personality: A practical solution*. Psykologisk Institut, University of Oslo.

Engevik, H (1993) Big five på norsk. *Tidskrift for Norsk Psykologiforening*, 30: 884–896.

Engevik, H (1994) *Manual til 5pf. Oslo: ISV-test og*. Psykologisk Institut, University of Oslo.

English, P and Sutton, E (2000) Working with courage, fear and failure. *Career Development International*, 5(4–5): 211–15.

Engstrom, T and Mykletun, R (1999) Personality Factors Impact on Success in the Mentor-Protégé Relationship. Dissertation.

Enomoto, EK, Gardiner, ME and Grogan, M (2000) Notes to Athene: mentoring relationships for women of colour. *Urban Education*, 35(5): 567–83.

Ensher, E, Heun, C and Blanchard, A (2002) Online mentoring and computer-mediated communication: new directions in research. *Journal of Vocational Behavior*, 63(2): 242–63.

Equal Opportunities Review (1995) Mentoring: a positive action initiative for ethnic minorities. *Equal Opportunities Review*, 60: 11–15.

Erikson, E (1965) *Childhood and Society*. Harmondsworth, Middx: Penguin Books Ltd.

Eysenck, HJ (1947) *Dimensions of Personality*. London: Routledge and Kegan Paul.

Eysenck, HJ and Eysenck, MW (1985) *Personality and Individual Differences: A natural science approach*. New York and London: Plenum Press.

Ezzamel, M, Lilley, S and Wilmott, H (1993) Be wary of new waves. *Management Today*, **October**: 99–102.

Fagenson, EA (1988) The power of a mentor. *Groups and Organization Studies*, 13: 182–94.

Fagenson, EA (1989) The mentor advantage: perceived career/job experiences of protégés vs. non-protégés. *Journal of Organizational Behaviour*, 10: 309–20.

Fagenson, EA (1992) Mentoring: who needs it? A comparison of protégés' and non-protégés' needs for power, achievement, affiliation, and autonomy. *Journal of Vocational Behavior*, 41: 48–60.

Fagenson, EA (1994) Perceptions of protégés' vs non-protégés' relationships with their peers, superiors, and departments. *Journal of Vocational Behavior,* **45**(1).

Farren, C, Grey, J and Kaye, B (1984) Mentoring: a boon to career development. *Personnel,* **61**(6): 20–24.

Febbraro, GAR and Clum, GA (1998) Meta-analytic investigation of the effectiveness of self-regulatory components in the treatment of adult problem behaviors. *Clinical Psychology Review,* **18**(2): 143–61.

Feeney, JA, Noller, P and Hanrahan, M (1994) *Assessing adult attachment.* In Sperling, MB and Berman, WH (eds) *Attachment in adults: clinical and developmental perspectives.* New York: Guilford Press.

Feldman, DC (1999) Toxic mentors or toxic proteges? A critical re-examination of dysfunctional mentoring. *Human Resource Management Review,* **9**(3): 247–78.

Fenigstein, A, Scheier, MF and Buss, AH (1975) Public and private self-consciousness: assessment and theory. *Journal of Counseling and Clinical Psychology,* **43**(4): 522–7.

Ford, RC and McLaughlin, FS (1987) Should Cupid come to the workplace? An ASPA survey. *Personnel Administrator,* **32**(10): 100–10.

Forret, ML (1996) Issues facing organizations when implementing formal mentoring programmes. *Learning and Organizational Development Journal,* **17**(3): 27–30.

Fowler, A (1998) How to: mentoring guidelines. *People Management,* **October**: 48–50.

Fraley, RC, Waller, NG and Brennan, KA (2000) An item response theory analysis of self-report measures of adult attachment. *Journal of Personality and Social Psychology,* **78**: 350–65.

Franks, DD and Marolla, J (1976) Efficacious action and social approval as interacting dimensions of self-esteem: a tentative formulation through construct validation. *Sociometry,* **39**: 324–41.

Franzén, C and Jonsson, J (1993) *Mentorskap som metod och möjlighet.* Stockholm: Workingpaper Arbetsmiljöfonden.

Furnham, A (1992) *Personality at Work: The role of individual differences in the workplace.* London: Routledge.

Gabarro, JJ and Kotter, JP (1992) Managing your boss. In Gabarro, JJ (ed) *Managing people and organizations.* Boston, MA: Harvard Business School.

Gaetani, JJ, Johnson, CM and Austin, JT (1983) Self-management by an owner of a small business: reduction of tardiness. *Journal of Organizational Behavior Management,* **5**(1): 31–9.

Gardner, C (1997) Mentoring: A professional friendship? A model of mentoring and friendship. Paper presented to the 4th European Mentoring Conference, London.

Garvey, B (1995a) Healthy signs for mentoring, *Education and Training,* **37**(5): 12–19.

Garvey, B (1995b) Let the actions match the words. In Clutterbuck, D and Megginson, D (1995) *Mentoring in Action.* London: Kogan Page.

Garvey, B (1995c) Peer mentoring, supported by a consultant: Jane Smith with John Jones. In Clutterbuck, D and Megginson, D (ed.) *Mentoring in Action.* London: Kogan Page, 175–88.

Garvey, B (1997) What's in it for me? *The Learning Organization,* **4**(1): 3–9.

Garvey, B (1998) Mentoring in the Market Place: Studies of learning at work. Unpublished PhD Thesis, University of Durham, UK.

Garvey, B (1999) Mentoring and the changing paradigm. *Mentoring and Tutoring,* **7**(1): 41–54.

Garvey, B and Alred, G (2000) Educating mentors. *Mentoring and Tutoring,* **8**(2): 113–26.

Garvey, B and Galloway, K (2002) Mentoring at the Halifax plc (HBOS): a small beginning in a large organization. *Career Development International,* **7**(5): 271–8.

Geertz, C (1971) *Myth, Symbol and Culture.* New York: WW Norton and Company Inc.

Gibb, S (1999) The usefulness of theory: a case study in evaluating formal mentoring schemes. *Human Relations,* **52**(8): 1055 ff.

Gladstone, MS (1988) Mentoring: a strategy for learning in a rapidly changing society. Quebec: Research Document CEGEP John Abbott College.

Glover, J (2001) *Humanity: A moral history of the twentieth century.* London: Pimlico.

Godshalk, VM and Sosik, JJ (2000) Does mentor–protégé agreement on mentor leadership behaviour influence the quality of a mentoring relationship? *Group and Organization Management,* **25**(3): 291–317.

Goleman, D (1996) *Emotional Intelligence.* London: Bloomsbury.

Gollwitzer, PM (1996) The volitional benefits of planning. In Gollwitzer, PM and Bargh, JA (eds) *The Psychology of Action.* New York: Guilford Press.

Gollwitzer, PM and Kinney, RF (1989) Effects of deliberative and implementational mindsets on illusion of control *Journal of Personality and Social Psychology,* **73**: 186–99.

Grant, AM (2001a) Coaching for enhanced performance:comparing cognitive and behavioural coaching approaches. Paper presented at the 3rd Spearman Conference, Sydney, Australia.

Grant, A. M. (2001b) Towards a Psychology of Coaching: the impact of coaching on metacognition, mental health and goal attainment. Unpublished doctoral dissertation, Macquarie University, Sydney, Australia.

Gray, WA (1988) Developing a planned mentoring programme to facilitate career development. *International Journal of Mentoring*, **2**(1): 9–16.

Green, SG and Bauer, TN (1995) Supervisory mentoring by advisors: relationships with doctoral student potential, productivity and commitment. *Personnel Psychology*, **48**: 537–61.

Greenwood Partnership (2000) *Mentoring Conversations*, video available from www.greenwood-partnership.com.

Grimley, DM and Lee, PA (1997) Condom and other contraceptive use among a random sample of female adolescents: a snapshot in time. *Adolescence*, **32**(128): 771–9.

Gutek BA (1985) *Sex and the Workplace*. San Francisco, CA: Jossey-Bass.

Hagenow, NR and McCrea, MA (1994) A mentoring relationship: two viewpoints. *Nursing Management*, **25**(12): 42–3.

Hake, B (1999) Lifelong learning in later modernity: the challenges to society, organisations, and individuals. *Adult Education Quarterly*, **49**(2): 79–90.

Hale, R (2000) To match or mis-match? The dynamics of mentoring as a route to personal and organisational learning. *Career Development International*, **5**(4–5): 223–4.

Hamilton, BA and Scandura, TA (2003) Implications for organizational learning and development in a wired world. *Organization Dynamics*, **31**(4): 388–402.

Handy, C (1986) *Understanding Organisations*. Harmondsworth, Middlesex: Penguin Books.

Hansen, C (2000) *Virtual Mentoring: A real-world case study*. www.usask.ca/education/coursework/802papers/hansen/hansen.htm.

Hansman, CA (1998) Mentoring and women's career development. In Bierema, LL (ed.) *Women's Career Development across the Lifespan: Insights and strategies for women, organisations and adult educators* (pp. 63–73). San Francisco: Jossey Bass.

Harrington, A (1999) *E-mentoring: The advantages and disadvantages of using email to support distant mentoring*. European Social Fund. Retrieved from www.mentorforum.co.uk/cOL1/discover.htm.

Harrison, N (2000) *Improving Employee Performance*. London: Kogan Page.

Harrison, R (1972) How to describe your organisation. *Harvard Business Review*, **Sept–Oct**.

Hateley, BJ and Schmidt, WH (1995) *A Peacock in the Land of Peacocks: A tale of diversity and discovery*. California: Berrett-Koehler.

Hawkins, P and Shohet, R (2000) *Supervision in the Helping Professions*. Buckingham: Open University Press.

Hay, J (1995) *Transformational Mentoring: Creating developmental alliances for changing organisational cultures*. Maidenhead: McGraw-Hill.

Hazan, C and Shaver, PR (1987) Romantic love conceptualized as an attachment process. *Journal of Personality and Social Psychology*, **52**: 511–24.

Hazan, C and Shaver, PR (1990) Love and work: an attachment- theoretical perspective. *Journal of Personality and Social Psychology*, **59**(2): 270–80.

Hazan, C and Shaver, PR (1994) Attachment as an organizational framework for research on close relationships. *Psychological Inquiry*, **5**(1): 1–22.

Higgins, M and Kram, K (2001) Re-conceptualising mentoring at work: a developmental network perspective. *The Academy of Management Review*, **26**(2), 264–88.

Hirschhorn, L (1990) Leaders and followers in a post industrial age: a psychodynamic view. *Journal of Applied Behavioural Science*, **26**(4): 529–42.

Hollenbeck, JR and Brief, AP (1987) The effects of individual differences and goal origin on goal setting and performance. *Organizational Behavior and Human Decision Processes*, **40**(3): 392–414.

Hollenbeck, JR and Williams, CR (1987) Goal importance, self-focus, and the goal-setting process. *Journal of Applied Psychology*, **72**(2): 204–11.

Holloway, A and Whyte, C (1994) *Mentoring: The definitive workbook*. Manchester: Development Processes (Publications) Ltd.

Hoschette, JA (1995) A mentor in hand. *IEEE Spectrum*, **32**(2): 56–8.

Howard, A and Bray, DW (1988) *Managerial Lives in Transition*. New York: Guilford Press.

Howe, SES (1995) The benefits of mentoring relationships. *Pennsylvania CPA Journal*, **66**(1): 16.

Hubschman, BG (1996) The effect of mentoring electronic mail on student achievement and attitudes in a graduate course in educational research. *Dissertation Abstract International*, 57–08A:3417.

Huczynski, A (1993) *Management Gurus: What makes them and how to become one*. London: Routledge.

Hughes, S (2002) *Exhibition interpretation of Shirley Hughes, children's illustrator*. Ashmolean Museum, Oxford.

Hultman, J and Sobel, L (1994) *Mentorn en praktisk vägledning*. Helsingborg: Lts Förlag.

Hunt, DM and Michael, C (1983) Mentorship: a career training and development tool. *Academy of Management Review*, **8**: 475–85.

Hurley, AE and Fagenson-Eland, EA (1996) Challenges in cross-gender mentoring relationships: psychological intimacy, myths, rumours, innuendoes and sexual harassment. *Leadership and Organisation Development Journal*, **17**(3): 42–9.

Hyrkas, K, Appelqvist-Schmidlechner, K and Paunomen-Ilmonen, M (2002) Expert supervisors' views of clinical supervision: a study of factors promoting and inhibiting the achievements of multi-professional team supervision. *Journal of Advanced Nursing*, **38**(4): 387–97.

Ibarra, H (2000) Making partner: mentor's guide to the psychological journey. *Harvard Business Review*, **78**(2) (March–April): 147–55.

Institute of Mechanical Engineering (1990) *A Guide to Mentoring*. London: IME.

Jensen, E (1995) *The Learning Brain*. San Diego, CA: Turning Point Press.

Joplin, JW, Nelson, DL, Quick, JC (1999) Attachment behavior and health: relationships at work and home. *Journal of Organizational Behavior*, **20**: 783–96.

Jung, CG (1971) *Psychological types* (HG Baynes, trans.; revised by RFC Hull). Princeton University Press (Original work published 1923).

Kadushin, A (1976) *Supervision in Social Work*. New York: Columbia University Press.

Kahn, WA and Kram, KE (1994) Authority at work: internal models and their organizational consequences. *Academy of Management Review*, **19**(1): 17–50.

Kalbfleisch, PJ and Davies, AB (1991) Minorities and mentoring: Managing the multicultural institution. *Communication Education* **40**: 226–271.

Kalbfleisch, PJ and Davies, AB (1993) An interpersonal model for participation in mentoring relationships. *Western Journal of Communications*, **57**: 399–415.

Kennedy, MM (1994) Good coach, bad coach. *Across the board*, **31**(8): 11–12.

Kirschenbaum, DS, Humphrey, LL and Malett, SD (1981) Specificity of planning in adult self-control: an applied investigation. *Journal of Personality and Social Psychology*, **40**(5): 941–950.

Kleinman, G, Siegal, PH and Eckstein, C (2002) Mentoring and learning: the case of CPA firms. *Leadership and Organization Development Journal*, **22**(1): 22–33.

Klingemann, HKH (1994) Environmental influences which promote or impede change in substance behaviour. In: Edwards, G and Lader, M (eds) *Addiction: Processes of change*. Oxford University Press, 131–61

Klohnen, EC and John, OP (1998) Working models of attachment: a theory based prototype approach. In Simpson, JA and Rholes, WS (eds) *Attachment Theory and Close Relationships*. New York: Guilford Press.

Knippen, JT and Green, TB (1991) Developing a mentoring relationship. *Management Decision*, **29**(2): 40–3.

Kram, KE (1983) Phases of the mentoring relationship. *Academy of Management Journal*, **26**(4): 608–25.

Kram, KE (1985a) *Mentoring at Work*. Boston: Scott, Foresman, and Company.

Kram, KE (1985b) Improving the mentoring process. *Training and Development Journal*, **39**(4): 19–23.

Kram, KE (1988) *Mentoring at Work: Developmental relationships in organisational life*. Lanham: University Press of America.

Kram, KE and Bragar, M (1992) Development through mentoring: a strategic approach. In Montross, D and Shinkman, C (eds) *Career Development: Theory and practice*. Springfield, IL: Thomas Press.

Kram, KE and Isabella LA (1985) Mentoring alternatives: the role of peer relationships in career development. *Academy of Management Journal*, **28**(1): 110–32.

Kutter, P (2002) From the Balint method toward profession-related supervision. *The American Journal of Psychoanalysis*, **62**(4): 313–25.

Lackoff, G and Johnson, M (1980) *Metaphors we live by*. University of Chicago Press.

Lalli, EP and Shapiro, ES (1990) The effects of self-monitoring and contingent reward on sight word acquisition. *Education and Treatment of Children*, **13**(2): 129–41.

Landau, E (1993), *Sexual Harassment*. New York: Walker and Company.

Lane, GM (1996) The competence of a mentor and implications for directors and CEOs. Paper to the 3rd European Mentoring Conference, London.

Lane, GM (1997) The developed model of mentor competence. Paper to the 4th European Mentoring Conference, London.

Lane, GM and Robinson, A (1992) Assessing work-based learning. *Journal of General Management: Manager update* **4**(1): 20–30.

Lankau, MJ and Scandura, TA (2002) An investigation of personal learning in mentoring relationships: content, antecedents, and consequences. *Academy of Management Journal*, **45**(4): 779–90.

Lao-Tse (1998) Tao-Te-Ching. iUniverse.com

Lave, J and Wenger, E (1991) *Situated Learning: Legitimate peripheral participation*. Cambridge University Press.

Lee, FK, Dougherty, TW and Turban, DB (1999) The role of personality and work values in mentoring programs. *Review of Business*, **21**: 33–7.

Leeds Metropolitan University (1995) *Mentoring: The 'working for a degree' project – final project report,* Vol I. Leeds: Leeds Metropolitan University

Levinson (1978) *Seasons of a Man's Life.* Englewood Cliffs, NJ: Prentice Hall.

Lobel, SA, Quinn, RE, St Clair, L and Warfield, A (1994) Love without sex: the impact of psychological intimacy between men and women at work. *Organizational Dynamics,* **23**(1), 5–16.

Locke, EA (1996) Motivation through conscious goal setting. *Applied and Preventive Psychology,* **5**(2): 117–24.

Luna, G and Cullen, DL (1995) *Empowering the Faculty: Mentoring redirected and renewed.* Washington: George Washington University.

Maidment, J and Cooper, L (2002) Acknowledgement of client diversity and oppression in social work student supervision. *Social Work Education,* **21**(4), 399–407.

Mainiero, LA (1989) *Office Romance.* New York: Rawson Associates.

Marrow, CE, Macauley, DM and Crumbie, A (1997) *Journal of Nursing Management,* **5**: 77–82.

Martinson, MG (1997) Human resource management applications of knowledge-based systems. *International Journal of Information Management,* **17**(1): 35–53.

McClelland, D and Burnham, D (1976) Power is the great motivator. *Harvard Business Review,* **54**(2): 100–110. In Vroom, VH and Deci, EL (first published 1970) *Management and Motivation.* Harmondsworth: Penguin Books.

McCrae, RR and Costa, PT Jr (1985) Updating Norman's 'adequate taxonomy': intelligence and personality dimensions in natural language and in questionnaires. *Journal of Personality and Social Psychology,* **49**: 710–21.

McCrae, RR and Costa, PT Jr (1989) The structure of interpersonal traits: Wiggins' circumplex and the five-factor model. *Journal of Personality and Social Psychology,* **56**: 586–95.

McDoughall, W (1936) *An Introduction to Social Psychology* (23e). London: Methuen.

Megginson, D (1998) Mentoring research overview. *Proceedings of the 5th European Mentoring Conference.* Old Windsor, Sheffield Business School and EMC, Sheffield, 113–19.

Megginson, D (2000) Current issues in mentoring. *Career Development International,* **5**(4–5): 256–60.

Megginson, D and Boydell, T (1979) *A Manager's Guide to Coaching.* London: BACIE.

Megginson, D and Clutterbuck, D (1995) *Mentoring in Action.* London: Kogan Page.

Megginson, D and Clutterbuck, D (2002) What's in it for the mentor? Plenary presentation, 9th European Mentoring and Coaching Conference. Sheffield Hallam University.

Megginson, D and Stokes, P (2000) *Mentoring for export success.* Proceedings of the 7th European Mentoring Conference. Sheffield Hallam University.

Mellon, N (1992) *Storytelling and the Art of Imagination.* Shaftesbury, UK: Element Books.

Mezirow, J (1991) *Transformative Dimensions of Adult Learning.* San Francisco: Jossey Bass.

Microsoft (1997) Unpublished research on line manager competence. Referenced in Clutterbuck, D (1997) *The Winning Streak Mark II.* London: Orion.

Miller, Andrew (2002) The way mentoring is going. Paper to the 9th European Mentoring and Coaching Council Conference.

Molvig, D (1995) Are you mentor material? *Credit Union Management,* **18**(6): 14–15.

Muller, CB (2000) *The Potential of Industrial E-Mentoring as a Retention Strategy for Women in Science and Engineering.* California: Blue Sky Consulting.

Mumford, A (1989) *Management Development: Strategies for action.* London: IPM.

Murphy, LR (1984) Occupational stress management: a review and appraisal. *Journal of Occupational Psychology,* **57**(1): 1–15.

Murray, HA (1938) *Explorations in personality.* New York: Oxford University Press.

Murrel, AJ, Crosby, FJ and Ely, RJ (eds) (1999) *Mentoring Dilemmas: Developmental relationships within multicultural organisations.* Mahwah, NJ: Lawrence Erlbaum Associates.

Nash, L (1994) Why business ethics now? In Drummond, J and Bain, B (eds) *Managing Business Ethics.* Oxford: Butterworth-Heinemann.

Neuhauser, P (1993) *Corporate Legends and Lore.* New York: McGraw-Hill.

Nietzsche, F (1990) *Beyond Good and Evil.* Harmondsworth: Penguin Classics.

Nieva, VF and Gutek, BA (1981) *Women and Work: A psychological perspective.* New York: Praeger.

Noe, RA (1988) An investigation into the determinants of successful assigned mentoring relationships. *Personnel Psychology,* **41**(3): 457–79.

Nonaka, I (1994) A dynamic theory of organizational knowledge creation. *Organization Science,* **5**(2).

Nonaka, I and Konno, N (1998) The concept of 'Ba': building a foundation for knowledge creation. *California Management Review,* **40**(3).

Nonaka, I and Takeuchi, H (1995) *The Knowledge Creating Company.* Oxford University Press.

Norman, WT (1963) Toward an adequate taxonomy of personality attributes: replicated factor structure in peer nomination personality ratings. *Journal of Abnormal and Social Psychology,* **66**: 574–83.

O'Connell, B (1998) *Solution-focused Therapy.* London: Sage.

O'Neill, R (2001) Gender and race in mentoring relationships: a review of the literature. In Clutterbuck, D and Ragins, R (eds) *Mentoring and Diversity: An international perspective.* Oxford: Butterworth Heinemann.

O'Neill, DK, Wagner, R and Gomez, LM (1996) Online mentors: experimenting in science class. *Educational Leadership,* **54** (3): 39–42.

Open University Quality Support Centre (1995) *Signposts for Staff Development (2): Workplace mentors.* London: Department for Education and Employment.

Ornstein, R (1977) *The Psychology of Consciousness.* New York: Penguin.

Parag, K (1995) Mentors and approved training organisations. *Chartered Accountants Journal of New Zealand,* **74** (4): 32–4.

Parker Armitage, M (1994) Using psychoanalytic theory in improving the mentoring process. Paper given at 1st European Mentoring Conference, Sheffield. Sheffield: Sheffield Business School and EMC.

Parkin, M (1998) *Tales for Trainers.* London: Kogan Page.

Parkin, M (2001) *Tales for Coaching.* London: Kogan Page.

Parsloe, E (1992) *Coaching, Mentoring and Assessing; A practical guide to developing competence.* London: Kogan Page.

Parsloe, E and Wray, M (2000) *Coaching and Mentoring: Practical methods to improve learning.* London: Kogan Page.

Pascarelli, J (1998) A four-stage mentoring model that works. In Goodlad, S (ed.) *Students as Mentors and Tutors.* London: Kogan Page.

Pasher, VS (1995) Women who own agencies overcome obstacles. *National Underwriter,* **99** (36): 3, 24.

Pauchant, T (1996) The Courage to Manage Complexity. Unpublished working documents.

Peluchette, JE and Jeanquart, S (2000) Professionals' use of different mentor sources at various career stages: implications for career success. *The Journal of Social Psychology,* **40** (5): 549–64.

Perry, D (1991) Mentoring amongst industrial managers. *Management Development Review,* **4** (6).

Pervin, L (1984) *Current Controversies and Issues in Personality.* New York: Wiley.

Piper, H and Piper, J (2000) Disaffected young people as the problem: mentoring as the solution: education and work as the goal. *Journal of Education and Work,* **13** (1): 77–94.

Polanyi, M (1958) *Personal Knowledge: Towards a post-critical philosophy.* London: Routledge and Kegan Paul.

Pope, ST and Jones, RSP (1996) The therapeutic effect of reactive self-monitoring on the reduction of inappropriate social and stereotypic behaviours. *British Journal of Clinical Psychology,* **35**: 585–94.

Popper, M, Mayseless, O and Castelnovo, O (2000) Transformational leadership and attachment. *The Leadership Quarterly,* **11**: 267–89.

Powell, GN (1986) Effects of sex role identity and sex on definitions of sexual harassment. *Sex Roles,* **14**: 9–19.

Prochaska, JO and DiClemente, CC (1984) *The Transtheoretical Approach: Crossing traditional boundaries of therapy.* Pacific Grove, CA: Brooks Cole.

Prochaska, JO and DiClemente, CC (1986) Towards a comprehensive model of change. In Miller, WR and Heather, N (eds) *Treating Addictive Behaviors: Processes of change.* New York: Plenum Press, 3–27.

Prochaska, JO, DiClemente, CC and Norcross, JC (1998) Stages of change: prescriptive guidelines for behavioral medicine. In Koocher, GP, Norcross, JC and Hill, SS (eds) *Psychologists' desk reference.* Oxford University Press, 203–36.

Proctor, B (1988) Supervision: a co-operative exercise in accountability. In Marken, M and Payne, M (eds) *Enabling and Ensuring.* Leicester National Youth Bureau and Council for Education and Training in Youth and Community Work.

Quick, JD, Nelson, DL and Quick, JC (1987) Successful executives: how independent? *Academy of Management Executive,* **1** (2): 139–45.

Raelin, J (1997) A model of work-based learning. *Organisation Science,* **8** (6): 563–77.

Ragins, BR (1989) Barriers to mentoring: the female manager's dilemma. *Human Relations,* **42** (1): 1–23.

Ragins, BR (1997) Diversified mentoring relationships in organisations. *Academy of Management Review,* **22** (2), 482–521.

Ragins, BR (1999) Mentoring in the new millennium: time to reflect, or party like it's 1999? Paper to the 6th European Mentoring Centre Conference.

Ragins, BR and Cotton, JL (1991) Easier said than done: gender differences in perceived barriers to gaining a mentor. *Academy of Management Journal,* **34** (4): 939–51.

Ragins, BR and Cotton, J (1999) Mentor functions and outcomes: a comparison of men and women in formal and informal mentoring relationships. *Journal of Applied Psychology,* **84** (4): 529–50.

Ragins, BR and McFarlin, DB (1990) Perceptions of mentoring roles in cross-gender mentoring relationships *Journal of Vocational Behaviour,* **37**: 321–39.

Ragins, BR, Cotton, JL and Miller, JS (2000) Marginal mentoring: the effects of type of mentor, quality of relationship, and program design on work and career attitudes. *Academy of Management Journal*, **43**(6): 1177–94.

Rawsthorne, LJ and Elliott, AJ (1999) Achievement goals and intrinsic motivation: a meta-analytic review. *Personality and Social Psychology Review*, **3**(4): 326–44.

Reynolds, L (1993) New Congress will tackle women's issues. *HR Focus*, **70**(2): 1–3.

Rigsby, JT, Siegal, PH and Spiceland, JD (1998) Mentoring among management advisory service professionals: an adaptive mechanism to cope with rapid corporate change. *Managerial Auditing Journal*, **13**(2): 107–16.

Roche, GR (1979) Much ado about mentors. *Harvard Business Review*, **57**: 14–28.

Roffey Park (1994) Promotional literature.

Rogers, C (1961) *A Therapist's View of Psychotherapy: On becoming a person*. London: Constable and Company.

Rosen, H (1982) *My Voice Will Go With You*. New York: WW Norton.

Rosenbach, WE (1993) *Contemporary issues in leadership*. Boulder, CO: Westview Press, 141–151.

Ribeaux, P and Poppleton, SE (1978) *Psychology and Work: An introduction*. Basingstoke: Macmillan Education.

Rothbard, JC and Shaver, PR (1994) Continuity of attachment across the life span. In: Sperling, MB and Berman, WH (eds) *Attachment in adults: Clinical and developmental perspectives*. New York: Guilford Press.

Rudy, IA (1996) A critical review of research on electronic mail. *European Journal of Information Systems*, **4**: 198–213.

Samborn, HV (1994) The buddy system. *Legal Assistant Today*, **12**(1): 78–79.

Sands, RG, Parson, LA and Duane, J (1991) Faculty mentoring in a public university. *Journal of Higher Education*, **62**(2): 174–193.

Scandura, TA (1992) Mentorship and career mobility: an empirical investigation. *Journal of Organizational Behavior*, **13**: 169–74.

Scandura, TA (1998) Dysfunctional mentoring relationships and outcomes. *Journal of Management*, **24**: 449–67.

Scandura, TA (2002) The establishment years: a dependence perspective. In Feldman, D (ed.) *Work Careers: A developmental perspective*. SIOP Frontiers Series. San Francisco: Jossey-Bass.

Scandura, TA and Hamilton, BA (2002) Enhancing performance through mentoring. In Sonnentag, S (ed.) *Psychological Management of Individual Performance*. New York: Wiley, 293–308.

Scandura, TA and Ragins, BR (1993) The effects of sex and gender role orientation on mentorship in male-dominated occupations. *Journal of Vocational Behavior*, **43**: 251–65.

Scandura, TA and Viator, RE (1994) Mentoring in public accounting firms: an analysis of mentor-protégé relationships, mentoring functions and protégé turnover intentions. *Accounting, Organisations and Society*, **19**(8): 11–12.

Schein, EH (1978) *Career Dynamics: Matching IIndividual and organisational needs*. USA: Addison-Wesley.

Schneider, RJ and Hough, LM (1995) Personality and industrial/organizational psychology. In Copper, CL and Robertson, IT (eds) *International Review of Industrial and Organizational Psychology*. Chichester: Wiley, 75–129.

Schrijvers, J (2002) *Hoe word ik een rat?* Schiedam: Scriptum Books.

Schur, TJ (2002) Supervision as a disciplined focus on self and not the other: a different systems model. *Contemporary Family Therapy*, **24**(3): 399–422.

Senge, P (1992) *The Fifth Discipline*. London: Century Business.

Shapiro, EC, Haseltine, FP and Rowe, MP (1978) A moving up: role models and the patron system. *Sloan Management Review*, **19**: 51–84.

Shea, G (1995) Can a supervisor mentor? *Supervision*, **56**(11): 3–5.

Sheehy, G (1976) *Passages: Predictable crisis of adult life*. New York: Dutton.

Simmel, G (1950) *The Sociology of Georg Simmel* (ed. KH Wolff). New York: Free Press.

Simosko, S (1991) *APOL: Accreditation of Prior Learning: A practical guide for professionals*. London: Kogan Page.

Simpson, JA (1990) Influence of attachment styles on romantic relationships. *Journal of Personality and Social Psychology*, **59**(5): 971–980.

Single, PB and Muller, CB (2001) When e-mail and mentoring unite: the implementation of a nationwide electronic mentoring program. In Stromei, L (ed.) *Implementing Successful Coaching and Mentoring Programs*. Cambridge, MA: American Society for Training and Development, 107–122.

Skinner, BF (1963) Operant behavior. *American Psychologist*, **18**(7): 503–15.

Sosik, JJ and Dworakivsky, AC (1998) Self-concept based aspects of the charismatic leader: more than meets the eye. *Leadership Quarterly*, **9**(4): 503–26.

Sperry, R (1968) Hemisphere disconnection and unity in conscious awareness. *American Psychologist*, **23**: 723–33.

Sproull, L and Kiesler, S (1986) Reducing social context cues: electronic mail in organisational communication. *Management Science*, **32**(11): 1492–512.

Stark, A (1993) What's the matter with business ethics. *Harvard Business Review*, **May–June**: 38–48.

Sully de Luque, MF and Sommer, SM (2000) The impact of culture on feedback-seeking behavior: an integrated model and propositions. *Academy of Management Review*, **25**(4): 829–49.

Sumer, HC and Knight, PA (2001) How do people with different attachment styles balance work and family? A personality perspective on work–family linkage. *Journal of Applied Psychology*, **86**: 653–63.

Swap, W, Leonard, D, Shields, M and Abrams, L (2001) Using mentoring and storytelling to transfer knowledge in the workplace. *Journal of Management Information Systems*, **18**(1): 95–114.

Taylor, SE and Gollwitzer, PM (1996) Effects of mindset on positive illusions. *Journal of Personality and Social Psychology*, **69**: 213–26.

Templeton, DW (1996) Mentoring. *Legal Assistant Today*, **14**(1): 89.

Thompson, M (2000) *Ethics*. London: Hodder and Stoughton.

Tokar, DM, Fischer, AR and Subich, LM (1998) Personality and vocational behavior: a selective review of the literature, 1993–1997. *Journal of Vocational Behavior*, **53**: 115–53.

Torrance, EP (1984) *Mentor Relationships: How they aid creative achievement, endure, change and die*. Buffalo, New York: Bearly Ltd.

Torrington, D and Hall, L (1987) *Personnel Management: A new approach*. Hemel Hempstead: Prentice Hall International Limited.

Trapnell, PD and Campbell, JD (1999) Private self-consciousness and the five-factor model of personality: Distinguishing rumination from reflection. *Journal of Personality and Social Psychology*, **76**(2): 284–304.

Turban, DB and Dougherty, TW (1994) Role of protégé personality in receipt of mentoring and career success. *Academy of Management Journal*, **37**: 688–702.

VandeWalle, D, Brown, SP, Cron, WL and Slocum, JW (1999) The influence of goal orientation and self-regulation tactics on sales performance: a longitudinal field test. *Journal of Applied Psychology*, **84**(2): 249–59.

Vallance, E (1993) What is business for? Ethics and the aim of business. *Business Strategy Review*, **4**(1).

Velasquez, M (1982) *Business Ethics: Concepts and cases*. Englewood Cliffs, NJ: Prentice Hall.

Velicer, WF, DiClemente, CC, Rossi, JS and Prochaska, JO (1990) Relapse situations and self-efficacy: an integrative model. *Addictive Behaviors*, **15**(3): 271–83.

Vertz, LL (1985) Women, occupational advancement, and mentoring: an analysis of one public organization. *Public Administration Review*, **45**(3): 415–23.

Vincent, A and Seymour, J (1995) Profile of women mentors: a national survey. *Advanced Management Journal*, **60**(2): 4–10.

Walker, A and Stott, K (1993) In Caldwell, BJ and Carter, EMA (eds) *The Return of the Mentor: Strategies for workplace learning*. London: The Falmer Press.

Watts, N (1996) *Storyscape*, www.ccweb.co.uk/telling.html.

Weiss, RS (1991) The attachment bond in childhood and adulthood. In Parkes, CM, Hinde, JS and Marris, P (eds) *Attachment Across the Life Cycle*. London: Routledge.

Whitely, W and Coetsier, P (1993) The relationship of career mentoring to early career outcomes. *Organization Studies*, **14**: 419–41.

Whitely, W, Dougherty, TW and Dreher, GF (1991) Relationship of career mentoring and socionomic origin to managers' and professionals' early career progress. *Academy of Management Journal*, **34**: 331–51.

Whittaker, M and Cartwright, A (1997) Learning to let go. In *32 Activities on Coaching and Mentoring*. Aldershot: Gower, 203–210.

Whittaker, M and Cartwright, A (2000) *The Mentoring Manual*. Aldershot: Gower.

Wicklund, RA (1975) Objective self-awareness. In Berkowitz, L (ed.) *Advance in Experimental Social Psychology*, **8**: 233–75. New York: Academic Press.

Wiemann, JM (1977) Explication and test of a model of communicative competence. *Human Communication Research*, **3**: 195–213.

Wiggans, J (1995) *Mentoring: the 'Working for a Degree' project*. Final report Volume II: *Issues and Debates in Mentoring*. Leeds Metropolitan University.

Wighton, DJ (1993) *Telementoring: An examination of the potential for an educational network*. Creighton University, Omaha, NE: USWEST Fellows and Telementoring.

Wilber, K (1985) *No Boundary: Eastern and Western approaches to personal growth*. Boston, Mass.: Shambhala.

Wilhelm, K and Parker, G (1988) The development of a measure of intimate bonds. *Psychological Medicine*, **18**: 225–34.

Williams, M (1982) Learning to learn from role models. Paper: School of Social Work, University of Texas.

Wilson, JA and Elman, NS (1990) Organisational benefits of mentoring. *Academy of Management Executive*, **4**: 88–94.

Wood, AW (1970) *Kant's Moral Religion*. Ithaca, NY: Cornell University Press.

Woodruffe, C (1990) *Assessment Centres: Identifying and developing*. London: IPM.

Yan Lu, R (2002) Mentoring in Belgian organisations: does theory fit practice? Paper to 9th European Mentoring and Coaching Council Conference.

Yin, R (1984) *Case Study Research, Design and Methods.* Newbury Park, CA: Sage.

Young, T (2001) *How to Lose Friends and Alienate People.* London: Abacus.

Zey, MG (1984) *The Mentor Connection.* Illinois: Dow Irwin-Jones.

Index

About the editors

DAVID CLUTTERBUCK

David Clutterbuck is Europe's foremost authority on mentoring practice and research. He has authored or co-authored more than 40 books and hundreds of articles on management themes, including the mentoring titles *Everyone Needs a Mentor, Mentoring and Diversity, Mentoring in Action, Implementing Mentoring Schemes, Mentoring Executives and Directors* and *Learning Alliances.* David has also been influential in developing mentoring across other forms of media, having developed several videos, including *New Chances, New Horizons,* in collaboration with Hertfordshire Training and Enterprise Council (TEC), designed a comprehensive mentoring diagnostics kit to aid mentoring scheme implementation and evaluation, and produced the e-learning CD-ROM *The Effective Mentor.*

David is co-founder of the European Mentoring and Coaching Council (formerly the European Mentoring Centre), a membership-funded organization to help further mentoring and coaching research and promote good practice in these areas (see www.emccouncil.org.uk). David's other academic posts include membership of both the Mentoring and Coaching Research Group at Sheffield Hallam University in the UK, where he is a visiting professor, and of the faculty of the Oxford School of Coaching and Mentoring. Outside of the mentoring arena, he is also co-founder and chairman of 'item', the UK's leading employee communications agency.

David has assisted hundreds of companies around the world to design, implement and sustain successful mentoring programmes. Much of this work has been carried out through his role as Senior Partner of Clutterbuck Associates (CA), the world's leading provider of mentoring scheme support, with franchises operating in five continents. CA pursues a constant programme of research and best practice development, and has developed the International Standards for Mentoring Programmes in Employment. The company is based in Buckinghamshire, England, and can be contacted on:

Tel: +44 (0)1628 661 667
Email: info@clutterbuckassociates.co.uk
Web: www.clutterbuckassociates.com

GILL LANE

Gill Lane has worked as a coach, mentor and trainer for more than 30 years.

With a personal philosophy of wanting to help people to develop themselves, she coaches mentors and trains senior executives across all sectors, types and sizes of business. The focus ranges from current challenges such as business strategy and managing change, to career direction and aspects of personal development including interpersonal skills and managing stress.

Gill began her career within the UK National Health Service (NHS), where she coached and mentored graduate trainees and all levels and disciplines of management over an 18 year period, culminating in a post as human resources director. During these 18-years she coached groups, teams and individuals in various management, interpersonal and inter-team aspects, in addition to her more general HR role.

Following her NHS career, Gill set up her own coaching and development consultancy, alongside a full-time academic role at Henley Management College, a post Gill held for nine years.

At Henley, Gill's main academic role – continuing to this day in an associate faculty position – is to coach and mentor chief executives, directors, senior managers and senior academics on Henley's International Doctoral and Executive Development Programmes, and to teach, supervise and coach MBA participants. Gill also led government-funded research into Standards of Competence of Senior Management and comparison of those competence frameworks with The Guide to Good Practice for Directors. Other research led by Gill included Work-based Learning, Training of Trainers and Computer-mediated Communication. She sat on Henley's Approvals and Accreditation Committee as accreditation adviser.

Gill consolidated her consultancy and academic roles with the formation of Gill Lane Executive Development in early 1998 to include the coaching, mentoring and training of senior executives, managers and professionals on a one-to-one, team and group basis. Gill Lane Associates was formed as a part of that consultancy in the year 2000.

Operating internationally, Gill is a member of the American Academy of Human Resource Development by invitation. She holds a Masters Degree in Public Sector Management, an Advanced Postgraduate Diploma in Consultancy, is a Chartered Fellow of the Chartered Institute of Personnel and Development, and is a non-executive director with an NHS Trust. She was also a member of the Institute of Health Service Management for 16 years and is a fellow of the Royal Society for the Encouragement of Arts (RSA) by invitation. Doctoral level research into competences of mentors has been a particular interest.

Gill Lane Executive Development and Gill Lane Associates can be contacted on:

Tel/Fax: +44 (0)1327 855572
Email: gill-lane@coach-mentor.co.uk
Web: www.coach-mentor.co.uk